Dark, Salt, Clear

DARK, SALT, CLEAR

Life in a Cornish fishing town

LAMORNA ASH

BLOOMSBURY PUBLISHING
LONDON • OXFORD • NEW YORK • NEW DELHI • SYDNEY

BLOOMSBURY PUBLISHING
Bloomsbury Publishing Plc
50 Bedford Square, London, WC1B 3DP, UK

BLOOMSBURY, BLOOMSBURY PUBLISHING and the Diana logo are trademarks of
Bloomsbury Publishing Plc

First published in Great Britain 2020

A catalogue record for this book is available from the British Library

ISBN: HB: 978-1-5266-0001-1; eBook: 978-1-5266-0002-8

4 6 8 10 9 7 5 3

Typeset by Newgen KnowledgeWorks Pvt. Ltd., Chennai, India
Printed and bound in Great Britain by CPI Group (UK) Ltd, Croydon CR0 4YY

To find out more about our authors and books visit www.bloomsbury.com
and sign up for our newsletters

To Denise and Lofty,
Don and Isaac

CONTENTS

Prologue   xi

1   The end of the line   1

2   Way down to Lamorna   9

3   Vesica Piscis   23

4   Guts   39

5   The sing of the shore   53

6   Lines through rocks   57

7   Wild beasts   69

8   Fish through fingers   81

9   Leather purses   93

10 Misways   107

11 Fish within fish   117

12 Careworn   133

13 Smoke   145

14 Sea-hab   149

15 Beaten copper   157

16 Local   171

17 A feast of seabirds   181

18 *Rosebud*   195

19 Dropped things   203

CONTENTS

20	Some old residents	219
21	Graveyard	233
22	Storms do come	243
23	Raymundo	255
24	Vortex	265
25	A passionate rage	277
26	'Ome	281
27	Fisherman's blues	295
28	Holloways	303

Bibliography	307
Acknowledgements	315

PROLOGUE

The life class model in Newlyn was nothing like the ones I'd come across back home in London. His body bore the marks of a life lived hard – his arms strong and sinewy, his face cross-hatched by wrinkles, his back and biceps scribbled all over with dark blue tattoos. I wanted to believe he had once been a fisherman, but he did not speak to us so I never found out. As we sipped tea there, in the bare studio room of Newlyn Art School up the top of Old Paul Hill, he stood in silence facing the large wooden windows, from where he could have seen the whole of Mount's Bay yawning out in both directions, if only the black night sky had not covered the view.

When he posed for us, he did not curve his body self-consciously across some chaise longue but looked at us head on, legs apart, arms outstretched as if to say: *Here I am*! Observing me as I sketched the man's outline – messily, hungrily, at break-neck speed, rubbing out lines, starting again, failing once more to capture his shape – the art teacher came over and asked me to put down my pencil. When drawing a body, she explained, do not look at the limbs themselves, the shapes and positions you expect the human form to assume, but instead at 'the negative space around them' – the triangles inside the crook of each arm, the crescent that emerges on the other side of where the waist slopes inwards. By following this method the figure will materialise on the paper of its own accord, not how you imagine it ought to appear, but how it really is: the flesh-and-blood person standing before the row of canvases.

I took a breath and relaxed. This was new; there was another way of looking at things.

It was not until I started drawing that I recognised the way I attempt to take the world in. When I sketch, I want the whole image to appear at once; I push the pencil hard against the paper until it is all but blunt, desperately trying to commit whatever is before me to the page. It is the way I speak, too, bloating each sentence out with as many exhaustive pieces of information as I can to ensure my poor audience does not miss a single moment of what I am trying to conjure.

That bare-boned man, built of so many negative spaces and unresolved marks and shadings, contained in his being all that I was yet to understand about Newlyn. What I had failed to see is that a place is alive; it too is flesh and blood standing before you, arms outstretched, mouth open, ready to call out: *Here I am*! – if only you would pause for a moment to listen.

John Steinbeck articulates the life of places better than any other writer I know, especially in his novella *Cannery Row*. I first read it on the advice of a good friend from Lelant, a village on the north Cornwall coast where the female line of my family has lived for generations. Since returning to London, it is this book that has found itself most frequently in my backpack as I commute, batted like a mouse in a cat's paws from one end of the city to the other to tutor children. I show each child the prologue to *Cannery Row* on our first English session together. I show it to them because I want them to know that there are writers who aren't afraid of admitting the near impossibility of transforming landscapes and people into writing, but who try anyway. I show it to them to remind myself of that same truth as I work on my own writing.

'Cannery Row in Monterey in California,' Steinbeck tells us, 'is a poem, a stink, a grating noise, a quality of light, a tone, a habit, a nostalgia, a dream ...' In one breath, he gives us the heavy, industrial percussion of a working fishing village which teems with life, and stinks and grates.

'That doesn't mean *anything*! How can a place be a *stink*?' interrupts one ten-year-old tutee.

It couldn't be, I tell her, if that were all Steinbeck had written of Cannery Row. Each of these sensations is necessary to the others – the way the light hits the warehouse buildings at different hours, the way the sounds intensify at dawn and fade away at dusk each day in time with the work beginning and ending, the potent stench of fish as it arrives into the factories off the boats, how it feels to stand right in the middle of a place where all these sights and sounds and smells occur together. What it means is that a place is every sense pricked, every sense activated at once.

Next, Steinbeck tells us of the strange, hushed magic left behind each evening, which is nostalgic, which is but a dream once more come the next morning. In this brief description of the workers who daily descend on Cannery Row he teaches us how places are nourished by those who gather in them, whose own multiple, contradictory parts render them just as complex and cosmic as the places themselves.

'How,' the book's narrator finally asks, 'can the poem and the stink and the grating noise – the quality of light, the tone, the habit and the dream – be set down alive?' He answers his own question immediately through a scientific analogy – a nod to Steinbeck's closest friend in California, Ed Ricketts, a marine biologist and the inspiration for Doc, the principal character in *Cannery Row*. Since 'a marine flat worm breaks and falls apart when you try to catch it whole', you must instead 'let them ooze and crawl of their own will onto a knife blade and then lift them gently into your bottle of sea water.' So too, in the telling of place, he advises, can you only 'open the page' and hope 'the stories crawl in by themselves.' After reading *Cannery Row*, I am mindful to greet each part of Newlyn as it finds me, letting it rush into me as the waves do against the ragged Cornish cliffs that stand before the Atlantic like custodians of the land, marking them, softening them, reshaping their boundaries with each rising swell.

A year on from my time in Cornwall, I have only the scruffy brown sugar-paper life drawings from that night at the art school to remember the unknown Cornishman by. More than any of the hundreds of photographs or diary entries or recordings I made during my time in Newlyn, it is these drawings that best capture, not just the town, but my relationship to the place, and the chiaroscuro shades it revealed while I found myself in the midst of all that living.

1

THE END OF THE LINE

'Do you like cats? Do you mind smoking? And, do you like a drink?'

It did not feel real at first, to be below the soaring ceilings of the scorched-red British Library, surrounded by flocks of tourists gazing up amazed at towers of books encased in glass, and then suddenly to hear, piped into my headphones, the rhythmic sweet timbre of a West Cornish accent. News had passed around the town of Newlyn that a girl from 'upcountry' was seeking lodging, and a couple – Denise and Lofty, who live right by the harbour – had offered their spare room.

Before this could happen, Denise had a couple of questions for me. A student at the table next to me was bashing furiously at his keyboard, so I turned up the volume on my phone to hear her better.

'Could you repeat that?'

'*Do you like cats? Do you mind smoking? And, do you like a drink?*'

Having replied yes, no, and then, very much, yes, it was settled. Denise, a fishmonger, and Lofty, a ship's chandler, would be greeting their first lodger, a twenty-two-year-old Londoner with a distinctly Cornish name at Penzance station in a month's time.

Paddington to Penzance, my ticket read: the beginning of the line to its very end. Virginia Woolf described the Great Western Train magicking her to 'this little corner of England' as 'the wizard who was to transport us into another world, almost into another age.' Every summer of her childhood it was this alchemical transformation that took her from the dense streets of London to the sea-edged wildness of north Cornwall. From Talland House, where they stayed each year – a cream building with large bay windows on the outskirts of St Ives – Woolf would have been able to make out the thin outline of Godrevy Lighthouse rising up from a dark mass of rock just off the coast, like a white candle stuck in a slab of cake. The lighthouse held on in her memory, a stubborn after-image that would later become the inspiration for the Scottish lighthouse around which the narrative of *To the Lighthouse* turns.

I have encountered the same magic Woolf experienced on the Great Western train countless times, shutting the pink-and-blue carriage door on bustling Paddington and, five hours later, opening it into the clear, salt-touched air of St Erth, from where my family and I would head on to Lelant for the Easter and summer holidays. All those journeys, my routine so perfected I knew which side of the carriage to sit (always the left, that way you're close to the sea) and when to eat my sandwiches (if I took the 10.03 train, then at Exeter St David's just after 12.00), but I'd never taken the Great Western line the whole of its extent before. Though only one stop further, it felt entirely unlike catching the train to St Erth – as if running over every track possible might provide some sense of finality.

As we pull out of Paddington, I look down the carriage which is now crowded with Easter holiday-goers; brightly coloured surfboards and wrapped-up windbreakers sprout out from behind almost every row of seats. Most of these tourists will leave the train long before we reach Penzance, travelling on from Plymouth, Par and Truro to the popular coastal resorts. You can tell instantly those passengers who are in it for the long haul: they have a certain look, with their books, notepads and snacks spread out the furthest from their laps.

I lean my head against the window and stare out at widening plains of unconcreted space. The last few tower blocks marking London's outskirts fall away. You still feel landscape on a train in a way that you cannot along long, homogenous stretches of motorway broken up by embankments, verges and identical-looking service stations.

The line from Paddington to Plymouth was opened in 1849. Back then, fishermen from Newlyn would send their fish in carts down to the station in Plymouth to catch the fast mail train to London. The great channels the Victorian railway engineers tore through the landscape provided nineteenth-century geologists with a view of the earth never seen before. For the first time, they were able to analyse the age lines of rocks long hidden beneath the skin of the land.

By 1859 the tracks the new steam trains travelled along had made it to Truro, crossing the Tamar River on the Cornwall–Devon border via Isambard Kingdom Brunel's Royal Albert Bridge. The bridge is an extraordinary feat of engineering, suspended thirty metres above the Tamar. Its design consists of two lenticular trusses – each an enormous, grey, iron-bound symbol for infinity leaning on its side. Lenticular describes a shape like a stretched oval lens. There are lenticular galaxies, ancient star clusters which have used up almost all of their interstellar matter and are gradually fading out of existence; there are lenticular clouds, too, which, when seen in the dark, look like flying saucers waiting to drop down to earth.

In 1867 the Great Western Railway made it all the way along the 'Cornish Riviera' to Penzance, covering a grand total of 79.5 miles. This line breached the ungoverned spaces between Cornwall and the rest of England, and brought some of the earliest tourists to the county. The Cornish called these new, odd-sounding visitors *emmets*, a term they use for all foreigners – that is, anyone who lives beyond the Tamar.

Newlyn is just on from Penzance along the sea road towards Land's End – where it was once believed the world of men drew to a close. Apart from its location and connection to fishing, I had little experience of the town, beyond the bare car park at the edge of its harbour where my parents would stop briefly at the start of each holiday to pick up fresh fish before we travelled on to more tourist-friendly destinations.

To provide my destination with some tangible shape I pluck random facts about it from my phone as we start along the final stretch of journey through West Cornwall. The population of Newlyn, coupled with that of neighbouring Mousehole, is around 4,400; Newlyn boasts one of the largest and most profitable fishing ports in the UK; it has five pubs, all within walking distance of each other; the mean gross annual salary in Penzance, of which Newlyn is part, was £26,788 in 2015, compared to £34,265 in England as a whole. In 2017 Cornwall had the tenth highest numbers of people sleeping rough in the country and the third highest suicide rate in the UK. It is the only county poor enough to qualify for EU emergency funding and has an average wage 17 per cent below the rest of the country.

That Penzance is the end of the line is often used to explain the high numbers of rough-sleepers in the area: people end up here because there is no place further to go. The phrase 'end of the line' at once loses its satisfying sense of completion, instead signifying something more oppressive: a lack of other options. This is the first impression I get of the darker shading around Cornwall's peripheries, largely unseen by the second-homers and sun- and beach-seeking tourists attracted to the county each year in their thousands.

The holiday crowds have thinned out by the time we enter the final, halting stages of our journey, the gaps between stops shrinking to a matter of minutes. When we come to St Erth I notice the absence of my family sat across from me. I close my eyes and try to forget my nerves about my new home, instead imagining what it would be like to flee the train now – to go where I know, where it is safe and certain. I let my mind blow briefly onto Lelant's melancholy stretch of sand. Lelant beach is where my mother and I have always got on best. Whatever mother–daughter fight we were in the midst of would cease as we launched ourselves through the curtain of marram grass that pulls apart to reveal the beach below the sand dunes. The place where our understandings have met, our lives briefly aligning along the shell line running parallel to the sea, with its long streak of purple and green mussels, cochlea-curled sea-snail homes, and light pink shell halves, joined together by a hinge, which she calls fairy wings.

The train crosses over to the south coast, leaving St Ives Bay behind. I receive a text from Denise saying she'll be wearing a blue-striped top so I can identify her at the station. I look down at my own blue striped top, not sure if I'm embarrassed or amused by the coincidence and send her a message back saying: 'Me too! See you soon.' Later she will tell me that a weary-looking middle-aged woman in a blue-striped jumper came out of the station just before me, leading Lofty to joke: 'Maybe the kids from London start looking older earlier.'

The sea – which on oceanographic maps is not the same Celtic Sea that I had thrown myself into each holiday in Lelant on the north coast but is now the English Channel – appears through the train window and with it, the magisterial, fog-ringed outline of St Michael's Mount, an island just off the coast you can only reach by foot when the tide is low enough to reveal the granite causeway connecting it to the land. We chase along the shoreline, past the large green-grey corrugated-iron structures that make up Long Rock industrial estate, and begin to slow down for the final stretch into the station. The buffer stops at a line's end never seem very convincing to me: the tracks slope upwards to meet them, as if tempting the driver to take the train on to further dimensions once the passengers have departed.

As I drag my case along the empty carriage and step down onto the platform, all I can see in front of me is a rusted vending machine emptied of snacks and a passengers' waiting room with a few rows of plastic-backed chairs. Though I have tried numerous times since to conjure up the image of us regarding one another as strangers, I cannot remember what it felt like to see Denise and Lofty for the first time. When I try to think of them standing there just inside the arced cover of Penzance station, side by side – Denise little, strong and tanned, with shoulder-length brown hair; Lofty in his work fleece and, true to his name, the tallest head amongst those waiting at the station – the image fractures: I imagine Denise erupting into the mischievous expression that spreads across her whole face just before she is about to play a prank on some unsuspecting friend, and the way in which Lofty's booming, open-mouthed laugh joins in with hers, revealing his missing front tooth.

Driving away from the station, I turn my head to look through the rear window and watch as St Michael's Mount disappears behind the evening sea mist that encroaches upon the bay.

The sky is fired red with its last light as we drive over Newlyn Bridge – passing on our left the large, grey-walled fish market and car park packed with heavy-duty lorries, behind which I can just make out the tall, pale masts of fishing boats swaying like a forest of leafless trees. Denise swivels round in her seat to point out an inviting-looking mustard-yellow building across from the harbour, the warm glow emanating from its windows drawing squares of gold on the pavement, with several dark figures standing at its entrance smoking. 'That's the Star, our local. You'll find yourself in there soon, no doubt,' she winks.

We turn off the main road to snake our way through the alleyways that make up Newlyn's fishermen's quarter and park alongside a small front garden decorated with potted plants. Through a low doorway, under which Lofty has to duck, is an immaculately kept cottage with a living room that opens out onto a patio garden facing the harbour. From the sofa, two of the biggest cats I have ever seen eye me with suspicion as Lofty and I strain to drag my huge case up the narrow stairs to my new room.

That night we sit together in the lounge, trays piled high with buttery baked potatoes balanced on our laps, engaging in uncertain, polite chatter in the silences between the soaps playing on the TV. Worn out from the journey and my mind's ruminating doubts about the coming stay, I finish as much of the meal as I can and head up to bed. Out in the darkness below my window, I hear the low clunking of heavy machinery, as crates of fish are unloaded from boats to be weighed and prepared in the market for the dawn auction, and a couple of nocturnal seagulls squawking over fish guts. A strong wind picks up and whips through the alley. Above it all I hear the sea, raging against the harbour walls.

2

Way down to Lamorna

I wake to the same muffled booms coming from the harbour that had lulled me to sleep the previous night. The spare room is pale green, the duvet patterned with geometric fish, the tail of one becoming the body of the next. On the wall opposite the bed there is a blue imitation of a captain's wheel, the interior spokes replaced by a small, round mirror. The smell of cooked bacon rises up the stairs and I dress quickly to join Denise and Lofty for breakfast.

My entrance startles them, as if they had momentarily forgotten the stranger they had accepted into their home the day before. It is not until I see them again – Lofty's head slightly bent so he can fit under the low ceilings, Denise by the stove and their two round cats, Teggy and Izzy, lolled out across the sofa – that I am entirely certain it is real, either.

Over our bacon sandwiches Denise tells me that today, Good Friday, happens to be the day of the 'Lamorna Walk', and might I like to go, as it's always 'a right laugh'. The Walk is a long-standing Newlyn tradition, I find out, that involves almost the whole town taking the coastal path up to Lamorna Cove for a rowdy piss-up at the Lamorna Wink pub, before everyone, much merrier than they'd been on the journey there, unites once more to kick a football back to Newlyn. No one seems to know the walk's origins, but it accrues more ridiculous elements every year.

As my first day in the town falls on the same day as a traditional walk to my namesake, it feels serendipitous and too good an opportunity to miss. I grab my coat and head out towards the harbour, agreeing to meet Denise and Lofty in the Star after, where the festivities will continue late into the night.

I take the sloping Cliff Road that leads up to the outskirts of the town, passing along the perimeter of the bay, and join the flowing crowds heading to Lamorna Cove. After just a few miles the coastal road draws you back down into one of the prettiest villages on the south coast. My parents would often take me to Mousehole as a child. We would sit together in the Old Coastguard Hotel which looks out over St Clement's Isle: a hermit was once said to have lived on the isle, though what kind of hermit would choose to place himself so near to the temptation of the land I cannot imagine. My mother would read *The Mousehole Cat* to me, its swirling blue, purple and green illustrations still so evocative: the cat's storm-striped paw taunting the fishing boats; the quiet fishing hero, Tom Bawcock, going out alone to catch fish for his starving village when no one else will risk heading out in such fierce conditions; every inhabitant of Mousehole waiting with bright torches along the harbour walls to guide Tom's red-sailed fishing boat home to safety and, finally, the whole village coming together for a triumphant fish feast crowned with the Cornish staple of Stargazy Pie, decorated with fish heads and tails.

Mousehole looks exactly how you would paint the idealised fishing village. And yet, in the smoothing brush strokes the artist has applied to it, it seems all the messiness of life has been wiped from it. There is none of the clamouring unruliness that I am immediately confronted with in Newlyn: no rough edges, no tangled nets or thumping machinery, and rarely do you actually see the fishermen walk by in their fish and blood-smeared oilskins. When boats do leave Mousehole's harbour they can be seen *dolling* – a Cornish word used to describe boats moving idly up and down the sea. One of the Newlyn fishermen, 'Cod', lived in Mousehole for a while (I ask about his nickname, expecting some dramatic fishing tale, but he simply replies that as a youngster he wore a jumper emblazoned with 'Cape Cod' and the name stuck). He tells me that nowadays Mousehole has become so flat, so without life, that once an American couple in matching shorts, flip-flops and baseball caps came up to him and said: 'Do they pay you guys to be here, or what?' The cottages are perfectly quaint but when you look closely, most have signs in the windows indicating which Cornish cottage website they can be booked from.

The tidal harbour has been drunk dry this bright Good Friday morning, leaving the boats naked, barnacles exposed, their tapering rudders driven into the mud; it feels almost rude to stare at them in this state, without the sea protecting their modesty. Up until the sixteenth century, Mousehole, not Newlyn, was the principal fishing port in the Southwest. In 1595 a Spanish naval squadron landed at Mousehole and sacked it, burning down almost every building, before continuing their violence upon the coast in Newlyn and Penzance. Mousehole never quite recovered from its destruction and Newlyn's port, from where boats could come and go at any hour uninhibited by the passage of the tide, soon assumed dominance.

I leave the village and cut up towards Lamorna. The single-decker Mousehole bus, bright pink with a cartoon mouse painted along its side, careers past me on its way back to Penzance. The landscape becomes harsher the further you travel towards Land's End, the cliff path climbing up and up until the glimpsed sandy coves look little more than fingernail clippings; lavender-coloured spring squill, heather in blue and green bushes of every shade, and pink tufts of thrift, erupt from the cliff side. And, opening out in the distance, Lamorna Cove itself – a recess cut back so deep into the coast that the precipitous granite cliffs surrounding its crescent of sea look out of scale. On clouded days the cove can feel like one of the most foreboding places on earth, as the land and sea turn black and the many boulders left high up on the cliff face from previous rockfalls look ready to descend to the Atlantic, taking the few seaward cottages with them. But today, with the sun gleaming, the whole cove is lit up, rendering the sea a deep, vivid blue and the carpeted cliffs a verdant green. The cafe is filled with visitors enjoying chips and ice creams and watching for the occasional scuba-diver breaking the surface of the deeper water out beyond the rocks.

At the beginning of the Second World War a London-born constructivist artist, and one of the founding members of the Abstraction-Création association in Paris, fled France on a tanker and found herself in Lamorna Cove. This was not the first time that Marlow Moss had run away to Cornwall. While studying at the Slade School of Art in London she had suffered an emotional breakdown and escaped westwards for her recovery. It was after this retreat that she replaced her given name Marjorie with that of Marlow and moved to Paris to start a Bohemian life there, living amongst a group of avant-garde artists that included Piet Mondrian. That second occasion Marlow Moss came to Cornwall, this time as a result of global rather than personal turmoil, she did not leave again. She found a cottage and a studio in Lamorna and remained there for the rest of her life, the village gradually becoming accustomed to the androgynous figure she cut – with cropped hair, riding breeches, silk cravats. After she died, her ashes were sprinkled into the waves at the edge of the cove.

Moss chose Lamorna for herself. My connection to the cove was established before I was even born. It is strange finding yourself in the place you were named after, experiencing some inexpressible affinity with such a wildly unpredictable stretch of coastline. In her decision to name me Lamorna, my mother unwittingly bound me to Cornwall. I think it was her way of retaining a link to the place of her birth once she had dug her seventeen-year-old roots from the sands of Lelant and replanted them in the cracked pavements of London. My name has defined the way I conceive of myself. Every time I meet a new person and they say: *Wow, sounds exotic! Is that Italian/French/Spanish...?* I am asked to acknowledge and, in doing so, reaffirm the ties between myself and this part of Cornwall, explaining to blank nods of encouragement: *Actually, it's a small cove in far southwest Cornwall – near where my mum's family is from.* This is how a land enters your psyche.

It was my mum who first taught me Cornwall. She showed me how to let it become an antidote to unhappiness and an opening leading back to one's childhood. When I used to look out across Lelant beach – a few minutes' walk from the cottage that had once been my great-grandmother's, next to the bungalow where my mother grew up and my grandmother lived out the last years of her life – my mind would plunge below the sea to find imagined monsters and mermaids. I would put my ear to the cliff cracks, split open by time, and listen to the dull hammering of the Cornish Knockers – malevolent, cave-dwelling spirits, 'three-feet high with squinting eyes and mouths from ear to ear', who would fold back into darkness any time a tin miner tried to catch one of them in the act of bringing the walls down around them. And each time I returned to London, I would feel the absence of that ancestral land sitting deep in my body for weeks, a sense that nothing looked quite right, that the light was wrong somehow.

The day before I left London for Newlyn, I had sat down with my family to examine our Cornish ancestry via various old documents and letters that Mum had kept stuffed in a cabinet in our living room. It is a genealogy that grows uncertain in its backwaters: great-grandmother Ginna, who played bridge at Lelant golf club and dressed in long slacks in the style of Marlene Dietrich while the other elderly ladies of the village were still in long dresses and shawls; generations before her, brewers who made beer in Redruth and sold the company to St Austell Ales; prior to that, hazily drawn figures wandering along Mousehole's tightly wound harbour, who we both like to imagine may themselves have been fishwives and fishermen. They are all there, sprinkled across the west of the county, waiting for the next member of the family to find her place along the Cornish archipelago.

As I approach the Lamorna Wink, a hum of voices echoes towards me and, beneath it, the unmistakeable sound of an electric guitar. Once at the pub's car park, I see that a stage has been set up and on it, a rock band is playing Eagles covers to a small gathering of grey-haired men and women, and a few smoking teenagers partially concealed behind a white van. Next to the stage is a marquee serving beer to the overflow from the pub, from where a queue is snaking all the way down the lane. Every few seconds bursts of laughter erupt from various groups arranged around the pub garden, their faces rosy, their pints spilling onto the grass unnoticed. Be brave, Lamorna, I tell myself. You've come this far; you can get a pint on your own.

I find a sunny spot to lean against the wall with my Doom Bar ale and tap my feet to the music, growing more confident with each sip. A few feet away from me I notice a tall boy wearing a pair of round glasses who seems to be staring right at me. I tap my feet harder, pretending to be immersed in the music. A moment later he comes over. 'This may seem strange,' he says, 'but are you Lamorna?'

I grin apologetically at the boy as if to say: *That's me!*, reckoning that agreeing yes, I am Lamorna, in the Lamorna Wink pub, in Lamorna Cove, on the Lamorna Walk will probably be the most absurd declaration of identity I'll ever have to make. The boy tells me that he is Isaac, a friend of a friend from university, whose family have been Newlyn fishermen for generations and who was informed by our mutual friend of my coming. I've only recently arrived, I tell him, and don't know a soul in Newlyn apart from the couple I'm staying with, who I met for the first time yesterday. Isaac, I soon learn, is one of the most generous, non-judgemental humans on the planet. Without a second's thought he pulls me over to introduce me to his circle of friends, who riotously call back: 'All right, Lamorna!' and in the same breath tell me I have a lot of catching up to do, so I better down that beer and buy another.

The afternoon passes in a spin of drinks, the sixties and seventies classics played in the background providing our score. I learn the lives of those around me through snippets of half-shouted conversation. Almost all of this gang, and most of their close friends too, left Newlyn for university, proceeded to get jobs outside Cornwall and are only back now for the Easter weekend. It becomes a recurring motif; every person my age who grew up in Newlyn expresses a deep sense of longing when they tell the tale of their unavoidable migration from Cornwall,

14

like birds for whom the necessity of chasing new, more suitable lands does not make leaving where they were born any less painful. Each time you come back, they tell me, you are slightly less like the rest of the town. Your accent is that bit softer, your views more at odds with those of the people you knew in school who have still never left Newlyn and probably never will. 'I'm Newlyn. That's all I am,' one boy announces proudly, his foot raised up on a bench. And then, almost mournfully, 'But I can't stay here.'

Still, this continues to be your home. Where else, they ask me, could you find a place with a tradition like this one; where the whole town gets together for no good reason other than to drink, dance, laugh wildly and enjoy the landscape they have grown up in?

A pint or three later and I too have given myself up to the joyousness of it all, slipping into a warm haze that carries me along with the revels. We admit that not one of us feels steady enough to join in with the football-kicking back to Newlyn part of the ritual, so one of the boys, Taylor, calls his nan to see if she will give us a lift. A few moments later, Taylor's nan – a tiny, feisty woman – arrives to take the delinquents back home without batting an eyelid at the state of us all. I linger at the back of the group, uncertain if there is space for me, ready to say: *Don't worry, I'll walk...*, but the gang looks back and waves me over: 'Come on then, Lamorna!' I put down my empty glass and squeeze into the car after them. This is it now, I think, I'm in for the night.

Taylor's nan races along the steep country roads, winding down the window and shouting 'Cheers 'n' Gone!' – an old Cornish phrase apparently – at those unsuspecting cars who politely stop for her and, when someone dares to pull out in front of her, she screeches 'CHEERS 'N' DEAD!' We throw our heads back and bellow 'CHEERS 'N' DEAD!' to the countryside. It becomes our battle cry for the night.

As evening comes, I find myself in Newlyn's Swordfish Inn for the first time – the Swordy ever after. I am met with an onslaught of drunken joy, the whole town crammed into this hot blur of a pub. Bodies teeter and thrash to a jukebox in the corner of the room, turning through an eclectic mixture of hits. Newlyners, no matter their age, do not discriminate between music genres, equally roaring along to Ed Sheeran, Queen, ABBA, the Animals, Madonna, Katy Perry and everything since and in between. I take a seat at the bar to steady myself and gaze up at the mosaic of old photographs stuck up on the walls: there are men with long beards and missing teeth, the t-shirts under their oilskins rolled up to reveal countless tattoos; groups with their arms draped round each other wearing outrageous fancy-dress outfits and posing lewdly, and individuals with traffic cones on their heads dancing on table tops. All of the images have saturated and gone foggy at the edges and so it looks as if they are all from the same time. Following my line of sight, Isaac points out some of the jolly faces in the photos: most of them are old friends of his dad, each of whom has his own rich stories attached. They're almost all dead now, he tells me, but, when not out at sea, these men were the poets, singers, writers, intellectuals, artists and cross-dressers of Newlyn. There is no one quite like them left anymore. And yet they are remembered here in the Swordy.

I soon reach that level of drunkenness where journeys are truncated and you seem to shift from one location to another without having to move at all. I am head-banging with a middle-aged woman in a miniskirt and bushes of thick curly hair; I am outside in the cold, looking out at the black water of the harbour; I am in the Swordy's smoking booth, gazing up at a painting that appears to be stapled onto the roof of the hut. 'You like it?' comes the grizzliest voice I have ever heard. It sounds ancient, like it had to travel a long way through time to reach me. I peer into the depths of the dingy hut. The speaker who emerges from the darkness equally has a look about him that makes me think he has seen all ends of the world.

'I painted it,' the man tells me and I notice the other boys regard him reverentially. 'I'm Ben Gunn.' He lifts his elegant

Stetson to me briefly, saying his name with such conviction that I feel I ought to know who he is. The name sounds familiar, too, and when I tell my mother about him on the phone later she reminds me that Ben Gunn is the name of the character from *Treasure Island* who is left marooned all alone on the island for three years. The two men blend into one in my imagination, Ben acquiring the hollow, wounded look of the abandoned sailor with his straggly white hair and tanned face.

This Ben, the real Ben, is a retired fisherman, who gained notoriety in a TV show called *The Toughest Pubs in Britain*, in which the Swordy was, impressively, ranked second. A much younger, less gruff Ben tells the camera of the time when a Frenchman dared to set foot in his pub and threatened the Cornish fishermen with a knife drawn out of his boot. Ben and two friends turfed him out the pub, breaking the door down as they kicked him through it.

Ben's daily routine as an artist is to smoke, stick Creedence Clearwater Revival on his record player and then paint fifteen or so rapid, messy-stroked canvases – usually seascapes, 'but don't ask me which way up they go afterwards', he adds. He spends most of his time painting, putting his finished pieces up around the town, sticking them outside other pubs, above shops, in alleyways. 'I'll paint anything,' he tells me proudly, 'if it stays still long enough.' When I go to his house a few weeks later I discover this includes every wall and ceiling, slapdashedly splattered with bright paints, and also a few harbour rocks he can see from his living-room window – 'I just fancied it one afternoon' he says – and they are now bright blue. I take one last look up at the messy strokes of blue above our head, before I feel myself being pulled away with the tide on to the next pub.

Where the Swordy is the fisherman's pub, this second pub, a mere block away along the front, is the central sun (or the Star, in this case) around which the rest of the village, particularly those slightly older residents, revolve. I spot Denise and Lofty at the bar and rush over to introduce them to my new friends. Denise grins at me before straightening herself up to play the role of my new guardian. 'Who are you, then?' she says sternly to the boys in our group. 'And what are you doing with Lamorna?'

After that, Denise propels me round the pub, introducing me as: 'This is Lamorna, she wants to know about fishing', which prompts a wide range of responses as people helpfully give me a quick lowdown on the industry: 'It's a great equaliser, the sea ... I don't think at sea, I go blank ... You better watch yourself for seasickness out there, I know people who've got so dehydrated with it, they died ... That's not true ... It is: they had a heart attack ... But that's not the seasickness, then ... Yeah, but I bet it didn't help ... We're the last of a forgotten species ... Not like it was, though ... You wait for that pull, girl. You won't be able to leave this place ... EU've fucked us ... Haddock quotas pitiful ... Bloody Frenchies ... It's a relief when he goes out to sea, he becomes a right nightmare if he's on solid ground too long ... You're not planning on going out on one of those trawlers yourself, are you? It's dangerous out there ...'

The pubs of Newlyn are places of refuge for bleary-eyed fishermen just returned from sea. 'When you first come in,' one called Nathan later tells me while we drink coffee together in his galley, 'you literally do not know what to do with yourself. And you're tired; you are just so bleeding tired that the easiest way out is to go to the pub and turn your brain right off.'

Seeking sanctuary in the pub becomes a way of numbing your-self within an environment that itself does not feel quite of the land, more an extension of your time at sea – filled with gum-booted men straight off their boats who retain the strong aroma of fish. When I ask Ben Gunn if he misses fishing, he says: 'Why would I? It's all right here with me in the pubs.' He can enter into any conversation and immediately feel himself re-immersed in the world of fishing. On Ben's business card for his art, in lieu of an address, it simply says: 'Meet me in the Swordfish'. Fishermen can linger here, letting the time of fishing be drawn out and recreated through colourful renditions of tales from sea – that is, until their wives or partners come marching down the road and drag them home before they can spend their entire week's pay packet on beer.

Somehow, we have returned to the Swordy without my noticing. The mood has altered since we left. The children are gone and an uneasier spirit pervades the place. In every night out there exists that ineluctable shift towards darkness from which, try as you might, you cannot return. This particular darkness is the colour of most of my memories in the Swordy – a dim, melancholic tint washed over its interior. A woman ordering a drink next to me announces to the bar that, generations ago, before it was a pub, this was the home of a very severe woman called Granny Jenkin who was a staunch Salvationist. 'You better hope she isn't looking down at her old place now,' the woman leers, spilling her pint onto the already beer-soaked carpet. Only a few figures are left dancing, but it is not really a dance any longer, more an absent-minded swaying performed in isolation by each figure. A group of dead-eyed men, whom I am sure had not been there earlier, are slumped along the bar below the cheery photographs of departed fishermen. I watch as one of the men's eyes drift up the wall to focus on a particular image, which in the gloom does not look wholly unlike the man himself. Perhaps these are lost fishermen, the ghosts compelled to haunt the bars they knew when living.

Not wanting to go to bed just yet, our group forms a plan to continue the revelries at a club in Penzance. We pick a cab up from Newlyn Bridge, taking with us a fisherman who has inexplicably lost both of his shoes. When he offers to pay for the taxi the boys refuse: 'You're a fisherman, mate. You're not paying.' Though the times may change, fishermen retain their status as heroes of the town – complex and at times difficult heroes but heroes nonetheless. As the taxi sets out towards Penzance, we wind the windows down and howl 'CHEERSSS 'N' DEAD!' into the night.

Time flips forward again and we are at the armpit end of the night in a sweaty Penzance club. It plays cheesy chart music while, perplexingly, at the same time projecting music videos

19

of nineties songs onto a large screen beside the bar. We stomp about in trainers, still muddy from the Lamorna Walk, amongst girls tottering in high heels and lads in rugby shirts competitively downing beers.

A moment later we are stumbling back along Penzance promenade to Newlyn, each of us cradling a bag of curry sauce-smothered chips. My new friends skim rocks out into the sea and chase each other in and out of the broken waves pulling up the beach. I imagine an alternative adolescence in which I would have done this drunken journey every weekend, scuffing my feet along the pebble beach and letting the sea spray clear my booze-fogged head. It seems far more magical than the anonymous night buses I took home through sleepless London.

At the border between Penzance and Newlyn, in front of a giant, bronze statue of a fisherman staring out to the sea, we cheerily hug one another goodbye. And, after a few false starts along seemingly identical, unlit cobblestone lanes in the Fradgan, I manage to get myself to Denise and Lofty's front door and tiptoe up to my room. I go to sleep thinking of Marlow Moss's ashes scattered out from Lamorna Cove – wondering how many other people have requested that their ashes be thrown into the sea, to swirl ever onwards, each atom dispersed across the oceans. If we could track down those burned pieces, perhaps we would find that they do not swirl randomly at all. Instead, their place in relation to one another, blown through the waters, would comprise a vast, complex constellation, the ultimate map of their life expressed by the waves.

I find it hard to think of my time in Newlyn as *contingent* in the way the word has come to mean – fortuitous, down to chance, disorderly. If it is contingent, it is in relation to its scientific terminology – an affinity of nature, a close connection. The contingency I encounter while in Newlyn simultaneously acts upon everyone else in the town, drawing us one to the other. It was this that drew me towards the Lamorna Walk, to which Isaac was also pulled, to which the whole community was lifted up and borne along together, and towards which my mother's thoughts were similarly pulled when, approaching her forty-first birthday, she discovered she would be finally having a baby, and began to rack her brain for names. The physical world informs the pattern of our lives and we give ourselves up to it, marvelling always at the things it brings us.

3

VESICA PISCIS

Before I arrived in Newlyn I was told time and time again that to secure a berth on a working trawler would be nigh impossible – no fisherman would want some girl getting in their way, or worse, ruining the whole trip if her seasickness got so bad she had to be taken back to land. Luckily for me, the first fisherman I speak to, David, one of two St Ives brothers who take it in turns to skipper the twin-rig trawler the *Crystal Sea*, is known for letting scientists, artists and students come out for trips on his boat – 'Even if you're sick everywhere, livens the trip up a bit' – and agrees to my coming along for a week. I only learn after my trip of the rivalry between Newlyn and St Ives fishermen, the latter referring to themselves as Hakes, while the Newlyn men, who harbour a long-standing resentment towards the uppity north coasters, give them the more offensive nickname: Scaly Backs.

My first trawler experience is, however, cut short to a four-day trip due to the arrival of force 8 gales that batter the *Crystal Sea* from all angles as we head home. Despite its brevity, I feel content with my first experience of deep-sea fishing, proudly telling people I have *done* trawling. But fishing is more addictive than I imagine and the desire to go out to sea once more spreads like a rash across my body. This time I want to be out for longer, I want to get more involved, maybe with a more roughly hewn, typically Cornish, crew, on one of those rusting crafts I eye up on afternoon strolls around Newlyn harbour.

Months later, around dusk sometime in late November, I bump into the *Filadelfia*'s barrel-bellied skipper, Don, outside the Star pub. I know Don a bit already and reckon he and his boat fit the criteria for my second trawler trip perfectly.

'Don,' I ask, trying to make my request sound casual. 'Do you think there's any way I could come to sea with you?'

'Don't see why not,' he shrugs, scratching the grey stubble under his neck that he leaves unshaven when he's out at sea. 'When's good?'

'Next week?'

'Yep, sure, my darling.' He finishes his cigarette and heads back into the pub, calling back over his shoulder: 'See you next week then, Lamorna.'

And just like that the date is set, as if we were only going for a beer.

The next Monday I am walking down Newlyn's North Pier carrying a bag of wellies, several fleeces and a thick winter sleeping bag. There is a sharp bite in the air, which feels far more foreboding than the balmy morning that I headed out on the *Crystal Sea* back in May. The vague shape of the coming week on the *Filadelfia* looms before me, arresting and intimidating.

Each time I go on a new boat, I feel it is like meeting a stranger unwilling to give anything of herself away, just yet. I learn that the *Filadelfia* (PZ – Penzance – 542), is a 79-foot beam trawler. She was built in 1969, the same year man felt the Moon beneath his feet for the first time and, like *Apollo 11* she is a voyager, transporting man away from familiar landscapes into the unknown, protecting her crew from the mysterious waters existing just outside her thick, steel, yellow-painted shell. It is often said we know more about the entirety of space than we do of the oceans whose ebbing borders touch our earth, as if it were more natural that the human eye be trained upwards through telescopes than down into the world's depths. The partial nature of our knowledge of the sea feels almost a relief to me: there exists somewhere still that we have not mapped, whose every intimate part we have not inspected and dissected.

Originally worked by fishermen in Holland, the *Filadelfia* was not carried across the seas to Newlyn until 1987, along with three other fishing vessels hammered and riveted into existence in the same Dutch boatyard. While we are out at sea these sibling vessels stay close to us, their lights ballasts in the otherwise formless nights.

Your boat is much more than your office. It is where you sleep, eat, work, brush your teeth, smoke, laugh, watch telly and wait to go home. Each vessel becomes a figure to whom the fisherman feels deeply connected for the rest of his life. Before I set out on the *Filadelfia*, Perry, her previous skipper, tells me that if I go into the third bunk on the right-hand side of the sleeping cabin and look up, I'll find his name scored there, upon the ceiling. Like love hearts etched into tree bark, the impressions fishermen leave on the boats they have worked on throughout their lives is proof to future generations that they too once knew and loved them. In the French philosopher Paul Valéry's meditation on seashells, he distinguishes between a shell carved by a man, which must be carved from the outside in, so that it always bears some sign of its creator, and the mollusc, which 'exudes its shell', the two forming together, equally necessary to one another. Day by day the metal armour of each fisherman's vessel grows around them, the outside world less able to perforate it as they are enveloped more deeply into the folds of their shells.

Don stands on the raised wheelhouse balcony smoking, leaning right over the bulwarks while the *Filadelfia* spits out inky fuel into the harbour waters. As I watch him from under the shadows of the covered part of the harbour, Valéry's mollusc comes to mind – a creature of the sea, half-exposed from his protective casement, blinking up at the unfamiliar sight of the world outside his shell. Don spots me and yells out to sling my bag aboard and climb on over. I throw the bag, remembering mid-chuck that it contains my camera and wince as it lands on a coil of ropes on the deck. Before I follow it I take a moment to push my heels into the ground, holding on to the sensation of solidness, letting it steady me one last time. At last I jump down, missing the last few rungs of the harbour ladder, check my camera is still intact, and enter the galley.

The compact design common to almost all trawler interiors is uniformly satisfying. Tables are built into the walls, drawers fold away, fridges are tucked into corners and every door is kept from bursting open in rough seas by hinges locking them in place. In their streamlined sleekness, trawler galleys are a bit like Frankfurt Kitchens – the world's first fitted kitchens, devised in 1926 by the Austrian architect Margarete Schütte-Lihotzky, and designed to take up as little space as possible in order to fit in the small German apartments of the inter-war years. On fishing boats, appliances and cupboards hug the walls and handles are barely visible: each part of the galley is able to fold right in on itself like a person who is self-conscious of their body and manages to collapse themselves away into the corners of spaces. In the trawler galleys I have seen, tables are covered with sticky blue mats to prevent plates from sliding around and have racks fixed on top of them with holes to place mugs (these usually accumulate multiple packets of baccy and crucial condiments like mayonnaise during the week at sea). Benches lift up to reveal additional storage space for spices and multi-pack crisps. Ovens are usually dinky, with two hotplates on the stove, and this is kept scalding hot while at sea, so as to keep the whole space warm. Finally, each galley has a TV fitted above the doorway that stays on night and day, providing an unending background burble.

Considering our call time of 9 a.m. is fast approaching, I expect to see the crew rushing about unwinding ropes and checking gear on my arrival. But there is only one other person in the galley, rolling a fag and cradling a steaming mug of coffee. He doesn't seem remotely surprised by my arrival. I ask him where everyone is and aren't we meant to be heading off any moment now, while at the same time trying to match the fisherman to the names Don's provided me with. There is Kyle, the youngest member of the crew with bright red hair and beard; Scottish Stevie, and the mate, Andrew – 'the Lothario', so Don tells me. The man rolling a fag has a shining bald head, salt-and-pepper stubble around his jawline, a Cornish accent and the flirtiest smile I've ever seen. This must be Andrew. There is also something disconcerting about his appearance; he is the first fisherman over the age of forty I have met who does not have a beer gut. I regard his slim figure suspiciously as he looks out of the grubby porthole at Don, who is chatting to another fisherman on a boat nearby.

'When Don asks what time we're meeting,' Andrew explains, 'you always have to ask him "is that Don Time, or actual time?"' – 'Don Time' being a good hour behind Daylight Saving Time. I'd already experienced this warp in time in which Don operates. When we first met, back in April, he was an hour late and began with the excuse 'I don't believe in clock changes – what have the farmers ever done for us?', before jovially admitting a few minutes later: 'Nah, I was just hanging big time.'

I clamber down below to deposit my things and take a look at where I'll be sleeping for the next week, wanting to keep myself busy to prevent my nerves from catching up with me. At the bottom of the ladder I find a large cabin with maroon carpets and no portholes, darkness seeming to gather around its edges like excess material. There is an inveterate shabbiness to the cabin. Along its edges are six discrete cubbyholes, each the size of a bus window: these contain our bunks. There is also a larger, more conventional bed covered with a squashy pink duvet that awkwardly juts out into the middle of the room. Andrew informs me that this bed was built especially for Don because the other bunks were too small for him and hurt his back. Several of the cubbyholes have shiny curtains draped part way across them, while others have makeshift equivalents – towels or old t-shirts tucked into them. Each contains a pillow and sleeping bag from which some of the more personal items spill out: a few thriller novels, an extra jumper or two, a couple of Lion bars.

I duck my head under the third and final bunk on the right-hand side and see etched into the ceiling 'PERRY X'. Between Perry's old bunk and Don's superior sleeping arrangements is an empty bunk with no modesty hangings at all, which I assume must be mine. It is nothing like the luxury skipper's bed I was given on the *Crystal Sea*, which was separated from the crew's main sleeping area. Since no one is about, I squeeze myself into the bunk to get a better sense of the space. It is like being inside a coffin, but one in which the relatives of the dearly departed have massively undercalculated the length of the corpse and have folded the legs up in an undignified manner.

Curled up in the foetal position, I flick on the light switch directly above my head. It has the same two settings as the cabin lights in the *Crystal Sea*: either a clinical white or a seedy blue. I lie there for a while inside the *Filadelfia*'s dark stomach and listen to her groan slightly as she grinds back through her long memory of the changing crews and times in Newlyn.

Fishermen tend to speak of past time in terms of fish – from the pilchard days of the eighteenth century to the mackerel years of the 1960s, before pilchards were virtually wiped out, to the decades of cod wars with Iceland, through ling, hake and bass. When she first arrived in Cornwall in the late 1980s, the *Filadelfia* would have experienced the tail end of the heady days of British fishing. It was during this period that the excesses of the seventies – when fishermen across the globe were practically unchecked in their ravaging of the seas – came back to bite them with the resultant collapse in fish populations. After this, stringent quotas were brought in to regulate the amount of fish that could be caught: each country was given a yearly total catch limit based on a scientific assessment of the seas' resources, which was then divided amongst ports and the number of fishing boats in each port. This gave a maximum quantity of fish that a boat might catch yearly, though owners have been able to buy up more quota where available. In the 1990s, the *Filadelfia* would have heard her crew silently praying in their bunks for better times, as they despaired over the lack of fish and money to be made in fishing, which many thought spelled the end of the industry. Over 29 per cent of the UK fleet has gone since then. More recently she would have noticed the weary, furrowed brows of her men relax slightly as the graphs of fish stocks curved up once again. She carries the cares of all those who have slept in her cabin, who have dreamt the strange dreams you dream at sea.

I catch myself beginning to fall asleep as the *Filadelfia* gently rocks on her harbour moorings and sit up with a jolt, knocking my head against the low ceiling. By the time I re-enter the galley, squinting as my eyes readjust to the bright light coming through the porthole windows, I see the other two crew have arrived and are sitting around the table smoking with Andrew. Kyle, freckly and ginger as Don had described, asks if I am the new engineer. Andrew retorts at once: 'No, you great plonker! Does she look like an engineer to you?' – to which I take some offence.

There is still little sign that we are about to set off, so I make myself a cup of tea and take a seat in the galley. Waiting to go out to sea is not unlike queueing for a rollercoaster ride. You are aware of the intensity of the experience that lies ahead of you, and yet you cannot quite name or locate the origin of that fear until you are in motion, staring the loop-the-loop in the eye. 'On sailing day,' one fisherman told me, 'more than anything, you're just praying that something might go wrong that will delay you from leaving.' That way, you can get just a few more precious hours at home with your family.

Don tells me that we probably won't leave until the evening now, as he hasn't even done the weekly shop yet. He takes a brown leather notebook from his pocket and begins to write a lengthy list of supplies. This requires extensive planning, the crew constantly interrupting to make personal requests. Kyle and Andrew are particularly keen for more Twister lollies after they got through a whole packet in one day on the last trip. The list takes at least twenty minutes to compose, Don's notes sprawling across several pages, its eventual form complete with lists within lists and footnotes.

Curious, I offer to accompany Don on his supermarket mission. It turns out to be the shopping trip of my wildest childhood dreams – every sweet thing, every flavour of crisp and every pos-sible naughty treat that you could ever imagine wings its way into our trolley, most of it in vast quantities. We move through the shop in a kind of frenzy. No meat is overlooked, no aisle left unturned. The trolley heaves with towers of ribs, lamb shanks, pork chops, chicken burgers, whole chickens, bacon, sausages, beef, mince, pork pies, pork slices, ham slices and chicken slices – the high-rise city of a vegetarian's nightmare. Into a second trolley are slung chocolates and crisps, every kind of vegetable, five or six varieties of cheese, eleven huge cartons of milk, four bottles of arrabbiata sauce, four bottles of squeezy mayonnaise and thirty yoghurts – Don taking care to remove every cherry yoghurt from the industrial-sized box because 'cherry flavoured anything is disgusting'. By the end of our shop, in which we have covered every aisle of both Lidl and Tesco, the car is heaving with two mountainous trolleys' worth of jam-packed delights.

I head up to the heel-shaped wheelhouse and sit cross-legged on a maroon upholstered bench beside Don, who is making the last checks before our departure. This bench will become my main perch for the week – the place where I will sit slumped, my head resting against the wall, gazing out at a square of neatly portioned sea and sky through the wheelhouse window, listening to the yarning (storytelling) of whoever is on watch. The archaic term to *yarn* still abounds in Newlyn. Certain fishermen are renowned for their abilities to spin a yarn, amassing crowds at the pub as they offer tales about their time at sea. Don flicks some switches and the *Filadelfia*'s engine picks up from a low growl to an all-consuming roar. We pass the diminutive red and white lighthouse marking the harbour's edge, head through the Gaps – the thin opening between the harbour walls through which vessels come and go – and out into the dusky evening.

I have seen the sun disappear behind the land most days on my evening walks along the prom at Newlyn. Each time I wish it would set, just once, over the water, rather than sinking out of view behind buildings. I imagine the dark bay filling up with thick petrol and the sun a lit match, which, on touching the bay's perimeter, would set the whole sea alight. But as we round Land's End, with no coast left to obscure it, I finally see the sight I have longed for. The sun in its deep redness sinks down into the sea. I try to catch its last moment, the point at which the line of light is as thin and delicate as the space between an eyeball and an eyelid. And then it is gone entirely, leaving only a soft, red after-image. The performance is more rapid than I had expected, the sky dwindling from fire to dying embers in a matter of minutes. Kyle – affectionately referred to by the crew as either the 'ginger minger' or the 'ginger ninja' – sees my surprise and nods: 'It sinks fast, doesn't it? You don't notice how quick it goes on land.' At sea, your eye can trace the whole arc of the sun's path across the sky each day. There is rarely an hour when you don't look out at it, using its light to centre yourself against the undifferentiated sea.

I leave Don bent double over the many flickering screens before his skipper's chair and go out onto the balcony where Kyle and Andrew are stood in silence, watching the last remnants of the land fade into the gathering night. My stomach is tight, my nerves just holding, the rollercoaster clunking its way up towards the first drop. It is too late to ask to be taken back to land now.

The old Cornish word for the sound made by waves slamming against a fishing boat is *troze*. It mutated in form and meaning to become *droze*, the sound of multiple human voices speaking at once. The guttural notes of the *Filadelfia*'s engine almost cover it, but I can just make out the noise of the waves smacking her bow, the indistinct voice of the sea acting upon this man-made thing passing through it. To distract myself from the sense of dread I feel mounting at the back of my mind, I focus my attention on the diminishing coastline. I lean into the spray from the giddy heights of the wheelhouse balcony, echoing the position in which I found Don smoking first thing this morning. Looking back towards the land, the speckled lights of homes positioned along the very edge of the coast play tricks on me in the darkness. At times I am sure they are so distant that this must be the very last moment before they sink behind the horizon entirely, only for the lights from a collection of farms or a small hamlet to reappear again a second later, their distance impossible to judge.

There are several kinds of darkness. In cities the dark is not an absence of light but a variation of it: evenings are marked by the dusty orange washes from street lamps and the bright white strip lights from shops. Darkness in the countryside falls like a rich, thick shroud, complemented and intensified by the greenness of fields. At sea, darkness has a character of its own. It arrives from every angle, a vampire sucking at all sources of illumination. Colour drains from the world and the sky hardens to slate. As the last few lights of the coastline go out, all certainty vanishes; you can no longer distinguish up from down, sky from sea, but feel as if suspended somewhere between.

In the opening pages of *Moby Dick*, that most famous of fishing narratives, Herman Melville suggests that harboured within all men is an inexpressible desire to be near water. On a 'dreamy Sabbath afternoon,' his narrator Ishmael declares, 'posted like silent sentinels all around the town, stand thousands upon thousands of mortal men fixed in ocean reveries.' As we steam away through the darkness on the *Filadelfia*, each of us drawn by that same compulsion to voyage beyond the land's edge, I imagine the residents of Newlyn lined up along their harbour watching us disappear beyond the limit of the sea's horizon. So long as I stay out here looking back to shore, I tell myself, I can't really be about to spend eight days twenty-seven miles from the coast, working, eating and sleeping in the same room as a group of fishermen, most of whom I just met a few hours ago. So long as I keep my gaze fixed on where I imagine Newlyn to be, I have not really left.

A row of pale hands grips the rail of the boat's wheelhouse balcony, each of us looking out upon eternity. The *Filadelfia*'s derricks, the huge wing-like outriggers from which her nets drag, creak down until they are laid out parallel to the water. We are riding the seas on some prehistoric yellow bird, her skeletal wings the resting place for the multitudes of seabirds who have joined us on our voyage out. At this signal, the fishermen depart from the wheelhouse to set to work preparing the boat for her week at sea and I am left alone, the dome of the sky above me, the black waves far below. Dressed in their oilskins, the men head out onto the uncovered deck to spread the nets ready for the first haul. They will repeat this performance over fifty times more in the week to come. The ancient, bird-like being heaves her wings back up, pulling the chainmail-clinking nets high up into the air above us, before dropping them down into the water with a smack. They break its surface and disappear beneath. The nets will remain sunken for the next few hours, stroking along the seabed, gathering fish into their cod-ends.

The salt-licked wind makes my eyes red and I hold the rail tight until my knuckles turn white, in case a sudden wave should reach up and pull me over the side. I feel the thrum of the *Filadelfia*'s engines through the hard metal, the whole boat's energy seeming to course along the rail and up into my chest. Without warning, there's a yelp from the galley.

'Turn the boat around!'

'*What?*' yells Don, swivelling his torso around on his skipper's chair and elongating the *a* so that the word goes on for many seconds.

'There are no lollies! You forgot to get the lollies, you bastard!' Andrew cries with a cackle.

On nights like these, if viewed from a satellite, the open sea must resemble an empty blackness and the fishing boats dotted over its territory, auras of pale light. The only illumination comes from the boat's floodlights that bounce off the crests of waves as we break the water's surface, emphasising their brilliant whiteness.

In my journal I draw out these auras as leaf or teardrop shapes chasing across the page. It is not until much later that I read of *mandorlas* (the Italian for almonds) in Maggie Nelson's book *Bluets,* and realise that these were the shapes I was reaching towards in my drawings. 'Mandorla' is the term used for the halo of light that surrounds a holy figure. From the sixth century onwards scenes of Christ in transfiguration or ascension almost always included this radiant, gold-painted aureole, framing his person and raising him above the other figures in the scene. In mathematical terms, the mandorla symbol takes on the new name the 'vesica piscis', formed through the intersection of two identical circles, the centres of each lying on the perimeter of the other, like the circle of the sea and the circle of the sky, which the boat intersects and exists between. In Latin, *Vesica piscis* translates as fish bladder, after the shape of the conjoined dual air-bladders in fish. These so-called 'swim bladders', present in bony fish, are gasfilled sacks that allow fish to control their buoyancy, acting like a primitive lung that prevents them from sinking.

For me, the mandorla/vesica piscis is one of those satisfying, almost ideal shapes that once noticed can be found everywhere, its significance spanning art history, geometry and biology. The shape could also be said to resemble the frame of a fishing boat. Each trawler, pushing through the water in pitch black is surrounded by a mandorla, a glow that emanates outwards in an almond shape, protecting those inside.

My mind still lost in shapes, Don bangs the door open and yells: 'Dinner!'

I come in, my face red and my eyes wild from the sea.

'Chicken burgers and lovely fucking peas,' he announces. Don tends to use 'fucking' as a punctuation mark, a way to divide words and give certain ones emphasis.

Our first dinner on board is a comforting school-dinner-style meal, the chicken burgers and lovely fucking peas supplemented by chips cooked in a deep-fat fryer. Kyle assumes the role of cook, a job that involves scrupulous prepping to ensure each part of the meal is readied in between hauls. In the galley a stench of grease and fat and the strong disinfectant used to mask the lingering aroma of fish, circulate and intermingle with diesel and tobacco fumes to form a single and overwhelmingly potent smell.

I sit gazing at the huge portion of food placed before me, while the other men wolf down theirs in a few mouthfuls. Andrew teases Kyle about his cooking throughout the week, calling it 'kiddie food'. Tonight, it is the chicken burgers that are in the line of fire. He claims they are so far from being chicken ('the chemical rubbish they make those chicken burgers with!') that you would need to add a third option to which came first, the chicken or the egg? This fails to achieve the rise Andrew had hoped for. Kyle calmly takes it, looking down happily at his own rapidly vanishing plate of food. The crew polish off my last few chips and we sit together for a while cramped along the benches in the galley, each twisted round to face the TV, shouting answers at *The Chase* and jeering at contestants when they get obvious things wrong. Apart from our final dinner at sea, this is the only time we will all be together like this.

The show ends. Don returns to the wheelhouse and the other men split off to catch a few hours extra sleep before the first haul. I sit in the galley until the heady smells make me drowsy and I anxiously notice the first swirls of seasickness curling around my stomach. In an attempt to shake myself out of these feelings, I return to the wheelhouse. The haze of smoke hangs thickest up here. It is like entering a *fumoir* in a Parisian bar, all corners of the room dissolving in smog so that the space could be either endless or shoebox-sized. The men roll cigarette after cigarette to break up the monotony of the watch and keep themselves awake, each inhalation followed by a phlegmatic cough, the air becoming so dense as to take on the form of another fisherman.

One thing the men do not do at sea, though, is drink. It would be too dangerous, they tell me. Too much is at stake while you're steering a large boat across an open sea for your senses to be dulled by booze.

I stand next to Don's skipper's chair, an old leather car seat whose foam is leaking out along the seams, and lean upon its armrest for support, rocking back and forth on my heels with the motion of the boat. It is snug up here, the heater burning continuously. Next to us, Don's beloved money plant sways gently. He got her as a cutting three years ago and now she's a huge sprawling creature covered in deep green succulent leaves. Money plants are supposed to bring good fortune – Don says she's brought him a lot these last few years. 'In bad weather it proper dances,'

Kyle warns me, mesmerised by the waving plant, 'like it's trying to hypnotise you.'

I check my phone to find the last bars of signal have now gone. No new network message arrives on the screen. No *Welcome! You are now in the middle of the Deep Sea, you really are roaming now*. On the *Crystal Sea* we had our own Wi-Fi, so I ask Don what the *Filadelfia*'s account is so I can check in with my parents. 'There's no Wi-Fi on here!' he laughs. 'Do you know how much that costs at sea?'

'Right, yeah,' I say, feeling embarrassed and wishing I'd been able to let my parents know they wouldn't be hearing from me for the week.

There is no television up in the wheelhouse to mask the lack of human noise, no Wi-Fi to break up the monotony. As such, time is deeper here, the space widening without the endless flick of social media to flatten life down onto small, shiny surfaces. Long stretches of meditative quiet are occasionally broken up by conversations that are themselves nothing like the quickfire, get-to-know-one-another dialogues of the land. I have always believed that the freest exchanges occur when you are not facing one another: on walks, on benches, in cars with your feet up on the dashboard, and while staring at the sea. With your eye travelling freely, language becomes untethered. Each word is given the space to expand and drift. Here, the space between sentences becomes a kind of practised grammar that opens up between me and whoever is on watch. But for the next hour or so we do not speak at all. I stare at the variously whirring machines sending out readings that give a rough, brightly coloured sense of the world continuing beneath us. The Ground Definition Machine draws marks across the screen that resemble a red and green millipede slinking along the ground. If its body suddenly contorts upwards, suggesting the seabed rises dramatically, there is likely to be something large below us, such as an old anchor or submarine cables that we are in danger of pulling up in our nets, or, worse, the object could yank down one of the huge derricks and capsize us. On a trawler you are potentially only ever seconds away from catastrophe.

Don guides the *Filadelfia* along the course he has set using the compass that he turns by minute degrees, following the pink line mapped out along the AIS, the Automatic Identification System – a tracking device that plots the voyage of every water-bound vessel around the world. This first line leads to the location where Don made the first haul on his last trip. Beyond it the map becomes a chaos of spaghetti strings, the paths of previous trips criss-crossing over each other endlessly, along with markers of significance such as 'Transatlantic cables down here, keep clear', 'Huge turbot school here', or 'Carn Base: BIG ROCKS. AVOID!' The screen provides a spatial representation of the *Filadelfia*'s recent life history, the hundreds of voyages she has made layered on top of one other. If only we humans kept the same records – and could see the lines of our lives, observing those that become thick through repetition, the places to which we cannot help but return.

To take my thoughts off my mounting seasickness, I break the silence and lamely ask Don what he's thinking. 'I'm blank,' he tells me gruffly. I come to learn that Skipper Don is very different to the man I know on land. Out here he barely speaks. Here in the dark, the wheelhouse lights casting shadows across his lined forehead and eyes, he reminds me of a character from a Joseph Conrad novel.

In Conrad's narrative, centred on a boat called the *Narcissus*, the old sailor Singleton keeps himself apart from the other men on the boat. 'Alone in the dim emptiness of the sleeping forecastle,' writes Conrad, 'he appeared bigger, colossal, very old; old as Father Time himself, who should have come there into this place as quiet as a sepulchre to contemplate with patient eyes the short victory of sleep, the consoler.' Singleton is one of a dying breed of old mariners. 'He stood, still strong, as ever unthinking; a ready man with a vast empty past and with no future, with his childlike impulses and his man's passions already dead within his tattooed breast. The men who could understand his silence were gone – those men who knew how to exist beyond the pale of life and within sight of eternity.'

We have left the pale of life behind now. At sea, you enter into a kind of monastic existence: imprisoned and yet free, roaming, but in the most confined space possible. I slip off to bed, promising Don that I'll be up at dawn for the first haul of the day.

Lying in my bunk, I feel restless and try to draw my mind down to where the nets are trailing along the dark, clear waters below us. I imagine the huddle of fish building up inside the cod-ends. I will have to try and learn how to exist beyond the pale of life out here too, allow the sea to soothe my emotions and land memories, and make them more manageable.

4

GUTS

One of the frustrating side effects of seasickness medication is that it holds your body in such deep slumber that it becomes almost impossible to wake before its effects have worn off. Though I set my alarm for 5.45 that first morning on the *Filadelfia*, I sleep right through and rouse to find it is 9 o'clock and I am alone in the cabin. I imagine the crew glancing over at me sleeping soundly, while they have worked through the night – another dead-weight passenger they are bound to carry this week.

Sea dreams tend to be expansive and, more often than not, horrifying. My half-asleep journal entry from my first night in the hot, dark pink mouth of the *Filadelfia*'s cabin reads: 'Dreamt I was watching a chat show that got inside my mind' – and, as an afterthought: 'Sort of worrying it's still in there.' That is to say, within the dream, I could not shake the droning theme music that underlay this particular chat show, transposed directly from the trawler's own creaks and groans, until long after it was over. It was like a kind of tinnitus, a wordless tune that I feared would be stuck inside my head forever. The boat's music pierced my sub-conscious, undulating through my dreams.

It is strange trying to remember the experience of the dream now. Ordinarily my diary serves as the tip of an iceberg, telling me that there is some memory down there in the water and it is my job to dive below once more to rediscover its shape. With dreams it is the opposite: all I have left are the fragments I write down while cocooned in my sleeping bag, the ghostly blue light shining on my words. Even the handwriting of this particular dream entry is unfamiliar, as if a stranger snatched away my diary and wrote their own memory in it, leaving something impenetrable.

As I lie in my bunk, overheating in the tracksuit bottoms I'd been too exhausted to change out of, I try to calm my elevated pulse. I can still feel seasickness menacing somewhere about my person. And so, though I hate the way it muffles my senses, I take another pill before scrambling up the ladder to join the men upstairs.

I enter the galley to multiple jeers of '*Nice lie in?*', '*Get your beauty sleep?*', and '*You must have been so tired from all that work you did on the boat last night!*' I make a silent promise to myself that I will have at least proved to them that I am not completely redundant by next Monday.

Since everyone is seated about the table, I gather I must have woken up just after the Fishwife Call, when whoever is on watch puts the kettle on, makes mugs of coffee and then heads down to wake up the snoozing crew for the next haul. Every fisherman goes about the Fishwife Call in his own idiosyncratic manner. I hear of one skipper who screeches at the top of his lungs right next to the sleeping men: 'LET'S GET FISHING!' Don goes for more of an inaudible '*Alrightfuckers!*', while others risk their necks performing wild pranks, such as pouring water on sleeping fishermen's heads, before being chased up ladders by their victims as they swear they'll throw them overboard. Fishermen are also very particular about their mugs, I discover. Midway through my trip on the *Crystal Sea* I was quietly informed that I had been drinking out of the cup belonging to Sandris, a Latvian fisherman, and that he was very upset about it. On the *Filadelfia*, Don has the biggest mug, which has 'OLD MAN' painted across it in large blue letters; Stevie's declares 'CAUTION: I am horny'; Kyle's is one of those nondescript mugs that come free with some online purchase. I am given a blue, flowery patterned one for the week.

Each man takes two three-hour watches. They keep these same times for the rest of the trip to provide some semblance of structure to their days. Kyle has the morning and post-dinner watch; Andrew the afternoon and the so-called Dog Watch (from midnight to the witching hour at three); Stevie the early morning and early evening slots; Don fills in between these hours, returning to the wheelhouse to orchestrate most of the hauls.

The wheelhouse seems to transform into a new space during each portion of the day, the changing light passing through the line of windows somehow reconfiguring its interior. One crew member on the *Crystal Sea* – whose dad was nicknamed 'Force 8' because he was the kind of 'nutter who stayed out in huge storms and dodged waves rather than returning to the harbour' – told me how days are contracted into the two or so stressful hours it takes to haul, plus the watch you perform afterwards. As there are eight hauls every twenty-four hours, seven days at sea feels equivalent to fifty-six days on land. But it is a different kind of time; your family's lives go on, while you are frozen in this strange state of abeyance in the middle of the ocean.

Coffee downed, Andrew and Stevie pull their bright yellow oilskins and boots up over their clothes, snap on heavy-duty PVC-coated blue gloves and head out onto the open deck. In the Celtic myth of the selkie, seals shed their skins and climb up the sand dunes, shivering and holding their furless, pale bodies to them as they stumble uncertainly towards the world of men. In each of the manifold variations of the folk tale, the selkie is fated to fall in love with a person of the land while in their human form. Over time the selkie starts to forget the life they spent carving paths through the water with their strong flippers and settles into their human-shaped existence. And yet, in each tale, even as their partner tries desperately to keep them landlocked by hiding their sealskin or entreating them with love, the reader comes to realise that the selkie must at last return to their original form below the waves. There is no other ending possible to such stories.

Dressed head to toe in oilskins, the fishermen once more become creatures of the sea. I follow Don up into the wheelhouse. On the dashboard are a series of levers to slow the boat down, to put breaks on the hydraulic winches and then bring them up with a rattling whine. Every few seconds Don checks on the position of his crew outside – the machinery they operate is so heavy that, when fishermen have occasionally been caught unawares by it, there have been fatal accidents. In the skipper's log, kept in the wheelhouse of every boat, Don notes down the precise times of the haul, our position and whether we are with or against the tide.

Skippers' logs are intricate records containing the entire life of a fishing boat in degrees, time codes and numbers. Larry, a wiry ex-fisherman with a long grey beard, whose blog 'Through the Gaps' documents the daily comings and goings of Newlyn harbour, tells me that he thinks fishing is a 'three-dimensional profession – not like that lateral nine-to-five work in an office'. Skippers fluidly move between tidal time, the breeding and migration cycles of fish, crew meal and sleep times, and occasionally the social time continuing back home through phone calls or TV shows (I hear of one skipper who plans his haul times around *Emmerdale* and *Coronation Street* so that he doesn't have to miss any plotlines while at sea) – and, of course, the ever-ticking clock of economic time.

So tremendous is the pressure that Don barely sleeps at sea. There are skippers who respond to this burden by effing and blinding at their crew, raging at the smallest errors, and I'd half-imagined Don would be one of them. As it is, I never see him calmer than when he is stood before the wheelhouse window watching the haul. He stays well out of the general bustle of the boat, raising his voice on deck only to warn the crew if something has gone wrong. While the other men go down below, resting easy in the knowledge that their work is over for the next few hours, his mind turns over and over. At odd hours I find Don running through past trips in the log, roaming the AIS system, and plotting the *Filadelfia*'s next move.

The nets that have flowed silently below the water's surface for the last few hours, their loose strings floating outwards like the tangled strings of jellyfish, are suddenly wrenched up into the air. Both cod-ends bulge with a seething mass of fish. Sprouting in tufts from the nets are frayed orange plastic ropes called 'dollies', which provide buffers as the nets are dragged across the stony ocean floor.

There is something ridiculously flamboyant about their floppy, clown-orange hair as they rise up from the sea. Working in mirror-image synchronicity on both sides of the boat, the two men heave the nets up and over the deck, tug out the knots in the cod-ends so the contents cascade across the deck in a sudden expulsion.

The deck is now swamped with fish of all colours and kinds, shaking and fizzing across the floor. A popular saying amongst fishermen is: 'It all comes out the cod-end', which is a bit like, 'It all comes out in the wash'. There exists fisherman lingo for almost every species: 'morgy' are dogfish, sea urchins 'zarts', 'paws' crabs, 'gizzy' spider crabs. Those creatures that have survived being hauled out of the water make violent, blind bids for freedom. Looking down from the wheelhouse they appear as sparks splitting off from a central firework. Lastly, the men climb inside the net itself to shake out the last few tangled fish. As soon as they're emptied, Don shoots the nets back out behind the boat. ('Keep the gear wet; never waste a tow'.)

The *Filadelfia* does not have a sophisticated conveyor belt, as do some trawlers, so the crew drop to their hands and knees and begin sorting through the congeries of fish piled up on top of one another: lemon, megrim, Dover sole; monkfish, haddock, bream; John Dory, crabs, one shining turbot – currently the highest value fish on the market – and cuttlefish, called 'black gold' because there is no quota for them, meaning boats may catch as many as they wish. Since the numbers of cuttlefish in the Indian Ocean have declined due to disease, the Cornish fishermen currently supply the rest of the world.

During our whole time at sea the *Filadelfia* only pauses for those few minutes when the cod-ends are suspended above the deck. Then she's off again, dragging her nets up and down the seafloor in deliberate lines under Don's direction, like a farmer ploughing his fields. It feels disconcerting not to have an end point in mind, to pass back and forth over this vague territory for days and days like wanderers lost in a desert. When the *Filadelfia*'s bow points towards the west I am aware that the closest landmass is North America, thousands of miles across the ocean.

While the men work, Don turns on a large sound system at the back of the wheelhouse. The speakers with their multicoloured lights are his pride and joy, together with a library of eclectic music that he has spent years carefully cultivating. Each morning he chooses a different genre to boom out through the wheelhouse at ear-splitting volume. One morning we have a pub rock session, moving between the Eagles, Led Zeppelin and Dire Straits, another it is Dolly and country classics. Today he chooses 'Elvis with the Philharmonic Orchestra'. Don's slippered feet, usually left dangling from the high skipper chair, tap along to the rhythm, as he croons softly under his breath to 'Can't Help Falling in Love'.

The soaring music provides the backing track to the work going on down below. Andrew and Stevie fling the fish through the air into buckets. Every time they come across small sharks wriggling out of the pile and snapping their strong jaws, they fire them back into the sea like shot-puts. I lock eyes with one and see across its rubbery face an expression of utter disbelief as it flies right past the wheelhouse window. The speakers flash between pink, blue and red, making it look as if we have temporarily escaped trawler life and found ourselves in some downtown karaoke bar.

Leaving Don with his head sticking out of the wheelhouse window greedily looking out for more turbot, I put on my wellies and pick up a pair of thick blue gloves. Outside the clouds stand around the sky like a waiting herd and the sea is mute. Two of the crewmen are leaning over a metal table in the bow and have already started to gut. They regard me with bemusement as I stagger over to them: 'Can I help at all?' Andrew grins, before handing me a small knife along with a large megrim sole. Megrims are the fish we bring up in the greatest quantity and are also probably the easiest to gut. I hold up a silty brown one and feel it squirm in an attempt to escape. The sunlight shafts through its body, displaying an opaque line of detailed bones.

The men break from their work to show me how to gut, instructing me to turn the fish over and make an incision into the space just below the head on its flesh side. I find a horrifying kind of satisfaction in gutting. It is the most visceral experience. I make a gash with the knife in the shape of a thin smile and dig the knife deep inside. Being clumsy, it takes me several minutes to pull the glistening purple, pink and crimson guts out. They eventually come out in a single strand, like the magician's trick of bringing out a stream of coloured handkerchiefs from his sleeve in one flourish. The guts comprise intestines, the vesica piscis 'swim bladder', and a strawberry-yoghurt-coloured liver so soft it falls apart as soon as you touch it and has to be flicked out with the knife. Due to my inability to aim, most of this liver lands in my hair which over the week grows thick with unspecified blood and guts. I continue to find scales attached to my t-shirt and bare arms long afterwards, so that I look as if I am slowly transforming into a hybrid fish built up of multiple species.

To distract myself from seasickness during my first trawler trip on the *Crystal Sea*, I tried reading a book I'd brought with me: *The Rings of Saturn*, W. G. Sebald's account of his psychogeographic meanderings along the Suffolk coastline. I became fixated on a page included a diagram of the reticular structure of the quincunx that Thomas Browne, the seventeenth-century English polymath, considers in meticulous detail in *The Garden of Cyrus*, an entire treatise dedicated to examining the quincunx. Sebald notes that, for Browne, this 'decussation' (crossing of lines, as in the letter X) was ubiquitous. He saw it 'in certain crystalline forms, in starfish and sea urchins, in the vertebrae of mammals and the backbones of birds and fish'. Perhaps because of my seasickness, and the sleepiness the seasickness pills induce in me, the structure became imprinted on my mind. During that voyage, I grew convinced that I saw the pattern everywhere – not just in the nets hauled in and out of the sea, but in the streams of light crossing over the ripples in the water and drawn onto the backs of gutted fish. Now back on a trawler once more, I see the pattern again, this time in the tangled string of glistening guts I drag out of the megrim.

When I was younger we had a dog that loved to help my dad with the gardening. She would enthusiastically dig up each bulb he planted with an expression that suggested she felt certain she was being supremely helpful. I provide the *Filadelfia* fishermen with a similar level of support, working at approximately a sixteenth of their speed so that I am still gutting my last megrim long after they have begun on the other baskets of sole.

Once the megrims have been dealt with, Andrew pours the next two baskets onto the table: pale lemons and stippled-grey Dover sole. These are much more popular and attract better prices than megrims, which tend to be shipped off to Europe. Lemons are 'slippery buggers', as Andrew puts it, that require chasing around the table, a procedure only made more challenging by the fact that my PVC gloves are four sizes too big. Each time I get my fingers around a lemon's girth, it squeezes out like soap in a bath. I finally manage a firm hold by wedging my finger just below its muscular eye. Once I've clamped down on it, the men instruct me to make a minute incision slightly higher up the body than on a megrim, and then tear out its guts. Alarmingly, even after its insides have been pulled clean from its body, the lemon sole continues to flap and twist out from my hands.

Stevie watches me jab at the lemons. 'You're lucky they can't scream,' he says.

It takes years before new fishermen learn the *knack* of it, Stevie tells me. Out on fishing boats you hear the word *knack* constantly. The *knack* does not come easily; youngsters must work for years as an apprentice until the actions become natural and flowing. 'You can't just turn up here and say I'm gonna be a fisherman,' says Andy, a St Ives fisherman with an illustrated fish tattoo running down his arm that reads 'HAKE AND PROUD'. 'It doesn't work like that. You've got to grow up through the bloody ranks: can you mend? Can you splice? How fast can you gut? We was all brought up like that. You're always trying to get better at this, get better at that. Fishing never stops moving, you know?'

At such close proximity it is a joy to watch the men's sleight of hand as the intestines spill out in a single circling motion.

'I reckon I'd be a good surgeon,' Kyle announces as he pauses to slice through a thick string of guts from a particularly large Dover, which slop out onto the table. 'Only thing is I wouldn't know how to put it all back in again afterwards.'

After the gutting is over the men hose down the deck, washing back into the sea those last few living fish, gasping for water, and the foul soup of hacked-out innards, which causes a frenzy amongst the gulls. Andrew and Stevie pull up the weighted trap-door next to the gutting table to reveal a vertiginous ladder leading into the 'fish room'. As I clamber down, the boat jerks in response to a large wave, almost causing me to fall several metres. At the bottom, I am met with an arctic scene. The ceiling heaves with stalactites and there is a large wall of solid ice that will be broken up and used over the week to freeze the fish. Piled about the edges of the room are several teetering towers of green boxes containing fish divided into their particular species and frosted over with ice, all caught during the three hauls that I slept through.

After breaking off ice shards with a pickaxe, Stevie starts layering the fish into the boxes, being careful to place the fish all the same way up (as certain species drain of colour if they are laid the wrong way and then fetch less at auction), creating intricate tessellations that he then covers over with ice.

There is not a moment when I am specifically told that my main job for the week will be packing monkfish, but rather it is communicated to me wordlessly as it so often is in fishing – work portioned out intuitively. I am especially fascinated by monks. They are the bulldogs of the sea: huge and globular, horribly ugly with rows of pointed teeth. When they come up in hauls, monks often have multiple partially chewed up fish dangling halfway out of their mouths. By the time they reach the fish room their bulbous heads have been hacked off with a machete-like knife and all that is left are their great meaty tails.

As the towers of fish boxes grow higher over the week, I have to climb up to reach the ones that graze the ceiling, balancing precariously atop a high-rise of cuttlefish from whose boxes cling ominous, black icicles mixed with their ink. I stand with my feet on either side of a cuttle box's thin rim, knowing at any moment I may fall in and be drenched in the sticky black substance. The men tell me that sometimes, days into a trip, there will suddenly come a thrash from within a tower of boxes and an eel, waking up from a cold coma, will try to burst out from its frozen prison.

The hours rush by during gutting, in sync with the frenetic nature of the work. Working down in the fish room the sounds of the sea die out and time seems to freeze with it. After an hour there I begin to feel deeply uncomfortable, in a catacomb of dead fish below the sea's surface, the only way out being a sheer metal ladder leading to a heavy trap door.

When the monkfish are all boxed up I scramble back up the ladder, take a gulp of sea air and go to the galley for a cup of tea. A few minutes later the men come in, peeling their gloves off and washing their hands in a vain attempt to rid themselves of the fish stench. Finally, Stevie heads down to the engine room to check everything is still in working order. From the *Filadelfia*'s depths there comes a violent roar, as if there is a hidden beast kept captive below deck, and Stevie returns looking satisfied. The haul is over.

That afternoon the weather is bleak, the sea without shape and there is a dreariness that pervades the whole boat. It comes from an unspoken recognition that this is how it goes from here: seven days of uniformity ahead of us.

A telltale sign of oncoming seasickness is continuous yawning. As soon as Kyle begins cooking that night's supper in the hot galley I cannot stop the yawns from coming. I offer to work as Kyle's sous-chef to distract myself and turn to face the fridge every time I feel another retch rising in my throat. Chopping carrots, potatoes, onions and cabbage with a large blunt knife on a boat whose movements you are still not quite used to is challenging enough but knowing that at any moment you might spew your own guts up onto valuable food adds another layer of trepidation to the work.

As we chop Kyle begins to grow suspicious and asks me how I'm feeling.

'Yeah, yeah. I'm fine!' I say in far too high-pitched a tone. He eyes me sideways as I stifle another yawn. Seasickness covers you like a shawl, as if the rest of the world is occurring at a distance from you. A desperate wish to be back home, or at least to be back on the sofa at Denise and Lofty's, comes over me with such intensity that I nearly burst into tears.

I think about homesickness often during my time in Newlyn, but especially while I am out at sea: it is a longing for home that, at its worst, takes on physical manifestation, a gut-wrenching pain that becomes almost more real than your present circumstances. The word seasickness does not work in quite the same way. While equally often all-too-physical in its symptoms, it is not that you are sick for the sea, nor sick of it, but rather the sickness seems to come from not understanding it. Your body, unused to the unfamiliar rhythms of the water beneath you, physically rejects them. Back when we were steaming away from the land on the *Crystal Sea*, watching Newlyn harbour fade away, a crew member told me reassuringly: 'The penultimate stage of really bad seasickness is being terrified you will die. The ultimate stage...' he continued, taking a long, dramatic drag on his cigarette, '... is being petrified you won't.'

It is the most common question people ask me about my time on boats. 'Weren't you sick the whole week?' It is also the way people tend to conceive of their own relationship to the sea – either a smug 'I love the sea; I never get sick', or an admission that they dread even half an hour on the water because they get so ill they have to spend the entire trip with their head over the bowl of a toilet. Lofty always wished he could have been a fisherman, but the one time he went out on a trip he got so sick he couldn't leave his bunk and, not knowing where else to aim in his desperate state, ended up vomiting into his own boot.

Both Kyle and his cousin began fishing full-time as teenagers. During those early years, neither boy got seasick once. While older men would lean grey-faced over the side of boats in force 10 gales, the two boys would look pityingly at their nauseous crewmates, understanding nothing of their torment. And yet, Kyle tells me, as soon as his cousin went back to sea following the birth of his first daughter he was seasick for the first time. Ever since then he has been ill for at least a day each week he goes out fishing.

Seasickness is not simple; it is not a condition you have or do not have. Rather, it speaks of larger truths about your relationship to the world you leave behind and the watery one you enter into. Like a horse that senses its rider's fear the moment they pull themselves up onto its back, the sea, in some mystical way, gauges your emotional state. Fishermen tell me gleefully about the number of scientists, filmmakers and artists who have come out on trips with them and not left their bunks for the whole week, except for urgent trips to the toilet to throw up. These passengers return to the land with no better understanding of fishing than when they steamed off. On the *Crystal Sea* and *Filadelfia*, I try to follow the advice of the crews and practise a kind of meditative holding back of the land from my thoughts. Both times this only half works and only for the first few days. Still, I do wonder if part of the reason that seasickness did not completely overwhelm me is because, like Kyle and his cousin before they had children, I do not yet have anything that truly ties me to the land.

Unable to hold back the tide any longer, I hurtle out of the galley towards the bathroom. As soon as I lean forwards over the toilet, a great wave of sickness leaps from my body. It seems to keep coming and coming, my entire insides expelled into the toilet bowl. Tremors rip through my chest. I take deep breaths and steady myself against the bathroom wall.

The storm passes, I return to the galley relieved and enjoy a relaxed evening laughing and joking with the rest of the crew. It is only later that I admit to Kyle it took all my strength not to projectile vomit onto his carrots earlier. He laughs and tells me he kind of wishes that I had, as it would have been hilarious.

Before I go to bed I sit in the wheelhouse with Don, the window slightly open, allowing a cold draught to rush through it and mingle with the warm air from the blazing heater that stays on throughout. Sitting down beside him with my flowery mug of tea, I take out the book I have chosen for this trip. *Arctic Dreams*, by the American environmental writer Barry Lopez, charts the five years he spent as a field biologist studying the wilderness of the Arctic region. It is Lopez's account of narwhals – the grey, marble-patterned close relative of the beluga whale and the only other surviving member of the Monodontidae family, or white whales – that is of particular interest. We still know more about the planets of the solar system than we do about the narwhal, says Lopez. The creature is often considered to be the mythic root of the unicorn, whose horn was reimagined over time as coming from a land mammal. Perhaps because of these horns the narwhal has long unfairly been considered a harbinger of death. Their very name comes from the Old Norse *nar*, meaning 'corpse', and *hvalr*, 'whale'. In the eighteenth century the naturalist Georges-Louis Leclerc, Comte de Buffon, described the rare creature as one that 'revels in carnage, attacks without provocation and kills without need'. As Lopez writes, 'animals are often fixed like this in history, bearing an unwanted association derived from notions or surmise having no connection at all with their real life.'

On the *Filadelfia* I begin to associate the fishermen with the narwhal – both misunderstood hunters travelling quietly through the seas. Lopez suggests that 'perhaps only musicians have some inkling of the formal shape of emotions and motivations that might define such a sensibility as the narwhal.' Watching Don in the wheelhouse, his eyes tracking across the array of machines pulsing out their readings of the sea, I wonder if skippers too might have such an inkling of the immensely complex, ever-shifting world of the narwhal.

Just as I am settling into *Arctic Dreams*, Don blows the boat's booming foghorn. 'You better put in your book that we are plagued with shit-brained fucking seagulls,' he growls, startling the innumerable gulls hitch-hiking on the ship's bow.

I consider some of the details I've learnt about Don. One Newlyn fisherman told me that on the bus home from school, Don would never sit with the other children. He would stand at the front watching the road, chatting to the driver, and always with a packet of crisps stuffed in each pocket from which he would take alternate handfuls. Another remembers him as the only kid who, come rain or shine, would be in the harbour every day after school and at weekends, lending skippers a hand with their boats, covered from head to toe in fish scales.

5

THE SING OF THE SHORE

Early on in my stay in Cornwall I discover by chance, in the
Cornish history section of Penzance's Morrab Library, a small
book of Cornish sea words written in the 1960s. In the introduction its author, R. Morton Nance, explains that it was the
disappointing lack of specificity in the *English Dialect Dictionary*,
which translated the Cornish word *gijoalter* vaguely as 'part of
the rigging of the ship', that first spurred him on to create his
Glossary of Cornish Sea-words.

As part of his research, Nance embarked on a series of visits
to every harbour in Cornwall to hear first-hand from fisherfolk
'the old words and ways at sea as they remembered them'. There
is *cabarouse* – a noisy frolic or drinking bout; *cowsherny* – when
the sea looks as if it is discoloured by cow dung; *prinkle* – to
sparkle with phosphorescence in scattered points of light; *ouga* –
the stench of fish. These words, brimming with and redolent of
the sea, equip me with a vocabulary with which to articulate my
Cornish experiences. One night I see the whole sea *prinkle* as
a gleaming shoal of pilchards is brought to the water's surface;
ouga follows me everywhere, gets into my nostrils, not just on
trawlers, but for many days after fishing trips. Each voyage back
to the harbour is celebrated by a wild *cabarouse*.

But the phrase that acquires most meaning for me is 'the sing
of the shore' – defined by Nance as 'the sound made by waves
breaking, varying with the nature of the shore – sand, pebbles,
boulders, scarped cliff, or reefs and ledges of rock – and thus giving
the experienced fisherman an indication of his position when fog

or darkness makes land invisible'. As I say the phrase, I imagine old Newlyn fishermen leaning out over bulwarks to listen for the particular note sung between shore and sea, delimiting the coastline and guiding them even through the thickest of sea fogs.

I keep a Dictaphone in my pocket and begin harvesting sounds on it. After carefully labelling each recording I add it to my museum of littoral sounds until I have built up a whole musical sphere carried inside the device. Later, when I am away from Newlyn and am craving re-immersion in the place, I hold the Dictaphone up to my ear like a shell and hear again the rage of the sea on a black night captured from the balcony of the *Filadelfia*, the yarns of fishermen told to me in pubs muffled by the blaring jukebox, the fish merchants yelling prices in the early morning auction, the scuffle of pebbles as I make my way across a quiet beach on a wind-rent day. As I listen Newlyn becomes visible to me once more, the sing of the shore continuing to ring outwards.

There are two paths out of Newlyn heading towards Land's End. One leads up beside the main road to Penlee Point and the other down to the sea, where you find a rocky shore on one side and a concrete wall dense with graffiti – together with a half-roof structure to retreat under in a sudden shower – on the other.

I take the lower path. There is no one else around apart from an elderly woman in a dark coat down to her ankles and a long brown plait snaking down her back. She seems not to notice me as she looks straight out at the sun-dashed water, her feet practically curled over the edge of the rocks that border the sea. For a moment I consider turning around and going back the way I've come, but when I catch sight of a slender object raised to her lips, from which comes a haunting sound, I find myself compelled towards her. As I near her, I recognise from the kind of the sound and then from the woman's finger movements that the object is a small wooden recorder and that the woman is playing her melody directly to the sea. I move closer until I am standing right behind her shoulder, listening to her play. The woman does not break from her music or take her eyes off the sea for even a second and I wonder if she is aware of my presence at all.

I listen to her for a long while, her music filling the space between sea and land; a woman looking at a woman looking to the sea. I let my gaze follow hers, to where all eyes in Cornwall cannot help but turn. And as I look, there are words contained within the waves, etched out in shimmering lines, and I read them as an incantation produced by the woman's wordless song. When they touch the clefts of cliffs or pour into the sand these words are deposited there in small pieces. All that the sea comes into contact with has traces of these incantations, in the same way that music is scratched onto a record. This is how the water tries to tell us its ways.

I leave the lone figure enacting her own sing of the shore back to the waves – 'I am here. This is my nature. Are you listening?' – and continue up to where the paths meet once more on the way to Land's End.

6

LINES THROUGH ROCKS

At the very end of the prom, on the edge of the town's sea-facing green, stands the *Newlyn Fisherman Memorial*. Unveiled to the public in 2007, the 10-foot high bronze and granite figure, cast by local sculptor Tom Leaper, commemorates all those fishermen from Newlyn lost to the sea since 1980 – over twenty in all. A thin, dull green patina has already formed over the fisherman's exterior, giving him a weather-worn look.

Though dressed in the simple fisherman's attire of oilskins and a beanie, there is something of the warrior in the statue. At night, when he is lit up from below causing shadows to fly up his face and highlight his strong features, he has something of the Riace Warriors, the two life-sized Greek bronzes cast between 460–430 BCE discovered accidentally off the coast of Italy and dragged from their sea graves during the 1970s. Impervious to the water, each aspect of their muscular forms has been perfectly preserved. It is difficult to believe the warriors, known simply as Statue A and B, come from another civilisation. A, with the more youthful stance, is thought to have been sculpted first, and B, the older warrior, with a softer posture and gentler facial expression, thirty years later.

It is hard to place the age of Newlyn's bronze fisherman. His features are simple and, rather than wrinkles, the sculptor has roughened the metal to make it look as if his whole face is alive and in motion. Between his hands, the fisherman holds taut a line of rope that ends in a loop at either end, ready to cast. At first I had assumed from his stance – left foot ahead, the momentum carrying him forward – that he was casting the line out into the water. But I had been looking at the sculpture all wrong. The man is not casting out but coming home, ready to throw the noose of rope over the harbour wall and tether his boat to the land.

In front of the statue this morning leans a man with his back to the promenade, his gaze following that of the fisherman as he looks fixedly towards the horizon. This is Roger, a retired geologist from Newlyn, who called me earlier this morning to say we should meet here at noon so he can show me the long history of Newlyn.

I stand alongside him, gazing out at the almost perfect curve of Mount's Bay. As soon as he notices me he gives me a wave and introduces himself, before retrieving from his bag a plastic wallet containing several complex maps of Cornwall, with patches of various colours and gradations of shading illustrating the different rock types that have continually risen, eroded and been covered over during the county's creation. In cities such formations are suffocated deep beneath roads and pavements so that one almost forgets there ever existed a natural landscape in the first place. But the largely untampered Cornish coastline stretches for over 630 miles; its bald cliffs act like time exposed, their many layers – some with lines of dark orange copper running through them – recounting the story of the county's ancient past.

I soon realise that a geologist's sense of time is not like that of ordinary people. It is not even like that of ancient historians. Roger refers to the last ice age, over 11,700 years ago, as recent history. His arms rise automatically as he speaks, describing the dramatic landscape into existence before my eyes. He tells me about the Devonian age, around 400 million years ago, when the continents were just rising from the previously borderless ocean, and Cornwall lay in tropical latitudes south of the equator. It was in Devon that the red sandstone from the period was first found, but the era is also known by the more appealing name, the Age of Fish, marking the period during which the first ancestors of sharks and amphibians, as well as thousands of new species of fish, evolved.

We travel on through time, past the mass extinctions at sea that coincided with the end of the Devonian age, to the start of the Permian period, at which point every continent was united in the vast form of Pangea. In those ancient days, Roger explains, Cornwall's landscape resembled a red desert comprised of great sloping mountains. By the end of the Permian period, 280 million years ago, the continents had begun to split, soon forgetting they had once shared an undivided earth. Devon and Cornwall were first joined together in a granite landmass called the Cornubia, the medieval Latin name for Cornwall.

As we use tales gleaned from ancestors to make sense of the fabric of our own lives, so I hold onto this information in my understanding of Cornwall. There was a time when Cornwall and Devon were an island, a great, granite ship drifting through the seas. It was not until the Cretaceous era that Cornubia was bound to the rest of the British Isles and mainland Europe with it. Erosion gradually reduced its once imposing mountains to gentle plateaus. As told by Roger, these natural changes acquire an almost mournful tone, as if this land, once regal and violent in its contours, was pacified by the elements. Though much of the original granite has been long covered over by the slate and sandstone, there are places where it is still exposed today, like the Tors in Bodmin, areas in which the past cuts back up through time.

Where rows of houses lie neatly today, mountains burst up through the ground, and plains of desert stretch out into the sea, onto which I drop the fishermen of Newlyn, their faces covered by scarves to protect them from the heat and excoriating winds as they trek across red sands towards their distant ships. Time races on. I see oceans come in to envelop the land, before washing out again. I see whole ice ages crawl up through the dunes, allowing only the most meagre tundra to survive within their barren landscapes, and then I see them thaw once more. I see the trees of the now sunken, petrified oak forest below the waters of Mount's

Bay – still visible when destructive waves strip the coastline right back. Finally, Roger draws for me the first human inhabitants of the area, who initially occupied a small corner of the bay, finding shelter beside what was once Gwavas Lake – *gwavas* a Cornish word meaning winter dwelling. Through Roger I understand that humanity's mark upon the earth is truly infinitesimal; our claims of ownership over this peninsula that we have barely known, that has barely known us, laughable. As his timeline rolls slowly down into the present day, Roger packs his maps back up and we leave the fisherman's memorial behind to make our way down onto the pebble beach between Newlyn and Penzance.

The tide is at its lowest ebb for our rock tour, the water leaked right out, revealing the secrets of the beach's rocky bed. Today there are large swathes of sea mist draped over the two ends of Mount's Bay, the wind howls and the beach for once is clear of people. Roger starts by pointing out an almost imperceptible line of rocks jutting out of the water parallel to St Michael's Mount, which he explains is the top of a long dike (an inclined table of rocks that cuts through the bedding of the existing ones) of blue elvan – a greeny-blue, fine-grained rock almost exclusive to Cornwall. In the eighteenth century, multitudes of rich, black cassiterite (tin oxide) veinlets were discovered within this dike – which could be profitably mined, if only someone were able to get to them. It was not until 1778 that Thomas Curtis, a poor middle-aged miner from Breage, near Helston, sought to construct a mine right under the sea to extract the precious mineral. A retrospective piece on the mine, written in 1949 and published in the *Mineralogical Magazine*, describes Curtis's plan for the Wherry Mine with hyperbolic delight as being 'unique in the boldness of its conception, romantic in the extreme in its situation and execution.'

Most assumed that Curtis's scheme was the daydream of a madman, expecting him not only to fail, but most likely to lose his life in the undertaking. And yet, undeterred, he single-handedly set out to build a submarine mine using black gunpowder to explode the wet rock – a miraculous feat in itself. Curtis had to limit his work on the mine to the summer months since that was the only time of the year when the dike was exposed above sea level. It took him three years of intermittent but intensive work before his submarine mine was completed. During this time the sea burst through the mine on several occasions, destroying the shaft and forcing him to begin from scratch.

By Curtis's death in 1791, the subterranean 'Wherry Mine' – so-named because the mine had been worked using wherries, light flat-bottomed boats, to carry the ore to the shore – was one of the most profitable in Cornwall. Accounts tell that the mine was 17 fathoms deep and that while working in it you could hear the sea roaring above you, threatening at every moment to break through and drown all those inside. In 1798 an American ship cut adrift in a storm and struck the turret, destroying the mine – summers of work in extraordinarily precarious conditions lost to the sea in a matter of minutes. Despite several plans to reopen it, the Wherry Mine remains untouched. Its dug-out crater hides just below Mount's Bay, an Aladdin's cave filled with a 'ground-mass of pinkish fine-grained orthoclase with sparsely distributed phenocrysts of quartz and innumerable small cavities plugged with scaly crystals of secondary chlorite and occasionally minute prisms and radial aggregates of dark brown to black tourmaline.'

We set out along the beach. Every now and then Roger pauses to pick up a rock that has caught his eye in order to map out its complex composition to me. Each rock is a time capsule, he tells me. A dark, hexagonal rock speckled with white flakes is porphyritic. The reason you can see the crystals inside it, which look like ripped-up fragments of paper pressed into the stone, is because it is fine-grained. Roger holds the rock gently, feeling along its sea-smoothed surfaces like a palm reader, following the lines along it that lead to plains of elvan, which inform him this rock has itself come from the Wherry Mine. In between these moments, with our heads down scanning the rocks, Roger begins to describe to me the lines that have gone into making his own life.

'The time of the now,' wrote philosopher Walter Benjamin, 'is shot through with chips of messianic time.' The past runs in veins

through every present moment like the striated lines of minerals –
quartz, tourmaline, copper. Roger tells me that his father worked
at Penlee Quarry, just along the coast from Newlyn, and would
bring home rocks for him to study as a young child, instilling in
him a wonder in the knowledge that every rock can teach you
something about the planet. It was this spirit that Roger inherited.
He recently found a black and white picture of his mother and
father, taken long before he was born, grinning arm in arm while
deep below ground exploring an old tin mine. They made each
other adventurous, Roger tells me, a quality he not only admires,
but believes is paramount if one is to truly live in the world.

Finding a student who was genuinely excited at the prospect
of geology, Roger's teacher at Newlyn's Tolcarne School set up
an informal geology club during the dinner hour. It was in these
sessions that Roger would learn about the different ages of the
earth, the formation of its volcanoes and the glinting minerals
that traverse its rocks. After he finished school, Roger worked
briefly at the Penlee Quarry, as his father had.

At twenty-one Roger's desire for exploration took him on an
aeroplane to South Africa to work on a De Beers diamond mine
deep within the bush. He picks up another rock, much smaller
than the last, and holds it out to me. It is quartz and schorl, a
deeper black version of tourmaline, a rock-forming mineral. 'I
reckon it could have come down the Coombe River,' he tells me;
this is the river in Newlyn that flows from a reservoir somewhere
between the two coasts and all the way out to the sea. As soon as
he places one rock down, he finds another just past it that fascin-
ates him even more – 'You don't know where to stop!' The words
he uses to explain their compositions are pure poetry: granitic,
porphyritic, quartz, olivine and feldspar – itself a mineral that
varies from red, pink, and white (orthoclase) to green, grey and
white (plagioclase) – each speckled and pockmarked by flakes of
fine grains and crystals. There is always some trace, Roger tells
me, of the history of things, the impressions humans have left on
them. The term for the study of rock layers in geology is stratig-
raphy, but it is also used in archaeology to describe the technique

of seeking out the contexts of rocks, discovering the events that have left detectable traces on their surfaces – in the same way we might scan one another's bodies, looking for those distinctive lines and marks which tell us something unspoken about the stranger opposite us on the train, or the friend we grew up with but have not seen for years, or the person we are falling in love with. A geologist's task is to see beyond the ways in which time tries to smooth out difference, examining layers in order to iso-late each shift to our world, to feel every fault line. We discuss how hard this is to do this with people, to imagine our lives not as one continuous line, but comprised of hundreds of versions stacked up behind us, and hundreds more ahead of us too, like those pairs of facing mirrors that make your reflection curl up infinitely on either side of you.

It was during this period in South Africa that Roger first met Poppy. He says her name in a way that I have never heard anyone speak a person's name before. Without needing to mention their relation, that single two-syllable word 'Poppy', seems to stand for the whole earth, all matter. 'Who's Poppy?' I ask, faltering over the word, knowing, without quite knowing how, that such a question cannot be answered casually. 'She was my wife,' Roger tells me. 'She died this year.'

We walk on. Like most young people, I am not yet comfortable with silences and desperately seek a new thread of conversation amongst the stones below us and at last ask whether Poppy was a geologist too. Roger shakes his head: 'To her rocks were rocks. She liked beautiful things, though.'

The first time they met was at a party during Roger's first year working in the bush. When he asked the quiet seated girl to dance with him, the rest of the room fell away and the world turned back to the very beginning of time. They danced close together until the music stopped and all the guests had left. Just before they separated, Poppy whispered her address into his ear and asked him to come for dinner with her parents. Roger echoed her address the whole way home to make sure he would not forget it; he remembers it perfectly to this day. The following week

63

Roger went to see Poppy and continued visiting her regularly throughout his time in South Africa, soon falling deeply in love with her. Roger worked for a while as a diver in Cape Town, while Poppy trained as an acrobatic dancer, before they left the city to trek cross-country together, finding adventure through companionship in the same way Roger's parents had.

I pick up a rock that seems especially beautiful to me. It is so black that it looks like a hole in the ground. When I ask Roger what it is, he puzzles for a while. 'This is porphyritic too, but it's much darker.' He pauses. 'To tell you the truth, I don't know what that is … Well, you can't expect me to know everything!' He bends down and reaches for another, half-buried beneath the cement-like grey sand, digging his fingers around its edges to loosen it. When he finally lifts it, we see the rock is much larger than he had thought: a huge bulk of charcoal black stone, striated with thin golden lines. 'What do you think of that?' he asks me. And I, not knowing how one ought to talk about rocks, say something like: *It looks a bit like a tiger?*

Roger looks at me wryly. 'Got quite an imagination, haven't you?' He shakes his head. 'Looks like a tiger,' he smiles and carefully slots the rock back into the bubbling hole of sand he clawed it from, without telling me any more of its history.

Roger's story has its own cracks and fault lines. He and Poppy stayed in London for a while, a place she grew to love. So much so that, when Roger got another job at a goldmine in South Africa, Poppy did not want to leave, knowing there would no longer by anything for her out in the bush. She was not the kind of woman that could ever be her husband's assistant, Roger tells me, and he knew he had to let her go.

By the time Roger returned to London, Poppy had found someone else, the discovery of which sent Roger into a spiral of self-destruction. He lost himself entirely, not even his work giving him pleasure, and he was eventually diagnosed with bipolar, a condition he was told had been buried within him, waiting to be unearthed by some tremor across his life. A prescription of lithium helped to make his moods more bearable, but he found the chemical also shifted the way he perceived the world. Now and then a dreaminess would come over him and he'd feel himself slipping away from reality. It took him a long time to adjust to this new way of existing, finding meaning through work once more, this time in a goldmine in Australia.

The next rock Roger chooses is a piece of granite, bisected by veins of jasper, known as chalcedony, a cryptocrystalline form of silica: 'It's quite something, isn't it? You never know what you're going to find out here.' Just as he was becoming accustomed to his new life, Roger received a letter from Poppy. In it she wrote that she loved him, that she always had and that she was in London waiting for him. Roger left his life in Australia without a moment's hesitation. 'Love is love,' he says simply: it is not something you can compromise on, it's too big for that. They quickly started a family and moved to Newlyn, swapping their youthful adventures for a quiet life, staying in most nights, watching TV or listening to the blues. But then, while they were on holiday last Christmas, another earthquake ripped through their foundations, dismantling the life they had built together.

At one point in Californian essayist Joan Didion's *The Year of Magical Thinking* – the devastating meditation on the grief she experienced after the death of her first husband John and then her daughter Quintana – she considers the years she spent searching for meaning as a young woman. She often contemplated the episcopal litany, 'as it was in the beginning, is now and ever shall be, world without end'. The young Joan Didion interpreted the phrase as 'a literal description of the constant changing of the earth, the unending erosion of the shore and mountains, the inexorable shifting of the geological structures that could throw up mountains and islands and could just as reliably take them away'. It took several readings before I could see the similitude between these two ways of regarding time. The continuity in the world, the one principle that unifies each moment, is change. It is this mutability that holds life together, drawing a line between time's beginning and all that which is yet to pass.

Geology is not only the key to learning the earth's past, it is the holy book for how to live in the face of such shifts. It reminds us of the ever-turning nature of the planet – from which mountains appear from nowhere, before disappearing down into the sea once more; where red deserts roll back across the landscape to reveal beneath them green fields and villages; and in which one day your wife is bounding through life, and the next can barely stand. In this way geology teaches us to see ourselves as we really are: finite landmarks within an infinitely shifting world. When we use the phrase 'natural disaster', geologists remember that these events are only coloured *disasters* for and by humans. When we talk about ice ages or huge storms at seas, they are not disasters themselves; the disasters are that humans become involved in them. They are just how the world goes. I look back at the town behind us at the edge of the sea. It remains a fishing port, as its community hopes it always will, and yet it changes every second too: the older fishing families die away; political diktats from afar transform its inner workings; new technologies wash over it, redrawing its landscape again and again.

Places do not hold still. I get an impression: I see a stone on a floor and its pattern is perfect. I pick it up, making certain of its shape in my mind and the shape of the space that I occupy in relation to it. I drop the stone to the ground again and try to draw how it looked. And then I pick the stone up once more and see its other side, which sticks out differently, has new lumps and colours, provides a completely divergent experience of the stone. I turn the stone back around again to rediscover that initial shape, but I can no longer find it. I cannot return to that first impression of perfection and two-dimensional certainty. In this way, we each of us try to grab the time of the world by the neck, holding it there tight to our chests for a second, before it skips away and we are swept onwards.

'That's a metamorphosed sediment,' Roger tells me, stooping and gesturing towards a line of light pink quartz that passes through a group of rocks leading out to sea. Minerals enter rocks through cracks that open up gradually over time so that the mineral is able to spread right through it.

It was during that Christmas holiday when Poppy suddenly lost weight, the first mark of an aggressive strain of pancreatic cancer beginning to consume her body. Within a month, it had taken her life. We start walking back up the beach towards the bronze statue of the fisherman. Now he is alone, Roger tells me he is having to teach himself once more how to be a person who is not joined to another body. He's started going out to gigs with his children and their friends, seeing the world through them and refusing to lose that spirit of enquiry he learned from his parents. The world keeps changing, parts are eroded and new formations grow out of their absences. 'You can't help it,' he says. 'You're walking on the planet and you're just thinking ...' – his eye traces along the line of the green elvan dike where the Wherry Mine is buried deep below – 'it gives you a sense of wonderment.' He picks up another rock and stares at it for a while, before chucking it back down. 'I think that one's a piece of a brick, actually.'

7

WILD BEASTS

The American poet Elizabeth Bishop lived out her early years beside the sea in Nova Scotia and much of her later life by the coast either in Key West, Boston or Rio de Janeiro. In the hundred or so poems she published, the word 'sea' returns sixty times, rarely just as a geographical backdrop, more often than not providing the mood of the poem or offered as a tool with which to contemplate larger ideas. In 'At the Fishhouses', she describes passing through a fishing harbour on a cold evening: 'the lobster pots, and masts, scattered/ among the wild jagged rocks',

> the small old buildings with an emerald moss
> growing on their shoreward walls.
> The big fish tubs are completely lined
> with layers of beautiful herring scales
> and the wheelbarrows are similarly plastered
> with creamy iridescent coats of mail,
> with small iridescent flies crawling on them.

Each aspect of this industrial scene is raised to a kind of splendour – fish scales 'iridescent coats of mail', moss turned 'emerald'. And yet, the image does not lose its everyday working quality. The speaker watches an old man accept 'a Lucky Strike' and then scrape away the last of the fish scales – which, to him, need not represent anything more than fish scales – with 'that black old knife, / the blade of which is almost worn away'. Near the end of the poem, the speaker turns her gaze out towards the sea, 'the same sea' that she has seen over and over. 'It is like what we imagine knowledge to be,' she declares: 'dark, salt, clear, moving, utterly free.'

Most mornings I head up along the Strand – the stretch of road alongside the bay, which leads up above the sea towards Mousehole. From here I can regard the whole of Newlyn harbour at once. I understand why Elizabeth Bishop made the place between land and sea her enduring subject. It is hard not to feel small and especially human gazing out at vessels that can ride upon the oceans. From up here, the boats resemble captive animals, straining against the ropes that tether them to the harbour wall. Each of them howls in the wind and clinks its chains, threatening to escape from the harbour and join the other wild beasts of the sea roaming out there beyond the horizon.

I take a quick turn around the concrete quays attached to which are row upon row of fishing boats. After skirting between the vans, forklift trucks, and plastic boxes brimming with frost-coated fish, the harbour opens up again before me. On its left-hand side are three piers where the trawlers, beamers and other large vessels moor; on its right the small boats pontoon. Each of the piers has its own distinctive identity. The Mary Williams, built in 1980, is the central and newest pier. Monstrous pipes pumping petrol snake down its main channel leading into open-mouthed trawlers, which guzzle it up thirstily. Engineers in masks dangle from masts and wheelhouse balconies, sparks flying from their welding, while fishermen kneel along the walkway mending still-glistening nets splayed out across the concrete. There is a coarseness to this pier, a hostility almost. I feel numerous eyes trained on me as I trip over pipes and net fragments on my way down to chat with fishermen over cups of coffee in galleys before their boats set sail.

North Pier is scruffier than Mary Williams. It is the pier I come to associate with Newlyn's harbourmaster, Rob Parsons. We stroll along it together while he fills me in on all the comings and goings. Rob leans against the harbour wall, surveying his domain and greeting almost every fisherman who wanders past by name – apart from the odd one who refuses him eye contact or make rude gesture behind his back because they have some quibble with the way he runs the harbour. Not that any of this fazes Rob. He is a former Royal Marine and takes no nonsense from anyone, which has already earned him a few enemies amongst certain old fishing families.

The boats that moor at North Pier are mainly those built in the sixties and seventies owned by the Stevensons, vessels grown worn and rusted in parts as a result of years spent contending with mercurial conditions at sea. This includes the *Filadelfia* herself, which I learn to distinguish from the other yellow-and-black-painted trawlers by the white cross of the Cornish flag painted along her wheelhouse, right next to where Don would lean out of the wheelhouse window and yell down: 'Where are my lovely turbot then?' This is also the quay where trawlers are left to die, boats sinking slowly down into the water, large holes growing in their sides and weeds sprouting from the cracks in their decks. They groan and wheeze as the fishermen they once knew pass by them and clamber onto newer boats, barely stopping to notice their hulls thinning out and their paint fade to grey.

I read in old newspapers about the extravagant celebrations that occurred every time a new pier was built in Newlyn. In 1885, to celebrate the foundation stone being laid of South Pier, John Hayter, the landlord of the Star, laid on a spectacular firework display. 'Batteries of Roman candles, rockets, fire fountains, mine of serpents, discharge of three monster shells and two fiery whirlwinds, fountain of fire, huge mine of serpents and crackers, illumination of surrounding country by 13 various coloured pyrotechnic compositions,' reported the *Cornishman* excitedly. I imagine these fireworks ripping across the bay, indiscriminately colouring the sea and sky in pinks, yellows, greens and golds, reflecting in the windows of the boats tethered on the pontoons.

Celebrations are still taken seriously in Newlyn. Any birthday, no matter the age one is turning, is an excuse for a messy party down at the Star where Stevie Wonder's 'Happy Birthday' rings out almost daily on the jukebox. Impromptu karaoke evenings happen every few weeks up at the Red Lion. Fundraising for the Christmas harbour lights switch-on party begins almost as soon as Christmas has ended. And Denise and Lofty once had such a long winning streak at the Star's weekly 'meat draw' (where you win vouchers to spend at the local butcher's) that their freezer overflowed with steaks for months.

Newlyn's original crumbling quay curves around the south side of the harbour. The first record of its presence is in 1437, according to a Church document offering indulgences to those who contributed to its repair. Nailed to the quayside is a plaque indicating that it was the *Mayflower*'s last berthing place in 1620 before her onward voyage to America. By the late 1800s, after the construction of the other piers, the Old Quay was barely used to moor fishing vessels. Rather, men would land their fish there so it could be carted more easily over to the fish buyers, many of whom conducted their business at the Red Lion. These days it is the most tranquil pier, occupied only by beautifully restored old luggers, traditional fishing boats with dark orange sails that largely disappeared from Mount's Bay after the emergence of mechanised boats by the Second World War. One I got to know particularly well in Newlyn harbour is the *Ripple*, whose underside I once spent an afternoon helping to paint in the sunshine with the old man who owns her. Below the waters gently pressing against the Old Quay, it is told, there lies an ancient village, a precursor to Newlyn, drowned in waves and now covered by Gwavas Lake, an area of calm water in Mount's Bay.

In 1896 the whole harbour was temporarily closed off and a chain stretched across the Gaps after a raging battle between Newlyn fishermen and the East (Anglian) Coast crews – known to history as 'the Newlyn Riots'. These upcountry fishermen from Lowestoft and Great Yarmouth had begun landing their catch at the Newlyn and Penzance markets every day of the week, ignoring the area's strict Methodist rules about not fishing on the Sabbath. By all accounts the riots were brutal: the Newlyn fishermen threw almost ten thousand mackerel back into the sea and rioted at Penzance to stop the East Coast boats from landing there too, and were only subdued in the end by the arrival of over three hundred soldiers from the Royal Berkshire Regiment and Royal Navy destroyers appearing in the bay. The Royal Berkshire Regiment fought the Newlyn men back with the flats of their swords, and one man's ear was sliced off in the scuffle. In a statement to the *Cornish Telegraph* the men of Newlyn declared: 'If they will not conform we are determined, cost what it will, that we will fight to the bitter end.' And yet, only ten years later, the religious commitment that had fuelled the riots had been forgotten and the Newlyn men could be seen fishing out in the bay most Sundays.

The place I go to whenever I am lonely or overcome by thoughts of home is the small boats pontoon. Its gentle pace feels a world away from the bustle of the main harbour. The boats that dock here are single or two-manned inshore vessels, as well as personal punts that locals take out on summer days for lazy fishing trips. Not long after I arrive in the town, Lofty and I take his bath-sized boat out around Mount's Bay. It is the first time I have been out through the Gaps, the first time I have seen Newlyn from the water. The town's shape immediately makes more sense to me when viewed from the sea, like seeing a cross section of a tree's roots below the ground and only then understanding how it can be so strong. Another day, Isaac, Taylor and I go hand-lining for mackerel down by Clement's Isle in Taylor's little punt. We catch nothing but spend the afternoon drinking beer and enjoy watching the sun radiating out across the bay while seals heft themselves over the rocks like fat slugs.

Protected by the embracing arms of North and South Pier, the water below the pontoons is like glass, reflecting perfect images of the multicoloured boats. On each mooring pole sit seagulls surveying their empire, their white-feathered bodies, plump with fish stolen from the fishermen's nets, spilling over the sides. Within the boats too are squads of seagulls, settled squat like fishermen waiting for the tide to change. I wander between the many branches that diverge from the main wooden gangway. From a bird's-eye view the pontoons look like slender trees whose leaves are the boats that colour and animate them, blowing slightly in the wind. I stop by each boat and imagined stories project onto me: which regions of the sea they have travelled through, what storms and lives have passed across them. Some vessels proudly display their polished decks to you, smart paint jobs and flowerings of red buoys at their sterns, their ropes and flags playing out percussive notes into the otherwise silence of the pontoon. Others retreat right back from their moorings, slipping into the shadows, sides rusting, their knowledge of the world beyond the harbour fading into distant memory. One, the FH52, has painted onto its black bow the upper row of shark's sharp white teeth opening to reveal a blood red mouth that, reflected in the water, opens up into a gaping mouth.

Newlyn has the largest number of vessels in its administration of any port in the UK, and 88 per cent of these are 'ten metres and under' inshore fishing boats. And yet, over the years, as with the larger quays, the pontoons' leaves have become sparser – a deciduous tree living a perpetual winter. Not only have many boats been decommissioned over time – the number of fishing vessels nationally has fallen by 29 per cent since 1996 according to government statistics – and the money required to purchase and maintain a boat, as well as paying for fuel and more quota grows higher each year, ensuring that young men or women hoping to enter the trade are put off before they have even begun.

A local fisherman called Mike Buttery, known affectionately as Butts, has compiled a catalogue of all 2,500 luggers, yawls and ketches (two-masted sailing boats) registered PZ between 1869 and 1944. Buttery has made it his life's mission to record in obsessive detail everything that has happened in the area (both the momentous and the mundane: one entry reads: 'Monday 1st March 1993, first wheelie bins in Mousehole') in his book, *Mousehole: a documented history*. Leafing through the records of fishing vessels is like reading the obituaries section of a newspaper. Many of their lives have been cut short – lost at sea or broken up for firewood during the war – while others have disappeared to far-flung places, like the *Snowdrop*, which was last seen some-where in the Far East. In his introduction, Buttery also notes the shrinking of the industry locally. The largest decline in registered fishing boats occurred in 1980, after the winter mackerel fishery was killed off by industrial fishing; the old luggers could no longer compete with trawlers that swept up the seabed, hunting many fish populations to near extinction prior to the introduction of quotas. Since that time, Buttery writes, 'it has been estimated that 1,000 boats and some 2,500 shore workers have lost their jobs in Devon and Cornwall'.

Before mechanised fishing, there was no pressing need to limit men's work upon the seas; they did not have the resources to make a lasting dent in fish stocks. The introduction of steam-powered trawlers near the close of the nineteenth century altered this, together with the arrival of new technologies such as more efficient nets, and long-line gear in the form of thousands of hooks sewn upon a single line. A *Cornishman* article from 1963 states: 'Newlyn fishermen have quite often counted over fifty large trawlers sweeping certain grounds – boats from Germany, Belgium, France, Spain and recently Russia or Poland.' These trawlers became a regular sight across the Cornish coast, siphoning off whole shoals of fish from the seabed in one haul. In time, the Cornish fishermen would modernise too, building or buying their own industrialised trawlers so that they could com-pete with boats from abroad. Under this new intensive approach, fishing ceased to be a sustainable activity, with stocks unable to reproduce as quickly as they were being fished.

One of my favourite stories included in Buttery's catalogue is of the 40-foot lugger, *What You Will*, owned by George Water and Samuel Harvey. 'The owners were painting up their boat and said, "What do we name her?"' writes Buttery. '"Call 'ee what you will. I'm off for a beer," said one to the other. When he came back with a glass of ale for his partner he had already painted in the name WHAT YOU WILL.' The boat names chronicled in the harbour here are often testament to the changing times and technologies arriving in the town. Early in the last century there was a fishing boat named *Telegraphy*, another called *Telephone* and another still named *Railway*. More recently there was a boat called *Nat-West*. When asked why, the owner replied: 'Coz that's where I get my money from.'

Before I started going out to sea on boats, I thought fishing was fishing. Whatever kind of vessel or whichever species they were hunting for, fishermen head out to catch what they're after and return to sell it. This simplification comes from a lifetime of seeing fish as a commodity – a supermarket product lumped together in a single aisle, neatly packaged and coated in a film of plastic. The fish itself is stripped down to a homogenous, skinless fillet, so that it is hard to believe it was ever a living thing, racing below the water. In reality, every boat I spend time on in Newlyn varies in size and age, has its own distinctive smell and sounds – the particular wheezing, spluttery cough of each engine – and functions in accordance with the unique habits and patterns of work dictated by its skipper. The *Filadelfia* and the *Crystal Sea*, despite nominally catching the same fisheries, are very different crafts. As one fisherman said to me: 'Every boat's got its own rhythms. That's why, no matter how long you've been a fisherman, go out on someone else's boat and you will get seasickness all over again.'

And each kind of boat, too – be it for hand-lining, crabbing, day-boating, gill-netting, trawling or ring-netting – attracts a different kind of fisherman. Gill-netting, for instance, involves casting out a large panelled net that stands vertically in the water, held in place by a lead line on the seabed and a cork line floating on the surface, in whose mesh the fish – particularly hake, cod, pollock and turbot, while smaller fish swim right through the holes – get caught by the gills. This type of fishing, where the boat stays out for four or five days at a time and the crew are some-times on deck pulling fish from the nets for over thirty hours, is regarded as a young man's game: gill-netting crews are usually the wilder, more volatile boys who have yet to settle down. On the Newlyn-based *Joy of Ladram* the men are almost all in their twenties and listen to aggressive techno music while they gut.

A Penzance boy named Richard Hicks tells me one night in the Star that he came straight into fishing from the army and finds gill-netting far more intense and exhausting than the tours he did of Afghanistan and Iraq during his years active service.

Men grow old working on trawlers – like Don who has remained loyally with the *Filadelfia* for years. Though less physically demanding, trawler work itself is regarded as more technical and tactical than the static-gear fishing done by gill-netters. The trawler's method of dragging nets across the seabed has long been criticised, too, for leading to overfishing and causing unnecessary harm to the marine environment. As long ago as 1376 there was a petition to Parliament about a new kind of fishing vessel called a *wondyrchoum* whose mesh was so small that 'no manner of fish, however small, entering within it can pass out and is compelled to remain therein and be taken'. The author of the letter suggested that the *wondyrchoum* caused such destruction that its presence in the sea would lead to 'great damage of the common of the realm and the destruction of the fisheries'.

Day boats offer the most flexible kinds of fishing, though it feels like a misnomer to call them 'day boats' at all. Most crabbers and hand-liners have left the harbour long before the sun has risen and return after it has set, while the pilchard-hunting ring-netters, a cross between two other kinds of fishing gear, the purse seine (a wall of netting which hangs vertically in the water and is pulled in from the bottom like the strings of a purse to trap the fish within it) and the lampara (an older method comprised of a surrounding net with a central bunt), do not head out until dusk, in that greyish evening light that swamps the harbour, and are usually back before ten at night. Like gill nets, ring nets are weighted at the bottom with lead and held up by corks, but where the gill net stands like a wall in the sea, the ring net surrounds the fish in a wide circle, which then tightens and closes like a bag around the catch.

Day-boat skippers carve their own small paths through the world, quietly working inshore to their own schedules, and carrying a range of nets and pots for different fisheries: trammels (two layers of netting with a smaller mesh inner net between the two in which the fish become tangled) and tangle nets (single-walled nets like gill nets) for turbot and monkfish; hand-lines for mackerel, sole and the bit of haddock they are allowed to catch; nets for bass, gurnard, red mullet; pots for lobster and crab. Day-boat fishermen need to be acutely aware of their work environment, attuned to the changing of the seasons, feeling the way that the natural world shifts over the year.

For hand-lining, the most traditional fishing technique, a single line is attached with feather lures on hooks to catch mackerel by hand. Hand-line fishermen tend to work alone, often those men who most desire seclusion, keeping a distance from the main hubbub and rivalry of the industry. They are often more environmentally conscious than other fishermen. Newlyn's own 'Mad Dick', a self-proclaimed 'Environment Nut', who is in his seventies and wears shorts every day of the year, declares he would like to see all the technological advances that have wrecked the industry destroyed. He believes boats such as trawlers, which 'drag up the whole seabed', miss the essential intimacy of fishing: where you can literally feel each fish tugging on your line. These days there also exist long-lining commercial fishing vessels, which carry up to a hundred kilometres of line with hooks set at intervals along them. In this way the most environmentally sustainable mode of fishing has been transformed into a damaging one that results in far more waste, or by-catch – fish that you will not sell and may not have quota for.

There is fierce competition between the different kinds of fisherman. Every man I speak to has his own – often incredibly biased – opinions about the other kinds of boats, assuring me that his style of fishing is superior and takes a cannier sort of individual. One man, who was a gill-netter for all his career, describes trawling as 'kid's play – not proper fishing'. When I tell him about the huge monkfish we caught on the *Filadelfia*, he says: 'Yeah, huge for a trawler', and when I show him a picture of the great beast, he laughs: 'Nooo, that's a babby compared to what we gill-netters get!' Kyle, meanwhile, tells me he's never fancied the idea of day-boat work like crabbing because it is 'too much heavy lifting, not enough fishing'. For trawlermen the constant coming and going of day-boating is nightmarish: 'While you are out sea, you want to be properly gone – that way you know where you are.' Meanwhile some of the day-boaters say they could never imagine spending weeks away from their family. Another fisherman I speak to, who has worked both types of vessel, believes that the most skilled craft of all is trawling: it is an exact art, if even the smallest thing goes wrong, 'the whole trip is fucked'.

8

FISH THROUGH FINGERS

Most Saturday mornings Denise and Lofty's friend Nicky pops round for a coffee and a yarn. The three of them, several couples, and Don when he is ashore, are all part of what I come to think of as the Star crew, a group of long-time Newlyn residents, between forty and sixty-something, who spend most evenings laughing their nights away huddled around the table by the window at the Star, or playing sudden-death pool at the Royal British Legion Club round the corner.

I don't think I really knew what community meant before staying with Denise and Lofty. Because those who live in the town also work in the town and socialise here too, there is a depth to their relationships virtually unheard of in sprawling cities, where you are never served by the same cashier twice and your local is only your local for the year you live in that area, before your tenancy ends and you find yourself starting all over again in a new part of the city.

Despite never having played pool, I join the Star crew one night at the Legion. We take over the whole club, causing its older, more wizened members to grumble loudly about the youngsters coming in and causing a ruckus. 'You clearly didn't have enough of a misspent youth!' Nicky laughs as I miss yet another easy pot. There is a glass jar on the main bar, filled half the way up with 10ps. Every time one of our gang swears loudly, the old man behind the bar coughs disapprovingly, which in turn triggers a chorus of voices around the pool table to yell gleefully: 'We've broken rule fucking twenty-one again!' This is followed by a loud clattering as pockets are emptied into the jar for breaking the club's stringent swearing ban on the premises.

Denise and Lofty occupy a spot at the centre of Newlyn's community, loved dearly by everyone in town. Though they have both always lived in the West Penwith area, they didn't come across one another until later in life. Their relationship is the kind you hold up as a model to strive for. Each day during their lunch hour they walk home from their neighbouring places of work to eat and smoke together, living their lives side by side with an ease and sense of play that seems to come more naturally to them than I've ever seen in any another couple. While staying with them, I learn that the best conversations are not the big ones, the ones you are trained to reach for at university, all those long words with which to explain the world away; the best ones are the small chats that occur during the adverts between TV shows or while chopping vegetables for the Sunday roast, which make you laugh, which are repetitive and forgettable and need never be anything more than that.

Lofty works in the high-ceilinged marine equipment warehouse across from the Strand and just two doors down from the fishmonger's where Denise works, which means that Lofty is acquainted with almost every fisherman working in Newlyn. The shop, whose large front windows face the harbour, is filled with reams and reams of colourful rope, nets coiled up like snakes, oilskins and blue plastic fishing gloves spread out across the floor. I keep him company one afternoon, discussing the town and how it differs from where I grew up – our conversation punctuated by fishermen coming in every few minutes and calling out from the entrance: 'All right Lofty, I want you for oilskin trousers', or 'I want you for lifeboat cord'.

Sat there in the backroom office amongst half-inflated lifeboats, Lofty provides me with a list of some of his favourite 'Newlyn' phrases. 'Good as gold' is one he uses all the time to describe other members of the community, the goodness in this case simply meaning kindness and not needing to mean anything more than that. I can't believe so many people in one place can be as good as gold. One of my friends back home suggested that calling someone nice is practically an insult; when any of us gives a person a compliment, it is always that they are interesting or smart or cool, in recognition of some external factor rather than an innate quality or the way they treat others. But those words suddenly sound overwhelmingly hollow.

'What about *dreckly*?' he says. You must know dreckly?' I shake my head. Lofty explains that it's a quintessential Cornish time phrase. Though a near homophone of directly, its linkage to the word is perhaps ironic since *dreckly* tends to mean at some point in the future – a rough equivalent to *mañana* in Spanish. I soon hear it everywhere around the town. On one fisherman's kitchen wall is a clock that has word DRECKLY spelled out in block letters across its face, while the numbers themselves are suffixed by 'ish'. A St Ives-born fisherman has named his small day-boat collective 'Dreckly Fish'. And most texts I get from Newlyn residents I'm meant to be meeting imminently end with a vague: 'See you dreckly!'

More than almost anyone else in Newlyn I hear the phrase good as gold attached to, is Nicky. Perhaps counter-intuitively, he is also regarded as one of the grumpiest people in town. When you ask him how he is, he will inevitably say 'terrible', before – more often than not – breaking into a wild grin, so that you never quite know how to respond. I also hear rumours that he has the most beautiful singing voice. When he deigns to take the mic at karaoke nights in the Red Lion, the whole crowd falls silent in anticipation.

Nicky works at both the overnight grading in the market, a job requiring men to sort through all the fish that have arrived into the harbour that evening into sizes and species ready to be sold at auction the following morning, and on the fish auction itself. As a result, he is almost always exhausted. When I catch him about during the day, he is wearing the dreamy, absent expression seen on the faces of all those who are more accustomed to the uninhab- ited hours of the night. After we finish playing pool, he agrees to let me observe the grading one night the coming week, while the following morning I will come again to watch the auction, these two vocations providing the incomes of a significant number of people in the town. As I am so very often told: 'For every one man at sea, that's five jobs on land.'

Nicky meets me outside the imposing market building at 8 p.m., wearing a white coat, his hair tucked into a bright blue hairnet. The harbour water on the market's other side is already oil-slick black and the last few lights of crab boats can just be seen making their way back in through the Gaps.

The market is cavernous, damp and rattling; scaffolding climbs up its cement-coloured interior. Built in the 1980s, after years of complaints about its shoddiness the place is finally in the process of having its roof redone. We enter through a rectangular green up-and-over door. Above us harsh strip lights are suspended from corrugated iron buttresses fixed to the ceiling; their glow is so white that it seems to suck away all other colour, making the room appear like one enormous operating theatre. A large sign on the opposite wall declares: 'No smoking. No spitting. No eating'. Five men also dressed in white coats work silently at humming silver machines. They do not notice me come in. The atmosphere is especially low tonight, Nicky tells me. The men will be working flat out until six tomorrow morning: every fish must be graded before the auction takes place and last night over a quarter of a million fish came in from the boats. I look at the men working silently under the shadows of the market. I thought I'd met most of Newlyn by now, but I have never seen any of these night men with their purple-blue shaded eyes before, who toil all night in a decrepit building at the very edge of the harbour and who return to their homes before the rest of the town wakes.

Nicky gets to work on the large silver chute. He separates the clumps of icy fish that have just been unloaded from a trawler and sends them down the chute to be weighed and sorted into the appropriate red box. I ask if I can help and he gestures through a plastic curtain to a box of gloves, which I find are coated with a hardened layer of fish juice. I get to work, standing opposite Nicky, unpacking box after box of fish, sending them skidding down the chute.

No one speaks or even looks up, each of us retreating to our separate worlds as we work in sync with the monotonous background drone of the machines. Without a clock in the market, my only way of measuring time is through the arrival of each new boat's haul before the conveyor belt. I notice how crews cut the monkfish at different points, some of their slices cleaner, others more jagged. If the monkfish are the hardest fish to gut, then the endless numbers of tiny lemon sole are a nightmare to break apart. When a few boxes of monk tails arrive, the spark of variety it provides is a welcome distraction. I think of the men out on the boats, slinging these same fish into boxes and then stacking them up into swaying towers that move together with the waves. I wonder if I know the man who has caught these fish. Was it Kyle? Or Andrew? Or maybe David on the *Crystal Sea*?

The cold of the ice gradually seeps through my gloves until I can no longer feel my fingers. 'This is a bad job, Lamorna,' says Nicky, breaking the silence at last. 'It's a bad job.' He was a fisherman for most of his working life, but when you get older the strain the job puts on your body eventually catches up with you, he says. Grading and working on the auction seemed the only way he could avoid leaving the industry entirely. It is the same with a lot of retired fishermen. To lose your connections to fishing would simultaneously entail a loss of your place in the community. Still, grading is relentless, the hours unforgiving and, though the sea is at your door, you are bound to the land.

Within the rhythm of work we find moments to ask each other questions. Favourite music, favourite football team, what his daughter does, what my parents do, our relationships, our favourite fish.

'Monk. You?'

'I like John Dory.'

'Never had John Dory.'

Nicky stops. 'Are you pulling my leg? Fry it up in a little oil, a little butter and there is nothing better.'

Around 10 p.m., Nicky yells out: 'Okay you lot, tea break!'

Instantly all work ceases. The machines grind to a halt and a line of us traipse out along the edge of the harbour, our shadows long and slender in the lamplight. We pass alongside the rows of trawlers, lifted up and down by the gentle lap of water, their breath rising and falling in sleep. Down in their berths, fishermen from Eastern Europe, Latvia and the Philippines, are tucked up for the night in their sleeping bags; these men tend rarely to step foot on land for the six months they work on the Cornish fishing boats, as if not quite committing to the idea that they are far from home, in a distant country, before they return to their families for the rest of the year with their earnings.

Halfway round the harbour's edge we go through a door that I have never noticed before and enter a cramped room. The men at once sit themselves down and begin unwrapping lovingly packed snacks and sandwiches, mostly made by their wives. The kettle boils continuously and spoonful upon spoonful of instant coffee, with equal amounts of sugar, is heaped into mugs. The only sound comes from occasional yawns, noisy sighs and the munching of crisps. Then, apropos of nothing, someone makes an unexpected sarcastic comment, causing the company to shudder into wheezing laughter. After this, silence reigns once more, before the next joke comes in to slice through the solemn atmosphere of the room. It reminds me of the way that distinct moods seem to bloom out of different spaces on the *Filadelfia*, as if the moods themselves preceded the humans moving between them: the melancholy fish room and its silent stacks of iced fish; the contemplative still of the wheelhouse; the silliness of the galley.

The hush is broken by Martin who, I am told, is 'the driest chip in the whole of Newlyn'.

'How we all doing?' he shouts out, playing compere to the room, before responding to his own question with: 'Fucking great! Whoop-de-woo!' accompanied by a brief jig.

The men roar with laughter until Martin sits back down, his face settling back into a sullen vacancy and everyone looks down at their sandwiches again.

Then a huge, tattooed man called Leon, declares in a dead-pan voice: 'Life is what it is and then you die.'

One beat, a second, a third passes and then he slaps his leg, and the room erupts once more.

Next it is Nicky's turn. He cries out mournfully: 'What did I do in my past life to deserve this, then?' and the men howl with laughter.

After fifteen minutes of this pattern of laughter followed by glum silence, the men reluctantly down their last dregs of coffee and finish off the crumbs of biscuits and we make our way back across to the market. As we walk, Nicky tells me that none of the men sleep longer than a few hours after their shifts. I ask him why, thinking they must surely be knackered. 'Because then you would be a ghost,' Nicky replies.

We are close to ghosts now, I think, haunting the empty harbour in the dead of night. The graders are haunted by time, too: the white-coated men with clipboards joined at the shoulders who will march through the auction at precisely 6 a.m. the next morning to buy and then sell the fish onwards.

Just as we reach the edge of the market, Leon picks up a massive mouldy monk's head and chucks it into the harbour water. We all wait in silence as it sinks down. A second later, a fat dark smudge breaks through the surface and swallows the head whole.

'That's Sammy the seal,' Leon tells me, 'he's been living here long as I have.'

The hours draw out, and the boxes of fish keep coming. I find myself entering into a hallucinatory state, personifying each fish that passes through my gloved fingers. Two entwined monkfish tails are an old married couple, their feud forever frozen in ice. I pick up several glum Dovers and come to a huge, ugly ling, my least favourite type of fish. I am certain its gutless body twitches in my hand as it slips out of my fingers and tumbles down the conveyor belt. I tell Nicky that in a strange way I am beginning to enjoy the repetitious nature of the work.

He looks at me sternly. 'That's what they call novelty. And you know what happens with novelty?' – he throws another lemon sole down the chute – 'It wears off.'

He is right. Several trawlers worth of fish later, when I guess midnight must be approaching, I feel my eyes start to droop. He notices and laughs at me. 'You don't have to stay here all night, you know? Go on, get yourself to bed!'

I pause to watch the other men, each alone with their thoughts as they turn handles and weigh out boxes, their night of work barely halfway through. Then I throw one last monkfish down the conveyer and head off to unpeel my gloves.

'Oi, hang on!' Nicky jumps down into the room behind the plastic curtain and returns with a carrier bag containing two vast fish, their bristles poking out through the sides.

'John Dorys!' He grins. 'Little bit of butter, little bit of olive oil. You don't need anything else. All right? See you at the auction at six, Lamorna.'

I thank him and shout goodbye to the other men, who don't look up. Then I make the three-minute walk back up to the cottage in the Fradgan. Denise and Lofty's cats greet me enthusiastically at the door – smelling strongly, as I so often do now, of fish.

Six hours later and I am pulling my boots back on to meet Nicky outside the market for the auction. I notice his face has drained entirely as he gives me a weary half-smile. Around the back of the market I see the other graders heading for home now their part is over.

'Come on then, nutter,' Nicky says and beckons me back inside.

It is hard to believe it's the same building. The shape of the space, earlier defined by a spectral quiet that seemed to make the interior yet more gaping, now appears less intimidating as jovial Cornish voices boom across it. From the entrance to the furthest reaches of the room the market is packed with white-coated fish buyers, moving between hundreds of rows of red fish boxes laid out across the wet floor. Nicky inspects a few of the boxes and then checks his watch. The auction will inevitably begin late because, as another fish merchant interrupts him to tell us, the ageing auction supervisor 'can't supervise himself', letting one of the auctioneers know he'll be there 'dreckly'.

After ten minutes of no one knowing quite what to do, the supervisor arrives and the auction gets into full swing. Two auctioneers circle the room, a huddled group of white-coated men following them yelling out prices at each box. Like planets we rotate around the far-spreading rows of boxes. A mess of dark ink drips out from the cuttlefish boxes and is picked up and trodden around the market by the men's boots, painting trails all over the stone floor.

Every few bids someone will throw in a fake, ludicrously high bid, and another bidder will yell back, 'KERCHIIIIING!', after which the word continues to ping around the market for several minutes. If you were blindfolded you'd be forgiven for assuming we were still at the Star. Throughout the morning there is incessant bantering, catcalling and practical joking, men tripping each other up while dragging boxes off to the vans waiting outside to ship the fish off around the country.

Despite the chaos, the number of boxes declines rapidly. Nicky is bidding for Stevenson & Sons today and decides I'm bad luck because he keeps losing out on bids. Every now and then people leave to smoke and drink tea from polystyrene cups outside. Nicky and I follow a few of them to stand before the harbour's edge where you can just make out the horizon behind the sea walls. The water, pitch-black six hours ago, is clear as anything.

'It's a spring tide,' Nicky tells me, 'that's why it's so high and glassy.' We watch a man next to us get out a huge bacon sarnie from his back pocket and demolish it in seconds. A moment later he turns to run back in, shouting: 'Shit, I should be bidding on that turbot!'

As with almost every other aspect of fishing in Newlyn, an element of play runs through the auction. And yet, the constant fluctuation of prices at the market (set by the suppliers at the end of the chain) has a wider impact on the industry. The fishermen out at sea each week depend on their fish reaching adequate prices. When the prices drop suddenly, as they do after particular holidays such as New Year and Christmas, there is nothing the fishermen can do but accept that their week of precarious, exhausting work has earned them almost nothing at all.

After the auction, the men flow across to the Harbour Cafe on the other side of the Strand for their customary fry-ups. It is a bleak, windy morning. Streams of air rip down the road and the buyers drag their thick yellow boots behind them. The cafe's dark green, square-crossed window has fogged right up and its red sign with a copper trawler suspended above it swings back and forth in the wind. Inside it is snug and smells potently of grease. Along the sides of the room are fixed wooden benches like church pews. No one sits on the inside of the tables, preferring to position themselves with their backs to the wall from where they can see everyone else in the room and more easily jump between conversations. Each man has before him a white, unbranded coffee mug and a sausage sandwich on white bread dripping with lovingly and unsparingly squirted ketchup and HP Sauce.

Many of those present are retired fishermen. They spend hours here each morning, yarning about the years they spent at sea, or bent over page spreads from *Fishing News* and the *Cornishman*. When it gets to noon, they pick themselves up to make their way down to the pub, where they will continue the same conversations with the same lined faces.

Today the men are in the midst of a heated discussion about haddock quotas. Nicky sighs deeply, slipping into a seat beside the men to join in with their grumbles, a version of which they have had a thousand times before, which their fathers and grandfathers have had before them, revised to suit the frustrations of their own generation, and which their children and children's children will continue to have for many years, so long as the industry stays afloat in Newlyn.

We watch through the window as the last few fish boxes are sold and lugged out into the car park to be taken off in the vans. I hear the sound of plastic against gravel as one final fish merchant pulls a box across the Strand and into Stevenson's, where Denise will unpack it and lay it out across the display table to be sold that morning. Beyond the market, the meshwork of connections opens out across the country to endless supermarkets and suppliers.

In the introduction to *The Storyteller*, Walter Benjamin theorises on what it is that a storyteller does. He sees each story as first needing to be absorbed, sunk 'into the life of the storyteller' as he phrases it, so that they can then draw it out again in words that connect the story to their own experiences: in this way the 'traces of the storyteller cling to the story the way the handprints of the potter cling to the clay vessel'. The tracks and rhythms of the fishing industry too, told via the many hands through which the fish pass, cling to the creatures themselves; though the consumer can know nothing of the pranks, the storms and the struggles that their weekly fish supper has been privy to, these leave their mark, sunk there, within their sequinned bodies.

9

LEATHER PURSES

I wake to my alarm at 4.30 a.m. Outside it is *henting* it down, one of many Cornish terms for rain. It sounds appropriately heavy and unpleasant enough to describe the thick black drops illuminated in patches by the dim street lamps along the Fradgan. It is silent here in a way that it is not at any hour in London. The alleys that run alongside the cobbled ways behind the Strand, picturesque at day with washing strung up from one side to the other, by night reform themselves into foreboding passages filled with crudely sketched-out ghosts, whose peg-stretched arms reach out to draw you into their darkness.

I am up before daybreak to meet James and Will, the two-man crew of *Three Jays*, a 35-foot crabber, on the pontoons. I imagine the other day-fishermen around town hitting their alarms and lying still for a few seconds, counting those last moments of respite before they face the long hours of work ahead of them. At last, with a sigh, they reach across the bed to kiss their wives on the foreheads, slip out of bed, pull on their work clothes, grab a coffee and packed lunches, and leave, noiselessly shutting the front door behind them.

All along the pontoon, the white floodlights of boats are being turned on. Half-asleep fishermen prepare their vessels, and the juddering splutters of engines come to life one after another. James and Will are already on the *Three Jays* when I arrive, readying her for the sea without a word. They motion me to jump on board.

'It's going to be a cold day,' James announces.

From what I can make out through the grainy darkness, the *Three Jays* is an egg-yolk-yellow colour. She has a small wheel-house that is protected from the cold by a heavy door and down below I can just see a cabin packed full of ropes and equipment, which could just about be slept in if the occasion called for it.

Day-boats look like overgrown toy boats; there is something jolly about their tubby wheelhouses with their round-edged, oblong windows. James starts up the engine and steers the *Three Jays* around the harbour and over to the market, where he climbs up the ladder to pick up some frozen bits of by-catch from other boats. These chunks of fish will be used as lure in James's crab pots. As fish move through sectors of the fishing industry from boats to grading to auction and outwards, to retailers, they are also recycled between vessels.

Once loaded up with by-catch, we head off towards Wolf Rock, beyond Land's End, where James's 350 crab pots are lying in wait on the ocean bed. As we pass out of the harbour, I look back at Newlyn in darkness. There are a few more squares of light shafting across the town now. I imagine people sitting in their windows, peering out at the boats of their friends, husbands, fathers, children, passing through the Gaps – this whole town whose gaze centres upon the harbour.

The journey to Wolf Rock takes two hours. To prevent my body from slowly turning to ice during the trip out – James tells me that for some reason the heater only works in the summer months – I set to work with Will, chopping up the boxes of by-catch into more manageable chunks. He gives me a satis-fyingly large blade resembling a machete to hack through the various frozen rays and unidentifiable small fish. Their texture is entirely unlike that of the live fish I am used to gutting on the trawlers; it feels a bit like slicing through ice cream just out of the freezer. Once the bait is sufficiently broken up, the three of us sit together, still bleary-eyed, in the tiny wheelhouse with Radio 1 blaring out of the speakers to the empty sea.

There is something verging on the absurd about listening to a London-based radio presenter's 'shout-out to all those stuck in rush-hour traffic' while you are motoring through the running seas without another soul in sight. I think of all the long faceless offices of London that I have interned in, with their floor-to-ceiling windows designed to trick employees into believing they are almost outside. I imagine myself sitting there and quite suddenly those tall windows gracefully collapse downwards, computers and desks sliding away. The endless white corridors fold along new edges pulling them in towards me, the last person left in the whole building. The white corridors rise up and bend in until the space around me has been reformed into a sleek and streamlined paper boat. The concrete below the office slides up to meet me at the eleventh floor, where I have spent days dreaming of the sea, before melting into a body of water that picks up my paper boat on its tide and floats me away.

The *Three Jays* gives a cough and picks up speed. I am back here – in an old yellow boat tipping up and down through the waves, the three of us in oilskins and dark waters all around us.

Now and then there are spurts of conversation. I find out that James is only three years older than me, but he already has two children, a wife and a house to provide for. As well as working this boat for her owners, he also has his own boat, the *Bonnie Grace*, a day-boat with a dark blue keel and turquoise hull. Like many of the other twenty-somethings in Newlyn, James seems generations, rather than years, older than me and my friends back home. The work of fishing provides you with an immense sense of responsibility and obligation – the traces of which are just starting to show through the streaks of white in the hair around his ears. When he was seventeen, he tells me, he started going down to the harbour with his cousins to fish off the pier and gradually found himself spending longer and longer down by the water, before finally getting the chance to spend a day out on another fisherman's boat. Though the industry has changed over the years, fishermen's descriptions of their first days at sea are often the same; once they've experienced that first immersion in that world, they cannot imagine another kind of life for themselves.

For hundreds of years now, the sea's call has drawn young Newlyn lads away from school and a comparatively safe life on the land and out into its depths. 'It's in your blood,' Don tells me in the Star one night – after serenading me with a full rendition of the folk song 'Way Down to Lamorna' – 'it's the salt in your veins'. The phrase in Nance's *Glossary of Sea-words* is to 'go upon the water': 'I do b'long to go 'pon the water,' Nance quotes a St Ives fisherman telling him. Will, who is a few years younger than me, has fished for just one season. He has always known that he could only work on the sea though. The very idea of being kept within the four walls of an office appals him; from a young age, his evenings and weekends were spent angling with friends and drinking beers along the shore.

The *Three Jays*'s floodlights beam out across the waves as we pass Mousehole, Lamorna, Porthcurno and on to Land's End. I keep expecting the sky to lighten, but it remains a thick treacle colour until we are well into the actual work of fishing. On calm days on the *Filadelfia*, I would almost forget I was on a boat, the rhythm of movement becoming so steady and predictable. When the *Three Jays* rolls, her whole form lurches right over and it is hard to find any kind of balance. She is much lower in the water, too, which makes it feel as if the sea is drawing right around her in every direction and licking at her sides. If the boat jerks unexpectedly, you could slide right off the back in a way that is impossible with larger vessels. And yet she is less daunting than other boats I have been on; she seems easier to get to know somehow.

I tell James I think she seems a friendly boat. He laughs and tells me this bloody boat is anything but friendly. He complains about her throughout our trip, listing her problems on his fingers: she's old and difficult, rolls and creaks melodramatically, even in only marginally bad weather, and frequently refuses to work at all, spending days out of the water down by the Old Quay, the sickbay for unseaworthy boats, while James tries to find out what's wrong this time.

'She's bad luck,' he says, looking her up and down, resentfully.

James slows the engine as we get closer to the ominous Wolf Rock Lighthouse, near to where all his lines of crab pots are submerged – little buoys demarcating their place below the water. The looming lighthouse remains our lodestar for the day; whatever direction we are facing as we pull up each line, it is always there, swaying up and down together with the horizon line and in time with the *Three Jays*'s lolling motion. The lighthouse is eight nautical miles from the coast, a lone mark on the sea. Against the black sky, painted a solitary grey colour that is nothing like the jaunty, pleasant lighthouses from picture books, it resembles a thin man with a long bony nose, one of those stock images of death personified. Roger the geologist told me that the rock on which the lighthouse was built had been an active volcano during the Cretaceous period and that it produced phonolitic lava. I wonder if the land remembers its old power: this resting rock that once boiled and spat flames at the shore from across the water.

Before the arrival of the lighthouse, multiple ships were wrecked on Wolf Rock. The first attempt to erect some manmade structure on the rock occurred in 1791, when a 20-foot-high unlit daymark (mast), surmounted by a metal sculpture of a great wolf, was constructed. It was washed away only four years later, the wolf freed to roam the seabed. Each tale of the manmade daymarks or beacons placed upon the rock ends in a similar destruction: man's attempt to impose his vision on the sea, to claim a stake in it, forever failing and wiped away by the waves. Besides the lighthouse itself, only the engineer James Walker's cone-shaped beacon, which took five years to complete and comprised iron plates and concrete rubble, has survived to this day, and can still occasionally be seen just above the water amidst the waves that smash over Wolf Rock. Walker started to build the lighthouse tower itself in 1862 but didn't live to see its completion seven years later.

Nim, a retired shipwright from Newlyn who is now in his eighties, tells me that one of the best practical jokes he ever played involved the Wolf Rock Lighthouse. One day his young apprentice, Nigel, came upon several huge tins of paint outside their workshop down by Tolcarne near the bottom of town, and asked Nim what they were for.

'They're for us,' Nim replied, quick off the mark if ever there was an opportunity for a tease.

'What d'you mean?'

'We're going to paint the Wolf Rock Lighthouse tomorrow!'

The boy went white. That evening Nim turned up at Nigel's mother's house. As soon as she opened the door and saw Nim, she cried out: 'Just don't let my boy be the one on that ladder!'

Nim assured her he'd be the on the ladder, suppressing the urge to laugh.

'What will he need, then?' She asked.

'Tinned potatoes, butter, warm pyjamas and an eiderdown.'

The next day Nigel, who was only fourteen at the time, arrived at work with a huge bag carried over one shoulder.

'What the hell are you all packed for?' Nim remembers their boss asking the boy. 'We're going to paint Wolf Rock Lighthouse,' he replied, earnestly.

'Says who?'

'Says Nim.'

'I never said that,' Nim replied innocently and went back to work, leaving the boy stood before the row of half-built ships in utter bemusement.

Nim sighs, coming out of the memory with a thoughtful expression. 'Ah, he was a good lad. He got lost on the lifeboat, poor boy.'

Around 7.30 a morning gloom begins to spread across the sea revealing Land's End in the distance. The dark brown scraped edges of its cliffs look more severe from the *Three Jays* than they do from the higher vantage point of trawlers. James's plan today is to haul up the seven lines of crab pots that they 'shot' on their last trip, before refilling the emptied pots with the bait we picked up from the market and dropping them all back in the water for another few days.

To even find the buoy marking your line of pots can be a struggle, particularly when the first few hauls are completed in relative darkness. On his navigation map, James has marked the position of each pot like an 'x' on a treasure map. After circling these coordinates several times, he finds the flag that indicates the pots are below. As soon as the first flag is pulled up, the two fishermen wordlessly leap into their respective positions. A machine next to the wheelhouse winds up the line and the pots emerge from the sea like ancient drowned birdcages, black and gnarled and dripping with seaweed that twists around their steel frames. Inside each is a lattice of intricately woven wire-mesh pockets, so designed that crabs can scuttle into them to grab the bait but cannot escape again afterwards.

As each pot surfaces, James sticks his hand in to pull out the four or five affronted crabs that have found themselves unlawfully dragged from the water. The crabs themselves look to me like old leather purses, the kind you find in boxes at the back of charity shops or swinging from the arms of grannies. James holds them by their back legs, from where their pincers cannot spin round and grab a hold of your gloved fingers, and slings them into large cylindrical containers called bongos. When one bongo is completely filled with its seething mass of claws, James covers it over with a thick layer of material that pacifies the crabs beneath – though a few of them do still make almost successful bids for freedom. After James has emptied a pot of its crab guests, he hands the pot back to Will, who stuffs it with bait before carefully stacking the pot up in the back of a boat. The men do not speak at all during the forty-five minutes that it takes to raise and clear the pots. All the while from the small stereo in the wheelhouse Radio 1 plays, not ear-splittingly like Don's multicoloured sound system on the *Filadelfia*, but quietly. I love these profound silences of fishing. No needless word is spent. Rather, each person on the boat performs his individual tasks with a measured precision.

The two men harmonise their work perfectly, fish and gear crossing between them in a metrical flow. It is a symphony built of intricate parts that come together at the end of each haul in a satisfying coda. And it is musical, too: the whirring of the pulley system, the clatter of each crab in the bongo, the continuous beat of the sea against the boat and occasional squawk of seagulls from a great height. During the first cycle of work, I watch carefully to see where I might be able to slot into its rhythm. On the next haul, James instructs me to stand behind Will and take the bait-stuffed pots from him and line them up along the back of the boat. Easy, I think. And yet every task that seems straightforward on land becomes arduous at sea. I initially struggled just to walk across the deck of the *Three Jays* without stumbling, and now I must factor in the additional challenge of carrying an unwieldy crab pot, the size of a large dog.

Will gives me precise instructions about how to stack the pots. The first row should have two storeys of pots, the second three storeys, except for the two outside columns, and the next four rows all with three pots piled on top of each other, until the deck is covered with lines of neatly arranged pots. I try to keep a mental image of how this stacking had looked when Will had done it, and keep count in my head as James begins pulling up the second line of pots of the day. But the added weight of the pot unbalances me. Each time I try to make a straight path from where Will hands me the pot to where I ought to place it, I end up zigzagging across the back of the deck. The cold makes my heavy breathing come out in thick streams. Now and then, the boat lurches unexpectedly, sending me crashing into its side. If I were to fall in, I imagine that the pot awkwardly cradled in my arms would tug me down with it to the bottom of the sea. Luckily, both men complete their own work facing forward and are so immersed in their own roles that they do not witness the look of sheer terror on my face as I am flung right across the boat – or perhaps they do see me fall but save my dignity by pretending they haven't.

During the twenty minutes or so it takes to locate the next buoy marker, James tells me more about his time fishing. This last year has been especially trying. His decision to purchase the *Bonnie Grace*, hoping he could work both boats at once by taking on more crew and make a bit more money, has not exactly gone to plan. She has needed constant repairs, he has struggled to find extra people to crew her and it has been the worse year for crabbing in a while – the amounts we are bringing up in the hauls today should be far greater, considering how many days the pots were left on the seabed. Day-boat fishing is also far more limited by the weather: you cannot go out in bad conditions, as the larger boats do, but must wait on the shore for the seas to change, counting in your head the amount of money you have lost that you will not get back. And so you have to seize any opportunity you can to fish when the weather is good. This means that James sometimes works eleven days on the trot and often all night too, because that is the best time to catch mackerel. James tells me that day-boats are barely given any quota compared to the bigger boats, despite the fact that the trace they leave on the seas is negligible compared to the destruction trawlers cause. Trawlers have also been known to ravage smaller boats' gear, crashing right through it and causing thousands of pounds of damage to nets. This happened to James earlier this year and it cost him a couple months' worth of wages – another setback in a year when he needed to get his second boat going. 'That's just how it goes in fishing,' he shrugs his head philosophically. 'You just have to hope your luck changes soon.'

When I remark how calm he seems about all this, he shakes his head, responding quietly: 'No, no, it still makes me mad. Sometimes this job can be the hardest thing.'

James is quite unlike the rougher-edged fishermen of Newlyn I have met so far. There is something more measured about his approach to his work. He tells me that a lot of the younger fishermen are like this. They have come into the industry after the excessive overfishing of the eighties and the decline of fishing in the nineties with a greater awareness of man's potentially devastating impact on the oceans. Both Will and James speak with urgency about the need for conservation and their responsibility to the sea, telling me they would never leave broken nets in the water or throw their rubbish overboard. It is their job to protect the oceans for the future.

Around eleven o'clock the sun comes out. The clouds seem to fold back into themselves and everything is a shocking blue.

'Even days when you catch bugger all,' James says, 'it's so bloody beautiful out here that you don't really mind.' He tells me there have been dolphins beside their boat every day for the last month, and it doesn't matter how many times he's seen them, you still feel you have to stop what you're doing, just to look at them.

I begin to find my own rhythm. Leaning the pot against my knees makes it easier to carry. I learn to keep my body low to the ground and move sideways like a crab across the deck to prevent myself suddenly sliding forwards. I no longer have to ask Will again and again which rows have which numbers of pots but can hold the pattern in my head. Our faces are warmed by the sun gleaming off the water and we all peel more layers off, stripping down to t-shirts and oilskins. While Will sits on top of the pots smoking, I lean against the side of the boat and think, quite truthfully, that there is nowhere I would rather be.

Midway through the third haul, James stops to tell me to climb down below the wheelhouse for a second. I go down and, from the belly of the boat, hear that distinctive clicking sound of dolphins communicating underneath us. I rush back out and lean right over the deck, trying to spot them. My head flicks to the left and right and back again as I think I see a glint in one direction, or a disturbance of the water in another. Finally, just over the starboard side of the boat, barely metres from where I am leaning, I see a sleek grey body arc across the waves. A few seconds later I see another, and then four or five at once rise elegantly up above the water and disappear again without breaking its surface. They stay with us for the rest of our trip.

We do not see a single other fishing boat all day. It is just the three of us gently rocking on the ocean, silent apart from the low thrum of the engine, Radio 1 and the whirring of the equipment that drags the pots from out of the water.

Late in the afternoon a hulking great container ship passes along the horizon. With the declining sun right behind it, we are able to make out the silhouettes of two men standing on top of the ship's corrugated iron containers, which conceal the industrial cargo – cars, train carriages, lumps of metal – that have doubtless travelled halfway across the world. Will says that he's never seen a person on a container ship before and I realise that in all the times that I have seen them drifting ghost-like across the seas, I hadn't either. You imagine the men on them sunk somewhere at the bottom of the ship, mysterious night creatures who do this job because of its isolation, because for six months or so they get to be away from their everyday realities. Now and then they venture outside for the first time in weeks to blink at the sun and check their cargo, before slipping back into the depths.

At any one moment, there are tens of thousands of container ships gliding across the oceans. On MarineTraffic's online live map of the seas you can view them all at once via satellite tracking, visualised as arrowpoints to indicate their direction of travel. They draw precise lines between countries and continents, many hugging their perimeters so that the shape of the land may be defined by their progress around it. The proliferation of these sharp little arrows around the coasts reminds me of piranhas swarming around a lifeless mass, gnawing at its edges.

But container ships can also have devastating, world-altering consequences on the seas and the creatures that live within them. Each day at least four freighters are lost to the seas, their cargoes spilling out into the water to be dispersed by the waves and discovered on beaches years later – trainers, cogs from machines and plastic packaging mixing in with the seaweed and foam left by waves. In 1967, between 25 and 36 million gallons of crude oil spilled into the Cornish seas from the 974-foot SS *Torrey Canyon*, chartered to BP. It took several days just to float the container ship off Pollard's Rock in the Seven Stones reef between Cornwall and the Isles of Scilly. During this time, an oil slick spread out relentlessly across the seas, like blood from a shotgun wound. To disperse the oil, an untested detergent was used – 10,000 tonnes of it sprayed by various vessels, including fishing boats, onto the slick. This detergent was highly toxic and only added to the vast destruction of wildlife and marine organisms along the coast. Over 15,000 seabirds died, as well as huge numbers of seals, crustaceans and fish. When it was discovered that the detergent was simply sinking the oil rather than destroying it, planes were sent in to bomb and set fire to the container in order to hide the evidence before the tourist season began. There are still two colossal tanks down there, beneath the fishermen's nets and pots, filled with thick oil that one day may rupture.

All the pots back in the water now and the fish room below filled up with bongos of snoozing crabs, we race back towards the harbour with the setting sun. At this point, I can no longer pretend to myself that I am not desperate to use the loo. After giving the *Three Jays* a quick scan before we left Newlyn harbour, and seeing that there was no toilet or even a bucket, I made the executive decision not to drink anything all day. I watch jealously as the boys turn away to piss off the stern, one hand on the rail to prevent them from slipping unexpectedly into the water. I try to imagine myself completing such an elegant manoeuvre. Under my oilskin dungarees, I am wearing a layer of tracksuit bottoms, and another of tights under that, all of which would have to be pulled down around my ankles before I could even begin. I would then have to squat in my wellies with my bare bottom suspended outside the boat above the water, almost certainly risking being sprayed by icy cold waves, and all the while clinging on to the rail above me like a monkey so as not to topple off the back of the boat.

I shake the image from my head; there's no way I could face the shame. Instead, I sit cross-legged trying to think of anything but my bladder, which is easier said than done on a boat surrounded by water. I look back behind us at the mournful grey dash of the

Wolf Rock Lighthouse, a sole exclamation point to the sky. The clouds have almost knitted over it, but there remains a small tear in them, allowing a burst of late sunlight to cut through above the lighthouse.

As we follow the coast around to Lamorna Cove, James says that when we met this morning he thought he recognised me from somewhere and realises it was right here: a lone figure with loose hair looking back from the *Filadelfia* as the land disappeared and the sun set.

We pass Mousehole and James tells me that his grandparents have recently sold their cottage there, which they had lived in for almost their whole lives. He says they were desperate to sell to a Cornish person, but the amount was too much for anyone from down here, so eventually they had to settle for a holiday let agency. James's grandad was so upset that he could not speak for weeks afterwards, knowing that he is now, in some small way, part of the gentrification of the area that is cleaning it out of actual Cornish people. James laments that you can barely tell anymore that Mousehole and St Ives were once thriving fishing ports. The very thing that made them what they are today has been torn right out, leaving behind only husks, their harbours merely facades. Newcomers arrive in Cornwall wanting the beauty of the coast, the fishing boats lined up in the harbour and old men in oilskins smoking pipes, but none of what makes it a real, living industry.

As soon as James steers the boat alongside Newlyn market to land the crabs, I say a hurried goodbye, scale up the harbour ladder faster than I ever have before and dash back up the cobbled lane to Denise and Lofty's to go straight to the toilet.

I am in bed by eight. Outside, the town feels especially still this night. I wonder whether I would be lonely if this place became my home and I no longer had the roar of the city to return to. For one of the first times in my life, my body aches with physical fatigue. The next morning, I wake with the badge of pride of dark purple bruises all over my legs from carrying the pots, of which I proudly send photos to my parents and friends.

10

Misways

On an especially warm spring day, I sit on the patio sunning myself with Denise. The music from the radio in the kitchen carries across from the open back door, the cats loll beside us and the light wind rolling in from the sea gently blows the laundry hanging from a line between our cottage and the cottage next door. The peace is interrupted by a loud splattering noise on the cobbles.

'Not again! Not again!' Denise jumps to her feet crying out in anguish. 'Those bastards!'

A streak of cream and black seagull shit runs down the length of her sheets.

'They do it on purpose, I'm sure of it,' she tells me, her hand sheltering her eyes from the sun as she squints up into the sky in an attempt to spot the culprit. These battles between the seagulls living along the Fragdan roofs and Denise's freshly washed laundry occur at least twice a week.

Since the day is so fine, I plan to take myself off on a walk along the coast towards Lamorna and beyond to Porthcurno. Time spent in any new place is always characterised for me by what Virginia Woolf described as 'solitary tramplings'. Learning the landscape by first feeling its ways under my feet and letting it brush up against me from all sides. 'Here was the freedom I desired, long sought-for, not yet known,' wrote Daphne du Maurier of her teenage escapades in Fowey. 'Freedom to write, to walk, to wander, freedom to climb hills, to pull a boat, to be alone.' I imagine following these women out along the coastal paths of Cornwall, each of us trying to carve our own particular paths of freedom. They are also my way of staving off the sense of loneliness that comes over me at unexpected moments in Newlyn. Human feelings, or feelings for humans, dissolve on walks.

I often leave notes for myself on my phone when I go on these solitary walks, little inanities I wish I had someone else with me to whom I could say them out loud. This morning I write myself a particularly bold one: 'For someone who gets lost a lot, coastal walks are a godsend. Only if the sound of the sea disappears from your left ear, can you have possibly gone wrong.'

Finding myself behind a cluster of tourists, I veer away from the coastal path and take one of the many flights of stone steps that reach down towards the sea below the cliffs. It sometimes rushes on me without warning – the compulsion to be as close to the water as possible, like a needy lover for whom no amount of physical closeness to their partner is enough. I take the narrow steps two at a time and let out a long breath when I find myself in an unpeopled cove at the bottom. The sea pours into the spaces between rocks to create small pools, before rushing out of them again like lungs inflating and deflating. It comes up so high that I am forced to hug the dark green wall of the cliff as I make my way along the curve. The wet slick covering the rocks dyes them black. They are stained, sharpened teeth rising out of the water. I keep one hand pressed against the cliff side, my face right up close to its moistened surface so that I create a right-angled triangle between my slanted body, the cliff wall and the rocks below me.

I edge my way around the bight, testing each new seaweed-thick rock with my no-grip trainers before scrambling over it and on to the next one. I pull myself up and over the last bulk of granite in the far corner of the cove, only to find another identical cove with yet more treacherous boulders, boasting even smoother surfaces ready to fall away from my feet and send me into the depths of the sea.

In between the crevices of rocks, I see occasional washed-up polyps – stranded from a Portuguese man-of-war that they would have moved through the sea with as one mind. I eye them suspiciously: Portuguese men-of-war can still sting long after they have died. I imagine what it would be like if humans had a similar power – to leave some sharp trace, some electric pulse beyond death that would afford those who knew them one final, physical memory to remind them: *yes, I was alive and you were alive and that knowledge hurts.*

The man-of-war is a siphonophore, meaning it is made up of colonies of organisms. These polyps have recently appeared along the Cornish coastline in unprecedented numbers, blown in by south-westerly winds. They look otherworldly against the dull rocks: pale pink and almost glowing, shaped like partially deflated balloons or those plastic organs you find on models of the human body in classrooms with pretty, electric-blue frills along their bottoms. Before Hurricane Brian disbanded them and washed almost five hundred of them up onto Cornish beaches, fleets of polyps would have drifted without direction through the sea with their sail-like main arm rippling above the water: the lightest lace blowing in the wind.

I get out my camera and take a photo of one, delaying the point at which I will have to face the next round in my coastal assault course. Cupping my hand around the screen of my camera, I notice in the thumbnail version of the photo on my camera that the polyp has a slight discoloration to it: a yellowed stain curled over its body like a ring left by a mug of coffee. I zoom in closer, wiping the sea spray from the screen, and expanding the stain into a more complex form. A face emerges across the pale surface of the creature: the reflection of a woman whose hair blows outwards, her face filled with dark, uncertain features, like the craters of a moon. As in the famous Escher lithograph of the artist himself reflected in a glass orb, impossibly I see myself there, crudely drawn out upon the polyp's translucent skin. The stain seeps outwards across the polyp, veins of colour bleeding across it, and I see Newlyn harbour emerge in the background.

I shake my head. When I look down again, it is just a mark on the polyp, nothing more. I put the camera away in my backpack and continue scrambling along the rocks until my route is blocked once more by a sheer-faced boulder that marks the cove's end. I consider my options. Even to reach this perhaps unsurmountable rock, I would have to slide on my hands and knees down a sloped piece of blue elvan, whose furthest edge disappears down into the sea. Once at the very edge of this natural diving board, I would either have to spring into the air and claw myself up the side of the cliff or, if unable to make my leap, would somehow have to climb back up the blue elvan slide. Alternatively, I could give up now and return all the way around both coves to rejoin the conventional path with my tail between my legs. No, I can't go back yet. While slightly alarmed as to how quickly I have got myself into this perilous situation, it is moments such as these that a city dweller like myself, whose childhood was cushioned with asphalt, relishes. In 'The Romaunt of the Rose', Chaucer coined the term 'misway'. I like that it is a word of its own, as if a wrong way were itself a direction, a route one may choose to take through the world.

Scanning the cliffs for a potential other option that might save me from my rock and a hard place, I notice that the grass gets thick and stands in clumps above the rocks and that further up there is the vague sign of human activity: parts of bushes that look as if they may have been trampled down by adventurous feet, and a dark hole that might lead to another path parallel to the waterline. This could be my misway. Standing on tiptoe, I grab a hold of the grassy tufts above the rocks and hoist myself onto the soft grass above the rock, relieved to feel a more permanent and forgiving surface beneath my feet.

Up close, the way through to higher ground I saw amongst the thickets above me looks denser and I have to cover my head and force my way through. I feel the limbs of savage blackthorn bushes latch onto my clothes, piercing through my thick jeans and lacerating my ankles and hands. Midway through thrashing against these violent branches, I lose my footing and start to slide back down towards the cliff. The sea's bellowing seems to reach up over the top of the cliffs ready to embrace me into its open mouth. Just as my left foot slips right over the edge of the land,

I spot a thin length of faded orange rope tied between two trees like a handrail. Flailing, I manage to grasp it with the tips of my fingers and pull myself back up onto the grass. Hot and sweaty now, I look out at the seething waters below, sending out immense gratitude towards the unknown human who tied the rope there, perhaps long ago. Then I force myself back through the tangled thicket in search of a path.

The dense wood with its heavy aroma acts as a sound wall to the sea. Its angry cries disappear, replaced by the buzzing of flies and occasional rustling in the bracken to my right. The many layers of complex green seem to flatten out like an intricate wall-paper design that tricks the eye into thinking it is animated, leaves curling, fronds gently stroking at my sides and insects crawling over stems. I stumble with my back hunched right over through a claustrophobia-inducing path that looks as if it has not been traversed for many years. I decide to continue upwards, looking in vain for another way in. The brambles, heather and brown gorse become more matted, growing thicker and taller as I pull myself through it, eventually coming right up to my neck, so that it begins to feel like swimming through mud. Soon the ceiling of vines and branches blocks out the bright sunshine from earlier. Where the light does break through, it comes through in thin slants, as though the sun is being cast through a cheese grater. That impeccable observer of the natural world, Gerard Manley Hopkins, termed this phenomenon *shivelight*, an amalgamation of the Middle English word *schive*, meaning slice, and light, or as Hopkins himself explained it, 'the lances of sunshine that pierce the canopy of a wood'.

My trousers are now soaked through, my hands riddled with cuts. I barely notice the thorns any longer, whose long fingers pull at my backpack and jumper, urging me to return the way I came. At last, I find a slight break in the undergrowth and beyond it a clearing where I might sit and catch my breath. Along the edges of the clearing are a series of trees sprouting from the hedgerow and frozen into petrified wind-blown shapes. Each of their trunks is so twisted and bent towards the south that even on the stillest of days they would lean right out, tricking walkers just for a second into believing they are in the midst of a terrific gale. It is only when I have almost reached the clearing that I see the green hammock stretched across two trees. I stop moving. Staring intently at the hammock, I fancy I can see the outline of a body filling it up. Unbidden, my mind begins to build an image of this person, undisturbed by any other human for years, who each evening uses his faded orange rope to scale down to the sea to catch themselves a few mackerel to cook on a fire. At any second, the figure will leap up and attack this trespasser, before they have a chance to reveal their hiding place to the world. I imagine a face coated and cracked with mud, their eyes, which have not met with another human for many months, wild and raging.

I take two cautious steps backwards, then turn on my heels and run, not allowing myself to look back for a second to check if there really is a body there. All rationality long departed, I sprint back through the hedgerow with its violent thorns and lower myself back down into the cove. The sea has crept in closer and most of the rocks are now wholly submerged. The sing of the shore screams of the danger facing any human left in its way. For a moment, with my energy spent, I think I might just let it take me. And then, with the cry of a seagull, sense floods back, I accept that my only option is to admit defeat and return the way I have come.

The route back passes swiftly, as if the coast is hurrying to expel me. Once back up on the sandy cliff path, which is shotgunned with rabbit holes, I overtake multiple groups of slow-moving walkers and try to give off an air of insouciance whilst horribly aware that my trousers are ripped and sticky wet. I feel my face: there are hard patches of mud stuck above my eyes and twigs sticking out of my hair.

I look down far below where the undergrowth grows dense. How many other people might be hidden in woods along the Cornish coast, I wonder: those who have escaped humanity among the entangled thickets above the sea cliffs. I return to the notes on my phone, adding 'not true' to the bottom of my original brazen statement and giving the note the title 'Misway'.

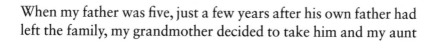

When I have not spoken to my parents for a while, I send them roughly drawn-up accounts of my adventures to reassure them that I am still alive. Unsurprisingly, considering my ability to lose myself along the simplest of paths, these tend to have the adverse effect. A few hours after sending my parents an account of my walk to Land's End, my father rings me as I am walking along Newlyn prom.

'I wanted to talk to you about that story you wrote.'

My mother, evidently standing just behind him, calls into the phone: 'Can you tell her that what she did was incredibly dangerous?'

'Your mother says she wants you to know that she thinks what you did was incredibly dangerous—'

'And stupid,' my mother interrupts.

'And stupid.' Dad diligently echoes.

'Does she realise that the sea is not a laughing matter?'

'She says, you know the sea is not a big joke—'

I say: 'I don't think…'

'She doesn't think…' my dad reports back.

'Well, that much is obvious,' I hear Mum say. 'Was she really wearing no-grip trainers?'

I watch a small girl in school uniform poking at a blue-frilled polyp washed up beside a plastic bottle on the beach below Newlyn prom. Her mother, seeing her daughter's close proximity to the alien creature, scoops her up in her arms and back to the safety of the pavement.

Eventually, I say something like: 'Look, if you just rang up to lecture me, then—'

'I rang you up because I know that story,' my father responds, leaving a mysterious silence to hang in the air.

When my father was five, just a few years after his own father had left the family, my grandmother decided to take him and my aunt to a Cornish cove during the Easter holidays. While there, almost exactly the same thing that I narrated in my story happened to them, he says. After our phone call, he sends me the typewritten transcript of the monologue his mother wrote about the experience, headlined 'September 1957, *Woman's Hour*, BBC: "The Murderous Innocence of the Sea"', which she read out on Radio 4 sixty years ago.

I know very little of my grandmother, Patricia Ash. She died when I was an infant, but from what I can remember and have garnered from my father, she was an austere, enterprising woman who lived alone for most of her life in the coastal hamlet of Shingle Street, Suffolk. Reading her transcript is the closest I have ever felt to her.

'There we were, scrambling, slipping over the low rocks guarding the edge of the bay and discovering smooth white sea-sticks, and better and better pools left by the tide,' she explains. 'The safe beach was out of sight – and out of mind too – and here was a stretch of rugged coast to take your sense away.' I recognise that desire at once: the need to reach the most desolate lines of coast, where you might obliterate your sense of self and be transported away from the known world.

But, as I did too all those years later, Patricia fails to notice the dangers of the route she has chosen and the changing of the tide. Below another yawn of cliffs on another piece of the Cornish coast, she is faced with a similar choice: 'Stay on those sharp cold rocks above tide level for 6 or 7 hours (why didn't I know the times of tides). Scale that leaning mass of rock to the beach where I couldn't even see first foot-holds. Or wade through the tunnel, where the water would be up to the children's waists and the force of the waves looked formidable. Up above, the green of growing things and the sunlit crest of the cliff looked the most inviting and possible – so I thought.' When I think back to my own foolish adventure I am no longer alone but see the two of us in parallel desperately trying to scale the same cliff, my aunt and father as young children following anxiously behind. I want to shout across to them: 'Go back! Don't do what I have done!'

'Occasionally,' my grandmother continues, 'the beauty and wildness of the scene did flash through my mind, and it was made more vivid because of the peculiar angle of the vision – and the horror. It seemed as though we might have died already.' Whatever danger it promises, to us the sea remains beguiling, almost enticing.

As they scrabble up the cliffs, the route gets more and more treacherous, while the tired, little bodies pulling themselves up behind travel ever more slowly. Her other options now gone, she decides to leave her children on the cliff and continue alone to get help. 'It will be all right, don't move an inch, don't look down,' she tells them, 'I'll be back' – and scrambled away out of sight torn by their cries of 'Mummy, Mummy' mingling with the gulls screaming and the pounding of the waves below.

Once over the clifftop, she races along the road, crying out for help along the empty track. Some way ahead, she spots a young fisherman and dashes over to him, gasping as she tries to explain her plight: the two children she has left on the cliff. They sprint back together; the fisherman nimbly clambers down the cliffs and retrieves first one and then the other of her children, who are now very cold and quiet. Thanking the man, who scolds her for the idiocy of her high-tide excursion, she takes her children firmly by the hand back to their cottage, murmuring apologies to them all the way home.

My grandmother describes how for the rest of the holiday, whenever her children felt frightened at night by the memories of their cliff-face escapade, she could only say: 'I know it was horrible, but it need never happen again. You can learn about tides and understand and watch the sea. The sea has a pattern.'

'So many of us seem to be out of touch with patterns of nature,' she concludes. 'The sea is just a summer playground and the cliffs a beautiful backcloth.'

Newlyners tell countless stories of naive tourists who have been stranded by the tide and have had to be rescued. In Mike Buttery's history of Mousehole, he writes of one time he and another fisherman saved a young girl trapped below Penlee Point: they found her 'only wearing a bikini and her body was "cut to rags" by brambles'. A *Cornishman* article from 1927 similarly describes how two Newlyn men risked their lives in order to rescue a ten-year-old boy from drowning: 'instantly people began to flock to the spot, drawn apparently by that mysterious influence that attracts to a scene of danger'. My own fateful adventure on that savage stretch of coastline between Newlyn and Lamorna was my first true facing of the sea. It betrayed a foolishness which, once I had begun to go out on fishing boats, and once I started to know the sea even a little, I would never allow to happen again.

11

FISH WITHIN FISH

You feel your whole body at sea. Its rhythms force you to notice the way you hold yourself, making minute readjustments every few seconds to keep yourself balanced as the boat rocks. There are six degrees of freedom on a ship that dictate the ways in which it can move: pitch (a port–starboard movement from side to side), roll (the back-and-forth tilt from bow to stern) and yaw (the boat's rotation). Every muscle learns to tense and relax in time with these motions in order just to keep yourself upright.

Once back down below, in my tiny bunk on the *Filadelfia*, it is a relief not to fight against these axes of motion any longer. The engine's bellowing softens to a croon and my body is gently lifted and dropped by the sea in a rhythm that is not regular but feels natural within the womb-like space of the cabin. I fall asleep in minutes, resting easy in the knowledge that there is always someone on watch, guarding our vessel as it carries us over the seas.

With my seasickness decisively over by Tuesday evening, I take no pills before bed that night and wake at six with a clear head in time to catch the sunrise on deck. My first sight of the day comes through the bathroom porthole (out of which window Don and Andrew, practical jokers both, like to stick their hands and grab my ankles as I stand outside taking photos). It always gives a foretaste of what will confront me as soon as I climb up into the wheelhouse, like looking through a kinetoscope and seeing a world in motion behind its round hole.

The view out of the porthole is still black this morning, but I can feel the day just waiting to spark. I take my toothbrush from where it is tucked at an angle through a wire running down the side of the bathroom wall with the other brushes and, to save time in case I miss the sunrise, simultaneously run my arms and legs under the burning hot showerhead, banging against one and then the other side of the wall as the boat lurches. And all the while I look out through the circle of window, waiting for the sky to arrive.

The only mirror on board the *Filadelfia* hangs spit- and toothpaste-stained in the bathroom. I don't like to check my reflection in it often and delight in the novelty of not having to bother with how I look out here. In cities, it is impossible to avoid the sight of your own face – it leers out at you from every polished car and shop front. There is not a moment when you are allowed to forget how you are seen, your appearance reified behind glass. Today I am taken aback by the wildness that greets me. There are flecks of cuttlefish juice across my face like black moles that intermingle with scattered sequins of flaking fish scales. My skin is a wind-burned red, my eyes somehow darker or deeper than usual, and my hair caked with guts and pieces of fish bone. The reflection returns a lopsided grin to me as I pull a fat glob of fish blood from my hair.

I hurry upstairs, shout 'Morning!' at Stevie, who is on watch, and throw open the wheelhouse door. It is all out there – not just a patch of sky framed by the interstices of skyscrapers; this is what the whole sky looks like, boundless in all directions. The sight still surprises me every time as if during the night my mind has unwrapped the sea's clasp from my memory. Sometimes I wake to find us in a flat, cool desert; other days amongst yawning black waves like caves; others still to arctic scenes, the entirety of the sea white, as if overexposed, and the sky revealing further snowcaps.

Today's pre-dawn blue is not a soft shade but an oppressive block of colour that seems to rush all the way up to our boat and slam against the deck, so vivid is its blueness. A heavy line of clouds has settled above the sea. Sandwiched between several blue tinted clouds, an expanse of golden light casts itself upwards and outwards. The light spreads across the line between water and sky, turning both a rich navy, the lapidary pattern carved out across the waves accentuated by the way the light falls on them. Horizon watching is the routine that steadies me on the *Filadelfia*, my fishing equivalent to reading the papers or listening to the radio over breakfast or watching television. And yet it is more than all those: all possible news expressed in a curve of blue. It makes me think of Newlyn, how this weather will blow back to them, and it makes me think of home.

Once I've had my fix, I make a coffee for myself and Stevie before settling in my seat beside the skipper's chair to wait for the first haul of the day. At 6.30 the 'booking out' system is broadcast over the VHF radio. One by one, in alphabetical order, every Stevenson's boat at sea calls to check in. The company brought this system in several years ago after one of their trawlers went missing. No one even knew anything had happened until two days after the ship had gone down. Now, each morning, whoever is on watch speaks the name of their boat back to those listening on land. In a firm voice the *Filadelfia* promises: *It's all right. We're still out here.*

The VHF also allows fishermen in range of one another to call each other across boats. Skippers use it to warn other fishing vessels not to come too close to their nets, especially if they have static gear below the water, and to let them know the coordinates of any rough ground nearby that might damage their hulls. But, more often than not, the VHF is used by fishermen to have a yarn when they're bored on watch – one fishing boat to another, the two of them speaking of known things from back home that for a moment make the land feel that bit closer, that bit more tangible.

The *Filadelfia* has two VHF receivers on board, which resemble nineties-style clunky black telephones with curly wires. While making my way up from the galley, I often hear what sounds like a raging party going on in the wheelhouse, only to find Don alone with a phone to each ear, shouting over two other croaky voices gossiping about market prices and turbot sightings. A few months ago there were so many Cornish boats out in the Channel that the VHF was 'bloody steaming', as Don puts it. Back in the eighties it became a craze amongst Newlyn's inshore fleet to yell catchphrases from the TV series *Happy Days* over the VHF. As soon as one fisherman yelled 'Perfectamundo!' into the radio, a whole host of 'Perfectamundos!' would ricochet around the bay, until someone eventually decided the joke had gone too far and would gruffly call out 'Shuurrup!' A moment later a new round of cheerful 'Shuurrups' would take over instead as the boats scooted around Mount's Bay.

This morning after breakfast Don is cut from his yarning by a great belch on the other end of the line. 'Better out than in', cackles the other fisherman from across the sea.

'Too right,' Don replies, and the man lets another rip. In these moments, it as if we have never left the Swordy at all.

In *Arctic Dreams*, Barry Lopez describes a moment when, staring out from a cliff above Lancaster Sound – a body of water between Canada and the Arctic – he sees a group of narwhals emerge from the sea, the clash of their great tusks creating triangular arches above the water. In that moment, he writes, 'the urge to communicate, the upwelling desire, is momentarily sublime'. Narwhals use clicking sounds deep below the water to communicate with their companions and locate prey and obstacles such as floe edges. The hollow, helix-shaped tusks, which they are famous for, allow the narwhal to navigate and feel the characteristics of the water acutely. For years there were various, imaginative speculations about the purpose of these swirled tusks, with most believing that narwhals clashed them against one another in displays of aggression. However, as these tusks contain about ten million nerve endings it is more probable that narwhals use them to communicate information about the seas they have travelled through with others – a creature's entire life journey passed to another in a single touch, a single crack of horn on horn.

Narwhals and whales are far from silent. Blue whales are the loudest creatures on the planet, communicating to each other in a series of moans and clicks and grunts at a volume greater than 180 decibels. These vibrations can travel along channels in the sea for thousands of miles, telephone lines between whales crossing over the breadth of the oceans. We cannot know for certain the biological reason why blue whales call to one another from such great distances, but I like to think that they, like the fishermen, are just yarning and burping across the vast regions of the seas, letting each other know: *It's all right. We're still out here.*

Don ends his morning yarn to prepare for the first haul of the day. I watch the derricks creak up, heaving with them the nets from the depths and the sea around them turns a muddy, olive green – the *cowsherny* hue from Nance's *Glossary*. Each haul is an unknown quantity, providing a moment of intrigue that breaks up the day. Whoever is on watch is arbitrarily chosen as the person responsible for the fish caught during that haul, receiving either great praise or a tumult of insults depending on the quality of the catch. While both cod-ends rise up and over the deck, the watchman and I lean out through the windows, rubbing our hands together saying: 'This feels like a good one!', and 'I can just sense the turbot down there this time, you know?'

We catch only one turbot that morning and a pitiful number of undersized monks. From the wheelhouse Don sends the nets back down into the water a little more forcibly than usual, his tone with Stevie that little bit sharper. Along with a baseball cap, an old sock and various other detritus that have somehow ended up amongst this first haul, the men have to throw vast numbers of dead fish back into the waters too. It is like watching a fish-monger take the freshest fish, or a baker his just-risen bread, and chucking it straight into the bin.

Around half the fish I saw caught on the *Crystal Sea* had to be thrown back into the sea, although they were dead, because of quota restrictions, and it is not much better on the *Filadelfia*. The immense frustration and sadness amongst fishermen regarding all this waste is plain. When I asked David, the *Crystal Sea*'s skipper, about it, he replied sparely: 'We don't talk about it; we try not to think about it.'

There is a belief held amongst many that the seas are common property, the shared heritage of mankind. And yet, like the serpent symbol of the ouroboros eating its own tail, our sense of the seas' commonality is chased by our desire to govern them, to territorialise the waters. The unpeopled spaces between land turn out to be far less neutral than we might imagine. It was by means of the seas that the first colonial missions set out over the world; deep below its surface, countries test out nuclear weaponry that damages marine life, while submarines prowl in wait for the first cries of war. And in every region of the world fishermen fight over the seas' fish stocks.

The Tongan and Fijian anthropologist Epeli Hau'Ofa describes how the dividing lines we have drawn through the sea reorder the land: 'Nineteenth-century imperialism erected boundaries that led to the contraction of Oceania, transforming a once boundless world into the Pacific islands states and territories that we know today. People were confined to their tiny spaces, isolated from each other.' The seas were mapped out and politicised, leading to terms of ownership like 'Our Waters' (as in 'Get Our Waters Back' the much-touted slogan of the Brexit Vote Leave campaign); and yet, though the sea is a site of damage, loss and corruption, it is also synonymous with life, generation and the flow of ideas between diverse places. It is all these things at once, every contradiction and inconsistency.

In 1968 the biologist and ecologist Garrett Hardin published a paper called 'The Tragedy of the Commons', in which he argued that individuals are motivated by their own self-interest to overuse common property. If the seas are left unchecked as a communal resource, Hardin explains, each man will ensure he spends as much time and effort at sea as to be certain no one else can take his share. The tragedy of the commons, as with most economic theories designed to make sense of an unpredictable world, is not as simplistic as first outlined; humans cannot simply be reduced to inherently selfish agents, as they cannot be reduced to purely good or evil. Rather, it seems clearer now that the rising competition over the produce of the seas is also intrinsically tied to the expansion of capitalism around Europe, the advancement in fishing technology and the more desperate conditions created by post-war austerity.

The introduction of individual fishing quotas (IFQs) throughout Europe during the 1960s was an attempt to tackle the tragedy of the commons, each fishing boat being allowed to catch their appropriate share of fish within the seas they hunted. Privatisation became a quick fix to the problems of commonly owned resources. The assumption went: if each fisherman had a property right over their share of the fish in the sea, instead of believing they were all chasing the same stocks, they would be more likely to conserve fish for the future. As competition over the stocks of the seas increased, agreements were drawn up that attempted to ensure each country was given fair fishing access to the seas. Before joining the EU, Britain signed the London Fisheries Convention (1964), which stated that every signatory nation (twelve in all) could have full access to the fishing grounds between 6–12 nautical miles from their coastline, as long as they had already been fishing there during the previous decade.

In the 1970s the Common Fisheries Policy (CFP) was introduced, which controlled the fishing rights of all EU member states. While the CFP's intentions were commendable, their strict legislation caused destruction and controversy too. Even today, despite their attempts to reduce damage to fish populations, 40 per cent of EU stocks are still overfished. Moreover, the rigorously enforced quota limits have led to increased waste from boats: returning dead fish to the sea because they are either undersized or the vessel does not have enough quota to keep them. Similarly, as happened with pollution quotas, fishing quotas could be leased, sold and auctioned off. Wealthier families and larger companies began buying out smaller boats and purchasing greater percentages of the quota until they held a monopoly over the area. This has increasingly happened in Newlyn, with young

123

fishermen struggling to enter the industry due to the price and demand for quotas.

That the percentages of quotas awarded to each member state of the EU has not changed since the CFP's inception is a large part of why the majority of fishermen in the UK voted to leave the EU (polls suggest the figures were as high as 92 per cent among fishing communities). Under the CFP's rules, though every member state has the right to manage the resources in its EEZ, or exclusive economic zone (up to two hundred miles from their coastline), the fishing area of all member states is considered one zone that everyone may fish in. For example, around 58 per cent of fish caught in the UK's EEZ was landed by fishermen from other European countries, with only around 16 per cent of British fishermen's catch coming from other European fishing zones.

Newlyn's fishermen, who play an active role in politics and avidly express their views on all things fishing via Twitter (most of their handles being the name of their boats rather than their own) are growing increasingly frustrated with the way in which fishing has become a pawn in political debate. The phrase I hear again and again is: 'We're being sold down the river.' They hoped that Brexit would allow them to readdress quota distribution and access to UK waters. However, while fishing rights played a sizeable role in Vote Leave's campaign, in reality the fishing industry only contributes 0.05 per cent to the UK's GDP and employs fewer than 12,000 people. There are concerns therefore that it will become nothing more than a bargaining chip if the EU ties fishing rights to other parts of trade deals.

It is not only the CFP who manage quota. The UK government is able to choose how quota is distributed amongst its fleet and for the last forty years has chosen to give the 'ten metres and under' boats (which make up 88 per cent of all vessels in the UK) only 2 per cent of their rights to fish quota. There remains a patent disjunction between legislation that attempts to protect fish populations and the complex realities of the industry: not only do fish populations frequently migrate, regardless of scientific advancements it will never be as straightforward to divide fish between fishermen as it is to apportion land and livestock between farmers. Legislation will always move more slowly than our awareness of the immediate issues facing the planet, and fishing legislation is particularly knotty. But in recent years the CFP has had successes in preventing further collapses in fish stocks and restoring those that have been almost wiped out; a discard ban has gradually been put in place to prevent more waste of fish, requiring fishermen to land all that they catch unless it is undersized or a banned species; recognising that inshore fleets are a more sustainable form of fishing than trawling, the quantity of quota they receive is also in the process of being readdressed.

To improve the mood on the boat after the dismal first day, Andrew fries us up some freshly caught lemon sole. We eat it piping hot with buttered slices of white bread. I have never tasted such fresh fish, the flesh pure white and flaking off on my fork.

'Just think, you might've gut those sole yourself,' Andrew says to me. 'And now you're eating them.'

'If she'd gut 'em, we'd know as there'd be half the guts still in there!' Stevie interjects wryly.

Kyle, with his indomitable appetite, passes up the offer of fresh fish for breakfast and chooses a starter of Pot Noodle followed by a ravioli sandwich. Afterwards, I follow him up to the wheelhouse and we get chatting. Kyle is only a year or so older than me and both of us are a good twenty years younger than anyone else on the boat. We take these mornings together during his first watch to discuss shared memories of the nineties and noughties as kids: TV shows we watched and computer games we played, the music we listened to, the terrible nightclubs we went to as teenagers and the outrageously stupid things we have done while drunk in them.

Kyle first went to sea when he was ten, skipping school to go out with his cousin. When he arrived back in the harbour his uniform was always filthy and covered in scales. This is it, he thought, this is living. Though he persevered with his schooling and got pretty good results, it was not enough to keep him from the sea. After leaving school at sixteen, he found a berth on a gill-netter. It made him grow up pretty fast – you can't mess about at sea like you can at school, he says. Kyle still has a huge amount of knowledge to mine from the *Filadelfia*'s older crew members. Any time they offer him some pearl of wisdom, he leaps up to follow them, learning while I'm aboard a new technique to mend nets and how to shimmy along the derricks so as to apply oil to keep out corrosion.

In fishing, Kyle has found a sense of purpose and a community. He remembers on his eighteenth birthday, climbing up from the cabin for the early morning watch and feeling miserable at the prospect of being at sea on his first day of adulthood. But, as he reached the wheelhouse he was greeted by the familiar sight of Lamorna Cove, on the final stretch home. 'Couldn't let you miss your eighteenth, could we!' the skipper called out from the wheelhouse, and led him down to the galley where the whole crew had gathered to present him with a birthday cake they'd smuggled on board. 'They did all that, just for me,' Kyle pauses and smiles out at the sea.

When they were still teenagers, Kyle and his fishermen friends would head straight from the sea, in their yellow gum boots and fish-stained tracksuits, to go clubbing in Penzance. He doesn't go out much anymore though, he says, since he and his wife are about to have their first baby together. I suddenly feel much younger and more immature than Kyle. Though we are practically the same age, my friends and I from our middle-class backgrounds in London get to act as kids much longer, messing about at university and believing the appropriate time to settle down and start a family occurs some time in your thirties. We in the cities are far less worldly than we like to think, just by the nature of our being in a cosmopolitan environment. Kyle told me he once visited Manchester. People kept asking him what he thought of Manchester and wasn't it a great city? Eventually he felt he had to be honest and just said to them, 'But, where's the sea?'

Kyle's stories are always left-field. He tells me that when he first started fishing, he used to write his phone number out on scraps of paper, seal them in old water bottles and chuck them overboard. Any time he got a call from an unknown number he'd excitedly shout down the phone: 'Hello! How did you get this number?' And they'd say: 'Have you been mischarged for PPI?' or something, and he'd say: 'No, but did you find this number in a bottle?' Another day his friend caught an electric ray, or torpedo fish as they are sometimes called, by mistake and the force of electric current passing through his body knocked him right off his feet. He grins at the memory.

Out the wheelhouse window, beyond where our feet are stretched out over the dashboard, a ghost of a sun is trying to break through the clouds. Kyle can't wait for the weather to improve again. Last summer they tied a fish box to the back of the trawler and water-skied across the sea. Another time, Kyle was on night watch after a particularly long week of fishing when a huge black monster suddenly erupted from the sea, water rushing off its dark sides. It turned out to be an enormous Danish submarine that had been hidden from the sonar. I can imagine Kyle, the sole member of the crew awake, standing on the edge of a fishing boat gazing up at this silent, menacing warship towering above him. While he couldn't see any of the boat's crew, he said he could feel on him the eyes of men who were not likely to have seen the outside world for three months or more. A moment later the submarine slunk back below the water, leaving a brief, foaming whirlpool. Kyle rubbed his eyes and went to make himself another coffee, unsure if he had imagined the whole thing.

Before Kyle can start on another tale, Don hoists himself up into the wheelhouse with a grunt, his face ashen and his eyes red from a few hours of broken sleep. 'You better have caught me some lovely fish while you've been gossiping away...'

Each time I return to the deck during the haul, my reward is to learn how to gut a new fish. Halfway through the week, on

Wednesday, I am taught how to gut hake, a round-headed fish that was recently declared sustainable by the Marine Stewardship Council (MSC), and is mainly caught by gill-netters. The MSC scientifically assesses whether fisheries are caught in a sustainable way and are not being overfished or damaging other marine populations in the process. I find that hake smell more acrid than lemon sole, and when I slice their bellies open they are often teeming with worms.

We also bring up scarred fish, their histories written out in their scales. Small nicks and bites in their sides suggest past scrapes with monkfish; roughness along their gills are signs that they have narrowly avoided the fate of being dragged up in a net once before, or perhaps that they were manhandled by a previous fisherman a few years ago and thrown back overboard for being too small. I inspect each fish with great care, opening up their mouths, tracing my gloved fingers over every fin and line and scale. It feels a privilege to get to see these hidden parts of a fish, like the inner workings of a clock. As soon as turbot are caught, the fishermen make a slit just above their strong, fanned tails to bleed them out so that they don't lose their bright white colouring. They stand out in hauls, like slices of the moon, cries of joy spreading around the boat if ever more than four are caught in one go. When you look under the flap of skin on a turbot, you can see their gills are bright purple and ruffled, like an Elizabethan collar.

At close proximity, most fish skin is fractalled with dark lines. In her poem 'The Fish', Elizabeth Bishop writes how the fish's 'brown skin hung in strips':

Like ancient wallpaper,
And its pattern of darker brown
Was like wallpaper:
Shapes like full-blown roses
Stained and lost through age.

The colour and shapes painted over the skin of each fish we gut reminds me of some aspect of the land. A particular Dory's back has echoes of the beige cubic patterns on the carpet in the Star, the dark circular mark on its side, known as 'St Peter's thumbprint', a faded spillage across one cushion; the pinks of a monkfish's gums are the exact shade of the cushions in the cottage in the Fragdan. Sometimes in the long gleaming strand of guts that you pull clean out of the fish come surprises, such as a second smaller fish in a translucent bag, as if my knife were a fishing rod diving into a second great sea, whose swilling waters were folded inside the first fish's belly.

On the deck of the *Filadelfia* I hold one of these gossamer-thin pouches drawn from the inside of a fish up to the sky and marvel at the completeness of the thing within, its dim gold eye just discernible, its body curved slightly as if caught in the motion of a wave. I wonder how it got in there. And then, dumbly, it enters my mind that these bagged fish must be the unborn babies of the fish I am gutting. The revelation sickens me and I almost drop my knife. For a while I can't continue gutting, the delicate, dead fish hanging limply from my hand like a goldfish won at a fair.

It is only after a few weeks back on land that I remember the vague details I do know about fish reproduction. Firstly they would be eggs, not fully formed fish. And secondly, most fish spawn eggs externally, which are then fertilised by the male fish (only cartilaginous fish, the jawed vertebrates with skeletons made of cartilage rather than bone, such as rays and skates, fertilise their eggs internally). It was not a fish embryo after all, but a smaller fish eaten whole by the larger one, its body undamaged in the process.

By dinner time I am starving and spoon myself out a generous helping of hunter's chicken from the stove (though still about half the size of the other men's portions). This is Kyle's speciality on board. He wraps chicken in bacon and cooks it in the oven for several hours, while it swims in an oozing layer of treacle-like sauce. The resulting meal is sweet and moreish. Food always tastes better at sea. Kyle says that sometimes he makes his missus the exact same recipe he prepares on the *Filadelfia* but it never tastes as good. After a day of being thrown about by the boat's lurching and with your body exhausted from the work of the hauls, to sit together out of the wind and eat hot, satisfying food is a feeling comparable to no other.

When I start to thank Kyle for the meal, he holds up his hand. 'Stop with the thank yous. Just finish your plate,' he tells me. 'That's the only thanks I need.' There are small shifts in behaviour one has to learn at sea: a kind of sea manners. I learn to put the toilet seat back up after I've used it; to help in the fish room without getting in people's way; when people need a coffee refill; which snacks are each men's favourites and so should not be finished off by anyone but them; and when someone wants to be left alone.

We sit with the telly on, our mouths sticky with hunter's sauce as the *Filadelfia* grunts and rolls over the waves. As I get to know her better, she seems to me like the kind of old woman who refuses to age gracefully, getting bits and pieces of herself Botoxed – a new engine, telly, more efficient nets – but still sagging in the neck, her external parts beginning to rust and flake, everything about her more rudimentary than the *Crystal Sea*. Most of the time no one says anything, too tired by this point in the week to utter more than a brief smattering of thoughts on a particular game show contestant or a question about tomorrow's dinner. Another fisherman tells me that when they're back on land, the reason fishermen like to gather together in the pubs is because 'We don't know what to say apart from fishing. The sea takes away everything else.' Nothing new happens on trawlers; the world does not change beyond the repeating cycle of hauls. Like the manners peculiar to the sea, a particular kind of vernacular emerges while fishing too, one that varies in each part of the boat. During the hauls on deck language is contracted, focused right in to convey instructions quickly, which are nonetheless always interspersed with at least one wisecrack at the expense of another crew member. This staccato dialogue is itself distinct from the more meditative, multi-directional conversations that occur on watch.

Describing life on the fictional *Narcissus*, Joseph Conrad reproduces the ways he hears men at sea interacting, the fragments of conversation captured perfectly through ellipses: 'Here, sonny, take that bunk! ... Don't you do it! ... what's your last ship? ... I know her ... there years ago, in Puget sound ... This here berth leaks, I tell you! ... come on; give us a chance to swing that chest! ... did you bring a bottle, any of you shore toffs? ... give us a bit of baccy... I know her; her skipper drank himself to death ... he was a dandy boy!' I imagine the sea and the engine beating over this punctuation, slicing through dialogue and causing the end of sentences to be washed away. That night, as the men come and go from their short sleeps, I stay in the galley with the TV still buzzing on. Like Conrad's narrator, I am privy to a whole host of fleeting exchanges between the men, while I lie slumped along the back bench in my tracksuit and thick socks, snug beside the hotplates burning away on the stove.

Up in the wheelhouse, I hear Kyle call up the *Billy Rowney*, skippered by Danny Fisher (nickname 'Fish') whose trawler lights we can just make out to our port side. Kyle asks the man on watch if his friend is about and the watchman replies: 'I think he's turned in for the night, why?'

'Oh,' Kyle looks dejected. 'Nothin' – just wanted a yarn.'

The watchman tells him he'll let the friend know once he's awake. A few hours later, Kyle gets his yarn. For almost forty-five minutes I listen to the two of them happily chatting, half a mile away from each other over the waves, reminiscing about the best steaks they've had in Penzance and Newlyn, their love of the Meadery restaurant and what they've eaten at sea so far this week. On the *Billy Rowney* last night they had a 'real rich supper' (rich means delicious in Newlyn) of breaded scallops and monk. Tonight, they're finally heading home after a gruelling week, so having the traditional '*Billy Rowney* Going Home Meal' of jacket potatoes and steak. The men sign off on the VHF, promising to speak again soon.

'Where are we going next, Old Man?' Stevie shouts up to Don.

'I know where the megrim is and the lemons, but where are the bloody monks and turbots?' I hear Don reply, and later: 'We'll try down south-east way tomorrow.'

If we were to continue our course 'down south-east way' eventually we would reach France. Some trawlermen reckon it's too hard and stony down that way, but Don loves those grounds, knowing that in those territories you're away from the other boats, pushing out alone into the sea. This knowledge runs through Don's blood; his great-grandfather was a fisherman and sailed all the way up to Greenland to hunt amongst the ice sheets. They talk of other boats they have had relationships with. Don was skipper of the *Sarah Shone* for thirteen years, she was 'a fucking gem', while Kyle has especially fond memories of the young crew on the *Joy of Ladram*. Once he and his mate went to the back of the boat when it was blowing a hooley and re-enacted the *Titanic* scene with Rose and Jack. When they get to talking about a fisherman who hanged himself the day we set out from Newlyn, I think of Conrad's dialogue once more, and the sadness that lurks between the ellipses: 'give us a bit of baccy … I know her; her skipper drank himself to death … he was a dandy boy!' The lines speak of how you can never know how much another person is really struggling inside their own head.

12

CAREWORN

Almost every cottage along the rounded bay on which Newlyn is seated has at least one window from where you can see the sea, so that from a distance the town appears like a theatre auditorium with rows of seats sloping down towards the stage that is the harbour – a grander version of the Minack Theatre a few miles further along the coast towards Land's End. The line between sea and land delineates Cornish experience. It seeps into every aspect of life, shaping its mythologies and slicing through any inflated sense of human grandeur by reminding its inhabitants that there is always something out there that is bigger than them.

To work within this environment is even more character-defining. Fishermen are shaped by the sea in the same manner that every coastline across the planet, though comprised of different rocks from various ages, has felt the presence of the oceans and been reformed throughout its lifetime by that encounter. When the Scythian philosopher Anacharsis was asked: 'Which were more in number, the living or the dead?' he responded: 'In which category, then, do you place those who are on the seas?' His retort speaks of a lasting conception about those at sea; while out there, away from the land, some vital part of their humanity is lost, making them fundamentally unknowable to those back on the land.

On the day of my twenty-third birthday, exactly a week after I return from sea, I meet Nathan at the Swordy over a couple of pints. As ever, I get more drunk than I intend to (it takes me a long time to admit to myself that I will never be as good at drinking as fishermen), I get back to the cottage late and wake the next morning to find the charred remains of my attempt at cooking one of the lemon sole I gutted on the *Filadelfia*. Nathan is thirty-one and one of the youngest men I've met who has a skipper's ticket (the qualification you need before you can captain a boat). He tells me that there's only one type of person who'll fit in that wheelhouse, and they don't come along often. A lot of the skippers Nathan reckons are really worth their salt are 'only-children', the kind of men who would have developed over time an insular strength which prepared them for life at sea. 'You gotta be tough as boots,' he says, 'and savvy enough to be able to control four other wayward men.' He pauses – 'a man amongst men' – and grins. 'I made that one up. Quote Nathan Marshall in your book, all right?'

You've got to be smart too. To get a skipper's ticket, fishermen have to complete a rigorous examined course that you can only take after you've fished for at least two years and requires you to attend three months of residential classes, working up to twelve-hour days. Another fisherman tells me that in the first class their teacher said: 'Hands up who's got a Maths A level?' After no one raised their hand he said: 'Well, you're all fucked then.'

Nathan shows me some of the questions he had to answer when he did the skipper's exam. Each algebraic or trigonometric question extends into a two-page sum comprised of letters, numbers and complex symbols. He explains how every calculation, every aspect of fishing – the winch, the nets, the position of your boat through the water, whether you are with or against the tide – must be measured perfectly so you don't damage the gear, or, worse, lose the boat or put your crew's lives at risk. A lot of the fishermen I meet say they couldn't handle the responsibility of being a skipper. Nathan only does it when he has to, preferring to be a mate.

Evening comes and with it the last of the day-fishermen tracing their way back along the coast home. The pub fills with oilskinned men yawning over their pints, and Nathan gets in another round: 'It is your birthday and all.' One Scottish fisherman, whose boat is presently moored in Newlyn harbour, explains to me that the community of fishing extends beyond borders. Many of the younger fishermen take time out from fishing for a year or two to travel around the world with the money they've made so far. In each coastal place they arrive during their travels, be it France, Australia or India, they somehow end up back at sea again with a group of foreign fishermen. Out on the water, the distinctions between cultures dissolve and the men share in that identifying mark: a sea language which is outside your native language and which feels more fundamental than your origins.

Nathan tells me that if I really want to understand fishermen, I'm going to have to learn some proper sea lingo. He mulls over some of his favourite fishing phrases, listing them on his fingers. 'Roughty tufty fishermen, man amongst men, and ...' He grins again. 'Furious wanking!'

'Wait, what?'

'Yeah, sorry.' He pauses for a moment, faltering in the list. 'That was one of my mate's. The one I was telling you about.'

The fisherman who took his own life the morning we set sail on the *Filadelfia* was one of Nathan's closest friends.

'Anyway.' He shakes his head and continues: 'My girlfriend at the time called me up on the satellite phone one night at sea, and she says: "Me and my friends were wondering, do you ever wank on the boat?" I go to my mate: "She just asked if I wank on the boat?" My mate says: "Say furiously." "Furiously!" I go.'

Nathan rubs his eyes, stretching the loose, bluish skin below them. 'That's probably why she's my ex and all.'

One of Nathan's friends, Big John – who, true to his name, is enormous, and also 'a funny, wordy one, like you', according to Nathan – joins us as we are both just finishing off our second round. Brave from beer, I tell Big John that I'd recently been trying to come up with a phrase that encapsulates what I think fishermen are. The men give me a funny look and I blush, realising how absurd that sounds; they have spent a week working at sea, while I have been sat in front of a laptop for a lot of that time puzzling over words.

Big John asks me straight up. 'Well, go on then, what are we?'
'Er, sea-sculpted...?' I say, wincing.

'Bollocks!' Big John responds immediately and Nathan shakes
his head in agreement. 'That's not it at all! Stop trying to roman-
ticise us, all right?'

I am ready to slide into my pint and never return from it again
when, still reeling from my blunder, Big John takes another glug of
beer and in the same beat that the glass hits the table says: 'We're
careworn' – as if it's the most obvious thing in the world.

'Careworn! That's it. Told you he was clever.' Nathan slaps
him on the back. 'Careworn!'

Regardless of my attempts to find words adequate to express what
it means to be a fisherman, there are a number of distinguishing
physical features that mark them out as men of the sea. These
tend to accumulate over the years so that the oldest fishermen
appear almost as caricatures of their past profession. Pretty much
all of them have at least one tattoo. Their chosen images have
a nice predictability: there are countless anchors, hearts with
names written across them in curly fonts, mermaids, pirates,
and the occasional registration number or drawing of a particular fishing boat they have grown close to – nothing too fancy,
nothing pretentious. Each of these is drawn in thick blue ink, the
lines spreading out like a fountain pen touched to wet paper so
that you can barely recognise where one line ends and another
begins. The most densely tattooed men accumulate dark clusters
of bruise-coloured islands running up and down their arms. Their
faces are weather-beaten (the word for this in Nance's glossary
is *towethack*). Their fingers are yellowed after years of rolling
endless cigarettes to pass the time on watch, their voices similarly
gritty and rasping from smoking. They often carry considerable
and impressive guts that stand as record to their bearer's ability
to sink innumerable pints given half the chance and a few nights
on shore. These guts look almost comically disproportionate,
protruding out above thick, muscled legs and alongside arms

made strong from years of handling heavy machinery. It is their faces that most betray their profession though. Every man I meet has heavily lined and intelligent eyes that somehow always retain some aspect of the sea within them. It is not a wildness in their look, but a wilderness that lurks somewhere at the edge of it.

At the end of the Second World War, *Life* magazine reproduced a painting by the artist Tom Lea entitled *Marines Call It That 2,000 Yard Stare*. A US marine, depicted in vivid, realistic detail, stands just off-centre of the frame positioned head on towards the viewer while behind him smoke billows, the land burns and engines of war are readied. It makes me uneasy to look at it – not because the soldier is staring right at the viewer, but because he is not. His eyes never reach ours; the wide whites and deep black pupils are hollow, empty and cold as space. This look has become a telltale sign of PTSD amongst returning solders, one family and friends must dread to see when they believe their loved one has come home, only to find a significant part of them has not.

Fishermen's stares are directed somewhere, though. It is not a kind of disassociation but an intent and profound attention to the water. I see it in Don sometimes, when even amongst friends during a raucous night out at the Star his usual booming voice fades and his expression returns to the one I have become accustomed to seeing him wear at sea each morning, after he has spent many hours alone in a smoky wheelhouse scanning the tar-black seas. Like the negative spaces that make up the human form, fishermen back on the shore feel keenly the absence of that other half of their identity, which, only when imagined together with their life on the land, can complete the portrait of who they know themselves to be. 'Some of these guys, if they didn't go to sea, they wouldn't last long,' Nathan tells me. Many fishermen are so used to their coming and going between the land and sea that, when injured or their boat is tied up with repairs, they cannot cope. Their identity becomes destabilised. There are men for whom being condemned to a life on the land, be it by injury, or simply by age, is a kind of slow drowning – or perhaps drowning is exactly the wrong word, but rather suffocation, like fish on a deck whose bodies flood with air. In *Quite Early One Morning*, Dylan Thomas's short narrative about a village in Wales, he writes of 'miscellaneous retired sea captains', who 'emerged for a second from deeper waves than ever tossed their boats, then drowned again, going down into a perhaps Mediterranean-blue cabin of sleep, rocked to the sea-beat of their ears'. Some retired fishermen never fully return from these sea-beating dreams.

In the same way that people brought up between two countries and two languages describe the feeling of being rent in half if they are suddenly prevented from returning to one of the places they call home, fishermen are no longer quite themselves without a sea to go back to. Don tells me that the longest he has been away from the sea since he was a teenager is about three weeks. Another trawlerman tells me of an occasion when he had been out at sea for a week, and the skipper was deliberating whether or not to do a few more days' work: the majority of the men quietly hoped that they could just go home, but one crew member who had recently broken up with his wife said: 'Well, I don't have anything to go back for, so we might as well stay out here.' Sea men are always on the verge of falling. If one of their two worlds collapses, either on land or at sea, that balance is lost, and he is in danger of losing himself.

For those lucky enough to have family, the day you have to leave them and go back out to sea is rarely easy. Even in my limited experience, the sea has never felt vaster and lonelier, the land never more appealing, than when you are staring out at it knowing that you are about to set out for long days and nights in comparative isolation. Nathan tells me that if there are crew members he doesn't get on with, he can go whole weeks without speaking, sometimes months. If you're in a real low patch, you can shut yourself off from everyone out there. He is hit with a case of 'sailing day blues' every time he passes that red and white lighthouse on his way out through the Gaps at Newlyn. He describes the experience of leaving as being 'torn away – literally torn from your home'.

Sometimes I cannot understand why it is that Nathan continues to fish. 'What do you like about it?' I ask him.

'I don't like any of it.' He pauses. 'I like the fact that it gives my family security.'

In that case, couldn't he find another job I ask? I should have known what his reply would be; it is the same as so many other fishermen have explained to me before.

'It's all I know,' he says.

Few of the skills on a fishing boat are directly transferable to any other professions. If men were to quit they would suddenly find themselves at the beginning of the career ladder again, earning comparatively little in a county with limited opportunities. Fishing is not merely a job; it is a way of life that you cannot unlearn, you are forever bound to it. As Nathan tells me, 'You know nothing else.'

The men cope with this sense of being wrenched from the land through what I come to see as a kind of mindfulness – a practised disassociation from the land while they are away from it. Perhaps in the same way that prisoners describe time dissolving while they are in confinement, fishermen have to let the outside world go while they're at sea, so as to not be driven mad by its absence.

In *The Need for Roots*, French philosopher Simone Weil speculates on the meaning of work in the twentieth century. She describes what she sees as a dearth of spirituality and a concurrent decline in civilisation that is endemic to the modern age. When a youngster first begins to plough a field by himself the work is 'pure poetry', she writes. The sense of elation he feels at being, for the first time in his life, truly active in the world soon descends into a weariness and he recognises that he will have to repeat this same monotonous routine day after day, year after year, with no hope of variation. At this point: 'The young man starts to spend the week dreaming about what he is going to do on Saturday.' It is from this moment onwards that the man is lost.

Nathan describes a sensation just like this: 'Soon as I go out those Gaps I start counting down the days, and the hours until I'm home. And as soon as I go ashore I'm counting down the days and the hours before I have to go away again.' The men grow detached, unrooted, from their present environment, their actions mechanised and performed abstractedly while their thoughts are fixed far away, back on the land. 'When you're away, all you can think of is home,' he continues, 'and when you're ashore you can't get it out your head, the feeling that you'll have to leave them again in a day or two.' You are stuck in a not-quite-place, a saltwater space somewhere between the lower world and the world of men.

For Weil, it is possible to move away from this spectral condition through resituating work at the spiritual core of life. In this way, we might root ourselves once more *in* the world. In fishing, as you stand before the sea, the brackish waters spraying your face, gripping a small knife in a thick glove, slicing into a twisting fish that has just come up from the water, you get the sense that you are engaged in a kind of work that is truly real. In these moments, you feel you are the closest to being in the world that a person can be. We cannot attain this spirituality within work without first acknowledging the burdensome nature of work, the monotony that 'hangs with an almost intolerable heaviness'.

Once this monotonous, dragging time is recognised, Weil believes that we might 'mount upwards'. For, she suggests, 'monotony is the most beautiful or the most atrocious thing. The most beautiful if it is a reflection of eternity – the most atrocious if it is a sign of an unvarying perpetuity.' Whether eternal or in perpetuity, Weil's sense of monotony is somehow outside of or beyond time, and there lies its potential for spirituality – for man to recognise that 'through work he produces his own natural existence' and therein accept the endless cycle between work and rest. She states that it is only 'when man sees himself as a squirrel turning around and round in a circular cage that, if he does not lie to himself, he is close to salvation'.

For fishermen, this sense of an endless rebounding between work and respite is brought into even sharper focus by their oscillation between the sea and the land. It is perhaps for this reason that they are especially attuned to the condition of 'turning around and round in a circular cage' and therefore closer to acknowledging the fundamental condition of work that Weil argues workers must strive towards.

In Newlyn, ex-fisherman Larry tells me that he and a crew were once left shelling langoustine on a Scottish boat for more than twenty-four hours. To pass the dragging time, they listened to music, but only had one CD. For an entire day and night, they listened to Fleetwood Mac's *Rumours* on repeat. When Larry hears the opening chords of 'Dreams' play on the jukebox in the Swordy it still makes him shudder. On the way home from the langoustine-shelling trip, the crew, delirious from exhaustion, began to giggle hysterically. I imagine Larry, his hands aching as he sits amongst thousands of flakes of pink shells with *Rumours* floating out of the boat's sound system, feeling suddenly that monotony fly outwards into a kind of transcendence.

'There's mornings out there when a gale's just ceased,' says Nathan, 'you're all on your own in that wheelhouse and the sun's coming up, the gulls are squawking away, and it's not too bad, you know?' He tells me that it's during these moments, when you are 'staring out at the sea, on your own, proper contemplative, that everyone has a little cry now and then – not that many fishermen would admit to it'. These silent moments are a kind of therapy. The boat seems to slip away and it is just you and the big blue yonder and nothing else. In those brief periods of sublimity, you encounter a kind of release that must be close to Weil's sense of 'mounting upwards'.

Nathan often prefers a force 8 to flat calm. 'You're out there in a screaming gale of wind and you think look at this, look at what the sea can do.' When the sea is like that you cannot help to feel a sense of reverence. Fishing is humbling, forcing you to confront your own insignificance. Out on the water, you witness sights daily while you work that people would pay to see, and which the vast majority of people will never even come close to experiencing. There are sunsets and sunrises out there so extraordinary that you cannot help but weep. You catch glimpses of basking sharks and mammoth whales that dwarf your boat and dolphins that arch through the water acrobatically with a single flick of their tails. Nature can do all this, you think, without requiring some 220-tonne metal thing that hefts and drags itself through the water, its engine belching fumes into the sea.

As I leaf through my sea diary entries, trying to find in them some kernel of information that might tell me what it is to be a fisherman, I notice a repeating pattern emerging in accounts. Almost every entry includes a burst of humour, something that happens on deck or up in the wheelhouse that breaks up the monotony of the work and in a sudden joyous moment draws the crew together like a family. Fishermen are some of the funniest people I have met, finding opportunity for play and silliness within almost every difficult situation at sea. This is something that Weil never mentions in her concept of work. And yet it is this sense of humour, the genuine companionship felt between the men, that stops them from being overwhelmed by the tedium of the work, allows them to keep going despite the many tragedies that they have experienced as an industry.

During his time spent on the remote Aran Islands, off the west coast of Ireland, the writer J. M. Synge saw how humour was used as a means of coping with melancholia. During an evening in a pub on Inisheer, translated as east island, he noticed a wildness to the men who would now and again break into a 'half sen- sual ecstasy of laughter'. In his meditation on where this kind of laughter comes from, he writes: 'Perhaps a man must have a sense of intimate misery ... before he can set himself to jeer and mock at the world.' There are times too when I think that the unending pranking and playfulness among the Newlyn fishermen, apart from easing the monotony and exhaustion of fishing, is born of a certain sense of desolation that comes from a life half-lived on the sea.

I hear of one brilliantly elaborate prank played on a decky learner – a fisherman who has just started out in his career – about to join them for his first week at sea. The crew set up the groundwork for the prank by telling the novice fisherman that a container ship of animals from a zoo had been lost at sea and they might see animals in cages floating along in the water. Meanwhile, another crew member bought a gorilla costume. Midway through the trip, while the decky learner was tucked up asleep, they dressed one of the men in the suit and jumped onto the bunk of the young man, scaring him half to death.

On the *Filadelfia*, Kyle made me laugh almost every minute, both of us cracking up for a good half hour after he tried to explain to me how navigation position systems work and accidentally asked me: 'What's your favourite position?' One afternoon, Andrew got a load of large tomatoes (which Kyle calls 'the devil's food – unless they're in ketchup'), and hid them in Kyle's wellies so that when he woke up after the Fishwife Call he squelched down into them and had tomato-drenched boots for the rest of the trip.

Another time, Andrew, the self-proclaimed Prank King, promised me that if you rub ray juice into your face it gives you a lovely complexion. After regarding him suspiciously for a minute, my slimy glove raised halfway up to my face, I cried out: 'No! Bollocks!'

Andrew, laughing his Muttley laugh, replied: 'Why else do you think fishermen have such beautiful, youthful skin?'

I had passed my first decky learner test.

A gill-net fisherman tells me that near the end of a thirty-hour shift your hands and back are often aching and you want to collapse, but then you look around the deck at the other men just like you. 'You're in it together, still cracking jokes and getting on with it – and you think to yourself: That's it. That's why I am here.'

13

SMOKE

One evening I head out to the Swordy to meet a girl from Newlyn a couple of years younger than me who I've seen hanging around the skate park below the promenade most evenings with other kids, doing tricks and playing music out towards the sea. A few days previously she had approached me out of the blue asking who I was – 'because everyone's clocked you, you know?' – and what was I doing disappearing off on fishing boats for weeks at a time?

In London the majority of my time is spent amongst young women. When I call them up after adventures in Newlyn, none of them can quite believe what I am doing, or why. Amongst my friendship group I often get branded with words like 'kooky'. This is my role; it is how my shape can be known – even though nothing that I have done has ever felt especially odd to me. I ended up in Cornwall because it was my mother's land and on boats because that gave me the opportunity to experience how other people live, not just hear about it and infer from that how it must feel. There was no other way of doing it.

The girl and I sit in the hut outside the Swordy underneath Ben Gunn's abstract painting, while she talks at a hundred miles an hour, I doing my best to match her, as she tells me of her fisherman dad, her certainty that there is nowhere better to live than Newlyn and of her Grandmother Lamorna – 'So I can't help but thinking of you as a really old lady with wrinkles!'

She makes me laugh constantly. I've missed talking to young women. There is a breathlessness and a joy to these kinds of first conversations that I've never managed to replicate when meeting boys on dates and the like. We are accommodating, eager to know things about each other. There is no power play, no need to display or present the best versions of ourselves. We just want to speak and be spoken to, about anything, about everything.

Two men at the next table come over to us to borrow a light. One is in oilskins and yellow gumboots, the characteristic garb of a fisherman just in from the sea, the other is his image, but as if that copy had been twisted through something painful, something sharp. This second man has two black eyes, the right one an old bruise – greeny-yellow to the left's blackberry – and a thin scar right across his forehead. He lacks the muscular, meaty build of his fisherman friend, his arms comparatively thin and white, his hands noticeably shaking. Both are drunk, but the drink covers the thinner man more; it wears him, pushing him around and causing him to stumble. The fisherman notices me watching his companion.

After lighting up, the fisherman tells us that this is his best friend – has been his best friend since they were kids, mucking about down by the harbour together. His best friend nearly collapses again and swears loudly at the ground, as if blaming it for rising up at him. As if I have said something, maybe my expression speaking words enough, the fisherman says: 'It's negative reinforcement, yeah?' He smacks the table and his friend ducks his head instinctively. 'He needs to be told he's doing a good job, not given a slap every time he tries.'

I nod, uncertain how to respond to this. The two men head back inside to get themselves another round, the fisherman with his arm protectively linked through that of his friend's and hoisting him up by the back of his hoodie so he does not fall again. I finish my drink and the girl returns to the flat where she lives with her boyfriend, promising to meet up again soon, and to think of me when I'm out on trawlers. It sounds so grown up to me, so secure, to already be living with one person.

Once adjacent with the harbour, I find myself compelled to walk right up to its perimeter. I stop at its very edge so that my toes are floating over its dark waters. Whether it is caused by the drink or the conversation we had with the fisherman and his friend, something doesn't sit right in my body that night. It is as if some part of me has become unsettled. I hang there for a moment, suspended above the black water, then turn up the Fradgan back to Denise and Lofty's, where they are still watching telly, both cats squeezed in beside them on the sofa.

14

Sea-hab

The strange feeling from the night before does not subside but carries over into the next day, as I set off along the promenade to Penzance to meet a newly trained fisherman called Harry. It is the day before his first week-long beam trawler trip, Harry tells me nervously as soon as I sit down. He has already had two trial trips – one on a gill-netter, the other a twin-rig trawler – but this will be the first time that he fully participates in the work of the boat, hoping that it will land him a permanent berth as a decky learner. Unlike the knotted-armed and wind-tanned faces of the fishermen I am accustomed to, Harry is thin, pale and somewhat fragile-looking. He checks the exits of the cafe we meet in several times and speaks with a habitual wariness, avoiding eye contact throughout. This is something most fishermen never do: they regard you with a fixed gaze, daring you to break focus. Nathan tells me that if a new crew member avoids looking him in the eye, he knows immediately the man is 'no good'.

Harry does not avoid looking at me because he is no good, but because his experience of life differs wildly from those men who have grown up in Newlyn, for whom fishing has provided them with a certain confidence and unshakeable sense of identity. Though born in the countryside, Harry has lived on the peripheries of cities for much of his adult life – loud places where people come and go too quickly to call them home and where trains only ever pass through. For years, he toiled in supermarkets and other long-shift work, but six months ago he lost his job as a result of continuing struggles with addiction and, finding himself homeless, hit one of the hardest periods of his life. He speaks to me with an honesty that is disarming. He is forthcoming about even his most private, painful experiences.

Harry tells me that during this period of darkness and before it, from childhood even, he dreamed of becoming a fisherman. When I ask him why, he seems to grow larger in his chair. He speaks of the pride that comes with calling yourself a fisherman, earning a respectable wage in an industry that is 'prestigious'. Most importantly, after years of being regarded not just as an outsider, but often entirely forgotten about by society, he will be part of a community. Lofty and Denise tell me how shocked they are when they go to London and find that people in need are just ignored. When they see a homeless person in Newlyn or Penzance, they always check that they're okay and ask them if they want something to eat.

Several weeks ago, with the help and support of his family, Harry got the money together for a one-way ticket to Penzance and enrolled in Seafood Training's three-week 'Introduction to Fishing' class. It's the best thing he's ever done, he says. He has never paid such attention in class before, nor found the lessons so rewarding. Many of the figures I have got to know over the last few months come up in his narration. Harbourmaster Rob gave the recruits a talk, informing the would-be fishermen that this was the very best time to be going into the industry; Andy Wheeler, an instructor and ex-fisherman, taught them about the environmental responsibilities of fishing and how it can enrich one's life; Clare, an administrator at Seafood, has called him up weekly since the training to check how his trial shifts have gone and to find out whether he has a permanent berth yet. Harry tells me that this is the first time in a long while that people have 'had his back'. In this way, it is much more than training. Mentor schemes are fighting to prevent the end of fishing in Newlyn, by bringing young men into the industry and nurturing those for whom fishing is not in their lifeblood.

Since Harry is the only other person I have met who is as much of a fishing novice as I am, we spend a joyous half an hour or so discussing particularly embarrassing mistakes we have made in front of other fishermen. Like me, every time Harry has had to use one of the thin, slippery metal quayside ladders and then jump across to a boat, he has been terrified that he will miss the boat completely and have to be pulled out of the harbour waters below. We both agree that this would instantly destroy any slight chance he may have had of gaining the crew's respect early on. Even worse, he says, he is terrified of heights. I admit what I have not to any other fishermen: that there were times on the *Filadelfia* that I felt truly frightened and alone, knowing I could not contact my parents and that there was nowhere I could escape to.

Crews tend to be hard on decky learners until they prove themselves. As Harry and I chat, I cannot help but think about the drinking culture amongst fishermen on land. Even for men who have grown up fishing, it is hard to retain the balance of the extreme vacillation between excess and teetotalism that Newlyn fishermen experience weekly. Many men have slipped under. I meet one skipper in the *Swordy* who tells me he had to bring his boat back early this week having found one of his crew – 'a young lad' – shooting up in the toilet. Sometimes, even when you're at sea, the land is not far enough away to escape the various problems and intoxicants it offers.

Harry tells me that, actually, the fishermen's self-enforced alcohol ban at sea has been a relief for him – many of the Newlyn fishermen jokingly call it their 'sea-hab' or 'sea-tox' because it ensures 'a week away from the piss'. While Harry knows that none of it will be easy, 'I will die before I give this up,' he tells me fervently.

In Walter Benjamin's essay cycle 'Nordic Sea', which emerged from his voyage to Norway and Finland, he describes how boats become 'the time in which even he who has no home lives'. For those who leave no home behind, the boat is no less than a palace. Fishing will give Harry a home; it will give him the opportunity to live and a new, clearly defined identity. I think about the way in which Newlyn has become a place that has helped me, too, or at least shown me that there are other ways of living: that there still exist communities for whom looking out for and fiercely defending one another is valued above all else.

Harry and I swap numbers, and I text him the following day to wish him good luck and ask him to let me know how it all goes. Fishing-related tragedies have left many holes in the fabric of Newlyn but talking to Harry I see that fishing can also bring salvation to those who are lost. 'Fishing can kill you,' I write in my diary that evening, 'but it can also save your life.'

The next morning, I go to a large open-fronted warehouse by the Strand to meet Simon Milne, who until very recently was the cook on the gill-netter *Governek of Ladram*. He proudly tells me that he is actually quite famous on Twitter because he was part of the crew filmed for the fishing reality TV show, *The Catch*. Where Harry is at the very start of his life as a fisherman, Simon's has been cut short. Though only in his mid-forties, the physical strain and intensity of gill-netting – spending great swathes of time bent double over nets – has left his body permanently damaged and has forced him to retire early. He now has carpal tunnel syndrome in both hands, the bones in his thumbs are wearing away and he has osteoarthritis to boot.

As we talk, Simon rigs nets, taking sheets of netting and stitching it onto leaded ropes, for the 'foots', and ropes with floats attached for the 'heads', so that the gill nets will stand upright on the seabed. The hake nets he works on are joined into tiers, each of about three miles long, comprising around fifty separate small mesh nets. Each hake net is worth about £10,000. I follow Simon up and down the warehouse, as he stretches the net from one side of the echoing room to the other, weaving a net needle in and out of a single tier.

'With fishing, you know what you're about,' he states simply. 'It's the very first thing you tell someone about yourself, if they haven't worked it out already, and after that you don't have to say anything else, really; people know exactly who and what you are.' He explains that he does not know another job in the world that gives you such a feeling of confidence and competence – 'not that I've ever been shy of confidence', he adds, which does not surprise me in the least – 'but it's turned me into a better person.' Through fishing, 'you soon learn your limits, you learn to push your limits and finally you learn that limits are just something in your head.' Simon is not yet entirely comfortable with working on land. He finds it mind-numbing spending his days in an unchanging, monochrome environment, faced with the oppressive quiet of a cavernous warehouse. For a fisherman, it is unthinkable – at times almost unliveable – to be away from 'that big wet thing out there – that life-giving, life-taking thing that is everything', as I have heard it called. To suddenly lose that illimitable world that is so beyond human articulation requires colossal readjustment.

Simon has started cooking more at home, he tells me, though his wife and daughter repeatedly complain about the vast portions he gives them. He says he can't help it; at sea he would make each man a whole roasting tray of food. 'You must have heard about my meals?': he sucks his breath in and starts to reel off some of his most famous fishing dishes, each of which sounds more extravagant than the last: Thai fish curry with whatever they had caught that day; hake and onions for lunch with thyme butter and a bit of fresh bread; fish mornay ('but not so French'), which would usually be haddock on a bed of shallots with Gruyère cheese and bacon on top; beef brisket, red wine, dauphinois and a bit of veg ('like beef bourguginon, but not so French' he adds emphatically once more); and a roast with all the trimmings every other day. He pauses in his net-rigging and looks out to where you can just see the masts of trawlers in the harbour and says wistfully: 'Kilo and a half of rice for six people. That's how you do it.'

Simon asked his wife recently: 'What am I now, then? I mean, are you all right being with a bloke, who's just a bloke?' In response she said she was just happy to have him home. It is those men who don't have this support once they can no longer go to sea who are in the greatest danger of becoming lost.

To prevent himself from becoming entirely adrift from the industry, Simon is studying at the Seafood Training School to become a fishing instructor, one of the people who will help teach novices like Harry to become fishermen. Unfortunately the dropout rate after the three-week course is extremely high. To find oneself confronted with the whole sea is something that no course can adequately prepare you for. Simon's role is to keep the trainees going, to say: 'If it doesn't work on that boat, then try something else: try crabbing, try day-boats.' He remembers when he returned to fishing aged thirty, after taking a few years out. 'It nearly killed me,' he says. 'I lost six stone in two weeks – even though we were eating like kings. One day, I was sweating my eyeballs out, and the skipper came up to me, patted my back and said: "Go on, you're doing all right lad."' It is such moments that mean everything, when an older fisherman whom you respect at last notices you aren't completely hopeless.

On his last ever trip out gill-netting there was phosphorescence in the water, Simon tells me. Dolphins and rays were weaving through it all night as they steamed back to the harbour, creating curling, luminous trails like streamers. It was hard not to believe, he says, that at least in some way the show was for him, a parting gift from the sea. 'They were like red arrows, or' – he pauses, trying to think of a more apt description – 'one of them sights that words cannot describe, you know?'

I don't hear back from Harry after his trawler trip. I soon forget that I made him promise to let me know how it went, and go home to London. It is only a few weeks later, when I return for a single, final weekend before the New Year, that I see Harry again. It is perhaps three in the morning: a few of us are drunkenly heading back with chips from Rami's kebab shop after a night dancing to cheesy music at Rumours nightclub in Penzance, and I spot him on the opposite side of the road. Noticing he is unsteady on his feet, as I am, I do not want to go up to him and ask how it went on the trawler. I fear he might tell me that it had not worked out after all, that the transition into fishing has been too much for him. The next morning I send him another text. He does not reply. I repeat to myself what I had written in my diary after I first met him – 'Fishing can kill you, but it can also save your life' – and try to make it true by saying it out loud.

In the *Rings of Saturn*, which I read while on the *Crystal Sea*, the version of the East Anglian coast that emerges out of Sebald's hallucinatory prose is perpetually on the verge of ruin. The decay of past grandeur is described with relish, fishermen are 'dying out' – as though they themselves are some ancient species destined to be forgotten. In Dunwich, once a prestigious port, every building 'one after the other, toppled down the steadily receding cliff face'. I didn't want to hear this while I was curled up in the wheelhouse of a Cornish fishing boat. I didn't understand how the collapse of an industry could be rendered beautiful in writing. Newlyn is fighting its future destruction every day. That fight can be loud and messy and misplaced, at times. But it is also hopeful and active. Though 20 per cent of the fleet has been decommissioned in Newlyn, contrary to Sebald, there is no such beauty to this potential ruin.

15

Beaten copper

Thursday is my hardest day at sea. The shore feels thousands of nautical miles and years away than it has done in the days previously. A close friend, who had been away on her first solo adventure while I was making mine in Newlyn, later asked me what was my most frightening episode at sea. After considering it for a while, I realised that there was no climactic instant on the *Filadelfia*, no moment I could isolate and say: 'Yes, here. I was afraid for my life here.' But all that did scare me was contained in that one grey Thursday.

Once dressed, I shakily make my way up into the wheelhouse, mumble hello to whoever is on watch and head straight out onto the balcony, hoping that the new morning will burn away the heaviness that has descended over me during the night. And yet the day provides no opening; the sun never rises. Instead, the greyness leaks across the sky, washing away every last blotch of colour until the world is the exact same pallid shade that you find under the eyes of a hospital patient in terminal decline, like that cheery line in *Woyzeck*, by the German playwright Georg Büchner that was left unfinished at his death: 'A nice solid grey sky. Makes you want to knock a nail in and hang yourself.' There is a Cornish dialect word for the sky that describes it exactly: *wisht* – pale and ill. I notice what I have not on the previous days: that there is no green, no thing with roots as far as the eye can see, except for Don's money plant bobbing beside me. And it is not just that there is no colour. There are no shadows either. Today the light is too weak for them. Annie Dillard writes that we need shadows in order to understand the world. 'They give the light distance; they put it in its place.' Without shadows, there is nothing to hold on to.

I find it hard to write about difficult moments. I tend to leave out sadness from my diary for fear of crystallising those feelings or allowing them to seep into other memories. Perhaps this is dishonest. But eight days is a long time on a boat and the concentration required to keep thoughts of home relegated to the nether regions of your brain can drain a person right out. I become Simone Weil's squirrel in a cage, turning around and around within the work of gutting, finding no chance of making headway. That day I shift between locations and activities on the boat as if unconsciously. Time progresses in a blue-lit blur like the droning screen in the galley as Don flicks between airport reality shows, *The Chase*, the news, and *Deadly Women*, an American true-crime show.

The monotony becomes annihilating. The mixture of intoxicating fumes, drifting through the cabins, sits right on top of me and the tightness of space makes me want to cry out. My resentment of the *Filadelfia* swiftly turns inwards. I feel embarrassed at my own redundancy, knowing that however much I try to participate in the work I am always, at base, a passenger here. The world becomes more blurred and I find myself unable to answer a single question on *The Chase*, which feels hugely important at the time. While the other crew do their usual jeering at contestants and yelling out of answers, it is as if it the world has switched to another language and I can make out none of it.

In old English, the compound *úht-cearu* translates as 'early-morning cares': those tiny worries that you can flick away like horseflies by day, but which gather at night and transfigure during the sleepless hours before dawn into weighty demons pressing on your skull. Cares similarly balloon on board trawlers to such a size that they obscure one's vision, preventing you from engaging with other beings. I remember Nathan telling me that this is a particular danger he associates with being on watch. If you are unhappy, your mind can start to unravel in those lone hours spent staring at the bare ocean.

Across the years I have accumulated a range of methods to cope with the undefined sadness that comes over me some days, sometimes lasting weeks – calling friends and family or finding ways to distract myself by visiting galleries and museums, anything to avoid having to listen to my own head. Unsurprisingly this is not possible on a boat in the middle of the sea. Over lunch, Don watches me slowly make my way through a colourful packet of crisps while half-slumped over the table. Without warning, he slams his hand down, shaking me up. 'I dunno why *you're* tired. You've been sitting on your arse all day!'

This feeds straight into my self-consciousness. In my heightened state, I am unable to take it lightly. I start trying to apologise for being useless, for being a dead weight, but soon lose my train of thought and lapse into silence once more. Don shakes his head and goes back to work. That day, Don continues to slam tables, doors and mugs of coffee whenever he sees my unfocused gaze, the noise becoming a beat that drills through me more violently than the engine below us or the sea outside.

In the cottage in the Fradgan, a blush of evening light skips across a pair of copper cats hanging on the living-room wall, which are perfect replicas of Teggy and Izzy. Lofty made them at the Newlyn Copper Works, which is run by Mikey Johnson.

Copper does not behave like other materials, Mikey tells me when I visit his workshop behind the Strand one lunchtime. Most become more malleable the more force that is exerted on them. The glass and plastics that end up in the sea are battered and whirled by the waves until their sharp edges are softened right down, their old forms barely recognisable. But copper starts out pliable. Coppersmiths continue to strike and beat upon the metal until its orderly particles become disordered, rendering it brittle and hard. With every piece of copper, there comes a point at which it can be worked upon no longer, when your ringing contact with the metal fixes its shape.

In 1888, a designer called John Drew Mackenzie moved from Scotland down to Newlyn. After some time spent living amongst the locals, he grew concerned about the effect erratic work patterns were having on the fishermen's wellbeing. Before the advent of mechanised trawlers, the men were completely at the mercy of sea conditions, sometimes losing a whole season without work. Hoping to provide fishermen with a productive secondary craft that would keep them occupied and provide an income during off-seasons, Mackenzie established the Newlyn Industrial Class Copper Works. Within a few years, his workshop was crammed full of fishermen spending their days hammering copper into intricate designs and learning refined techniques such as repoussage, where a sheet of copper is hammered from one side to create an image in relief on the other.

The copper works fell into disuse, until 2004 when Mikey moved into the town and set about re-establishing them. Like his predecessor, he began encouraging land-locked fishermen to come into his treasure trove of a workshop behind the Strand. Here French jazz can be heard dripping out of speakers like honey, rising above the sounds of hammer striking metal, while fishermen spend their days fashioning strange and wonderful objects as they wait for the seas to quieten. Mikey sees the two industries – fishing and art – as akin to one another, both requiring skill and close attention, while always being 'tangible, always gritty and real'.

Fishermen often come up with the most honest responses to Mikey's work, too – never appealing to his ego or trying to guess at what he wants to hear. When Mikey presented a new abstract piece he had been working on to a day-boat owner, the fisherman took it from his hands, turned it over a few times, then handed it back to him with a shrug: 'Pig's ear. That's the shape of a pig's ear.'

Mikey laughs. 'He wasn't trying to be a prick. He just looked at the shape and, rather than treat it as an abstract sculpture, he tried to see what it really was and turn it into something that was real; and the real thing he saw was a pig's ear.' He pauses to look at the piece again. 'I just loved him saying that. I thought it was perfect. Yeah, in many ways it is a fucking pig's ear! And you should be reminded of that when you're working in the arts. A lot of the time it is shit. Even if you think it's good.'

It is only later that I realise Don's gruffness, his slamming hand on the table, is not an attack, but an attempt to harden me into a shape so I can handle the sea and survive its difficulties. I am too lost in my own head to recognise this just yet on that Thursday morning.

Instead, I retreat into myself, endeavouring to dull my senses with an anaesthetic of my own design. The strong cocktail of drugs required to induce a general anaesthetic work by reacting with the membranes of nerve cells to suspend responses like hearing, sight and awareness. And yet, there is still debate over what actually happens in the areas of the brain that are numbed in this way. Scientists conjure up various visual images in an attempt to describe what it may be like – a total eclipse in the brain or a slow setting of the sun across the mind. Which horizon line do you disappear behind, then?

After taking a seasickness pill I pull open the heavy wheel-house door to be met by bracing sea gusts. I stand alone with my hands planted on the rail that skirts the wheelhouse balcony as I did on the very first night I spent at sea. The crew are hosing away dead fish on the deck, kicking them under the railings with their heavy boots and into the water to be feasted on by seabirds. I wait until the last few birds have got their fill and the men have returned to the galley. There is no one else here now. The whole outside world is empty, unmarked.

I don't know if loneliness has always looked like the sea on a colourless day, or if before that afternoon I just hadn't had the image in my head to describe it, but ever since then, whenever I have felt at my most alone, I see that flat stretch of ocean once again, feel it rise up and cover me over.

I look down into the water. The phantom bottom of the ocean is called the Deep Scattering Layer and comprises an entire eco-system of small fish and plankton that rise and fall each day. It was discovered accidentally in 1942 when an American coastal boat trying out its sonar read from its equipment, alarmingly, that the bottom was not 3,600 metres, but only 450 metres. After checking the sonar a few hours later and finding the seabed had sunk back down, they realised that the dense layer it had picked up was in fact a moving body of fish. In the ship's log, the captain wrote of the sounds they recorded from the Deep Scattering Layer: 'Some fish grunt, others whistle or sing, and some just grind their teeth.'

I watch the gulls make their circuits of the sky, noticing how often they seem to travel in pairs, describing figures of eights between themselves. When they reach the stern of the *Filadelfia*, they abruptly split and race one another long port and starboard before joining once more at the pointed prow of the ship. As the nets break the surface of the water, the gulls flap in great haste towards the boat's stern. They part into two channels when they get close to the boat, before swooping down to the nets to snatch at the flailing fish. If they fail in their pursuit, they arc back up into the sky, with no effort at all, as if massless, to attempt the circuit again. Trying to decode their patterns of movement, I form impressionistic figures of eight in my diary with various arrows showing directions of flight. Now and then I try to isolate a single bird, holding on to its distinctive markings and following its course. But, by their nature, the creatures function as one raging mass and elude my attempts at differentiation. Watching the ceremonial train of gulls following us, I wonder how long they have dogged Cornish trawlers, their hunting patterns rewritten to incorporate the huge metal seabirds that excrete fish whole. From his solitary position in the middle of the quarterdeck voy-aging in the North Sea, Walter Benjamin imagines the gulls as divided into two tribes: those on the east and those on the west, the eastern birds shimmering, still lit by the sun's last strokes; the gulls of the west appear dark, sharp, angular. Together they form 'an uninterrupted, ineffably shifting series of symbols, seemingly unceasingly; a whole, unspeakably variable, fleeting mesh of wings – but a legible one'. You cannot help but search for legibility in the precise marks these white birds emblazon across the sky, as their bodies seem to merge into a single streak of wings like the blow of a slow-shutter-speed camera. Perhaps this impulse comes as a result of the lack of communication with the outside world on board ship, making one more susceptible or willing to read design into their motion.

The other bird in great abundance while we are at sea is the gannet. They too complete ritualistic patterns of movement during hauls. But after weaving around the *Filadelfia*'s perimeter, they break the rules of the cycle enacted by the gulls and cut through the surface of the water, adding a third dimension to the shape. More magisterial than gulls, these are warrior birds, with faded ochre patches on their heads, like army caps, and striking kohl-black markings around their eyes which are painted with a bright blue line like a gas ring, that tricks one into thinking they have huge blue irises. Their wingspan is vast and when they are preparing to dive, they tuck their dark sheaved feathers right close against their bodies so that they don't make a single splash, and re-emerge moments later from the water with fish. Unlike the loutish grabs of the seagulls, they rarely miss. There is a brutality to them, too. They have seen more wars than the gulls, their bodies often raggedy and battle-scarred. I have heard many a yarn about fishermen being attacked on deck by 'monstrous gannets'.

In the *Metamorphoses*, Ovid describes how, unlike his brother Hector, Aesacus despised the city and escaped to the forests to climb the lonely mountains. One day, he catches sight of the nymph Hesperia resting in a sunny clearing. Alarmed at the sight of the unknown man watching her, Hesperia flees and is pursued by Aesacus all the way through the forest. When he is almost in touching distance to his object of desire, a snake darts into Hesperia's path and fatally bites her upon the ankle. Racked by guilt for the part he has played in her death, Aesacus throws himself from a cliff and into the sea. The goddess Tethys, unable to resist the chance to meddle with human lives, sees him fall and transforms him into a diving bird. Aesacus tries in horror again and again to dive to his death, but each time finds himself pulled back up into the upper airs. From my viewing platform, I look out at the strong gannets diving for fish, each of them a lover denied death and forced to forever leap without falling.

There are often bird stowaways on trawlers. When Andrew was working out in the North Sea a few years back, a flock of starlings travelled with them and for two weeks warbled outside the wheelhouse every morning. Kyle tells me that there was once a pigeon on the *Gary M* that got itself stuck in the wheelhouse and no one noticed until they were far from land. He tells me the pigeon was pretty unbothered by the adventure. In fact, he was really useful and ate up all the fish scales scattered across the deck and trodden through to the wheelhouse. When they got close enough to Land's End on the way home, one of the fishermen opened the window and let the pigeon free. Kyle says it got hundred metres away, then realised life on the boat hadn't been so bad, turned around and started flying back. Somehow, it misjudged the position of the wheelhouse window, crash-landed into the sea and died there and then.

This was not the ending I had imagined to Kyle's story.

'I know,' he says. 'Sad, really. I liked that pigeon.'

Another fisherman told me that after his father died, 'the same bloody seagull' followed him all over Newlyn. 'There's a story, see,' he said. 'Die a fisherman, come back a seagull.' This is why, despite their fish thievery, it is considered very bad luck to kill a seagull because you never know who they might have been before. Like Aesacus the diving bird, it is difficult to imagine deaths at sea as final. Instead, we imagine a transformation occurs under the waves, bearing these sad souls aloft once more along the sea winds.

I watch one last Aesacus dive-bomb the sea and trace a final seagull's path around the boat, before coming back to myself. My fingernails have turned pale blue and my eyes are watering. I hug

my arms to my body and am relieved to notice the outdoors has
wrung out most of my lethargy. Returning into the *Filadelfia*'s
hot belly, I go straight past the galley to the bathroom. Staring
into the crooked mirror, my face obliquely reflected back to me in
fragments, I tell myself: 'You can do this. These men do this every
week and you're here for eight days only.' I say it out loud. 'You
are tough – you're tougher than you think.'

I put the loo seat down and sit on it, listening to the *Filadelfia*'s
sounds. After a day or two at sea, you get a feel for what the
particular vibrations coming from the engine might mean. All is
silent now, suggesting we are in that brief period of respite when
the nets are hauled out, just before they are shot off once more
behind the boat. The gutting must be about to begin. I leave the
loo at once and pull my gloves and boots on, ready to resume my
bit part in the great show once more.

That evening, I join Stevie up in the wheelhouse before dinner. He
is less forthcoming than the others and I get the sense he is warier
of my presence on the boat. Not wishing to disturb him, I take my
place on the bench to his right, the two of us looking out at the
water without a word between us. Soon darkness vanquishes the
grey sky, the whites of our watching eyes lit by the restless machines
before us. Stevie turns on the staticky radio above our heads and the
Shipping Forecast starts to play out, the presenter's resonant timbre
reverberating through the room as he conjures up the incantatory
words that have come to stand for those squared-off regions of the
sea around the UK – Dogger, Humber, Fisher, German Bight. After
midnight on my last night on the *Crystal Sea* we listened to the
Shipping Forecast too and the echoing memories of those curious
words and the warning of gales we heard that night, not heard since,
draw the two occasions together more closely. I imagine David's
crew out here now too, half-covered in sea, sitting in silence in their
superior, two-chaired wheelhouse, just listening.

*And now the Shipping Forecast, issued by the Met Office on
behalf of the Maritime and Coastguard Agency at 00.48 today.*

I imagine other Cornish fishing boats besides hearing these
same radio waves thrown out across the water from the land,

and then send my mind further to visualise the many containers, cruise ships and solitary sailing boats crossing the sea's many paths, each of their radios altering the quality of the recorded sound, vernacularising its voice better to fit with the distinctive rhythms of their own sea lives.

Lastly, I think of those listening to the forecast back on the land, lying alone in their beds in dark, motionless bedrooms, letting the words smooth the edges of their insomnia.

Viking, North Utsire, South Utsire, Forties, Cromarty, northerly, north-easterly four or five becoming variable three at times: fair, moderate or good...

The radio seems to make the mood of the wheelhouse lighter, the distance between Stevie and me diminishing with each new verbalisation of the sea's current condition. Quietly, during forecast intermissions, and with longer pauses than I have with any of the other crew, we start to speak to each other about our lives. He and Andrew usually work together on the *Twilight*, but she's getting repairs done at the moment so they've been helping Don out. Once it would have been a mad scramble to get a berth on a Newlyn boat; from daybreak men would wander up and down the quay searching for any work going. But these days there are barely enough fishermen to fill the boats and it's a nightmare finding replacement crew.

Aged sixteen, Stevie was working as a potato-picker in Scotland when his brother came up and said: 'Oi, I've got you a job. Come fishing.' And that was that. A few years later, almost his whole family had moved down to Newlyn from Scotland. Stevie's way of living in Newlyn has changed a lot since he first came here. After he and his wife had their daughter, who is now two, he stopped going to the pub, finding he had little enough time at home with his family as it was. He strikes me as the most mature member of the crew, but he also has the sharpest, punning wit, his jokes always delivered absolutely deadpan.

Tyne, Dogger, Fisher, north-east four or five, increasing six at times: fair or good...

'I've missed a lot of life out here,' Stevie tells me in the dark wheelhouse: his daughter's first words, her first birthday. He'll probably have to miss her first day of school too. Every time you come back down the quay and see your children standing there to greet you, another fisherman tells me, they've changed in some small but fundamental way that you cannot put your finger on. They might have got taller or got a new haircut, but it's more than that. Perhaps something happened at school, which has made them that bit tougher, that bit harder. Perhaps they have seen something that has slightly shifted their view of the world, making them that bit less yours. You begin to fight over things you didn't even believe needed fighting over, concepts of the world that are strange and foreign to you, but your antagonism towards them seems to make your children hate you.

When my friend Isaac's father, Roger, came back after a month at sea with a beard, three-year-old Isaac ran away from the strange man to hide behind his mother's legs. From this point on, Roger knew his days of continuous fishing were over and he started to spend more time on land working as the ship's husband – the term for those who maintain the boat from the land. Often fishermen tell me that when they know they're only coming in for one night they silently turn up at home after their children's bedtime and return to sea once more before they wake. It's easier that way, less upsetting than having to say goodbye all over again. In between the sea and the land you are but an apparition, a ghost in your own home.

German Bight, north-east five or six, occasionally four later, occasional rain: moderate or good...

Fishing destroys a lot of relationships. There are not many fishermen out there, Stevie tells me, who haven't had relationships breakdown due to the pressures imposed by fishing. The difficulty of retaining the balance between land and sea is not just felt by the fishermen, but by the families they leave behind each trip. Once, I was with a fisherman when he rang his wife to ask if she wanted to come down and chat about her own experience of fishing to me. 'I don't want to talk about fishing,' she told him down the phone. 'You know exactly how I feel about what you do.' Simon from the *Governek* reckons it's actually easier for the fishermen to deal with their time at sea than it is for their wives. 'We disappear off the face of the planet, sometimes for weeks at a time,' he says, 'and we just leave them behind.'

I hear similar sentiments time and again – often second-hand from husbands – of wives growing to despise their husband's jobs because, even when they are back on dry land, it feels as if they are always on the verge of leaving again. Fishermen's wives must be tough, forever asked to hold on, to hold the family together on their own for that while longer. The readjustment once the men have returned from sea is not straightforward, either. Women accustomed to running households alone, practically as single mothers, are suddenly faced with a knackered, unshaven, fish-smelling, stay-at-home husband sprawled out on their sofas. It can take ages to get used to one another again, to remember how to live with each other. A skipper's wife tells me that when her husband's beamer was hauled up for repairs, he was stuck at home for two months and it was the closest they've ever come to a divorce – 'Our relationship is not built on nine-to-five, home every night, you know?'

Stevie has been contemplating quitting the industry for a while. But, like so many men, he reckons he could not stand to work indoors after so many years at sea. To leave fishing would mean completely rewriting your identity. There is a reason that so many fishermen continue working up until they are practically old men. The idea of a life imprisoned by the land frightens them, the way that one lived at sea sometimes scares me.

My melancholy passes like a weather spell. After the Shipping Forecast is over I stay in the wheelhouse late into the night, while the men rotate between watches. Kyle and I see an enormous cruise ship in the distance, lights blazing from every window, so that it looks like the whole ship is on fire. Kyle tells me he always fantasises about one day taking the *Filadelfia* right up close to an ocean liner, climbing aboard and having a cocktail at the bar and a quick splash in the pool.

Robert Hichens, the man at the helm of the SS *Titanic* when it made contact with the iceberg on its way to New York, was a Newlyn boy. In fact, there were five Newlyners aboard in total. They are there, these Cornish men born of salt, in so many of our stories about the sea. Hichens was one of those lucky rescued few, on Lifeboat 6 to be exact. After his near-death experience on the *Titanic*, Hichens's life was not easy; other surviving passengers attested that he had refused to help rescue other people in the water, calling them 'stiffs', a fact that he denied during the US inquiry. Despite these accusations and the traumatic nature of his experience, Hichens continued working on the sea for the rest of his life, dying of heart failure aboard the merchant ship *English Trader* in Scotland when he was fifty-nine.

A cargo ship follows the cruise ship a few minutes later, drifting morosely across the horizon. Though at a great distance from us, it still appears monstrously large, its white containers spaced out in tall columns so that its outline resembles the jagged bones of a carcass blown across the seas.

Just after midnight, having packed my last monkfish for the night, I go back up to the wheelhouse to say goodnight to Don. He swivels around in his chair at the sound of my voice. 'You know I'm only teasing you? Don't take everything so seriously!' he says and goes to the back of the room and turns on the sound system. I recognise the emotive tones of Adele at once. We listen to both *19* and *21* in their entirety, first uncertainly muttering the words to ourselves, before belting out the last chorus of 'Chasing Pavements', side by side, into the night. Don has an almost inexhaustible supply of female power ballads. He tells me that when he needs a good cry sometimes, it is these songs that help him to get to that place. I nod, and stand beside him in silence, the two of us looking out at the formless black sea.

It takes time to learn another person's ways. This is the beauty of fishing. You can move beyond a simple, two-dimensional understanding of those around you, discovering that, of course, we each harbour deeper emotions than can be spoken. I think back to the first day when I asked Don what he felt about heading out to sea and he replied, 'I'm blank'. Like me telling myself 'You're tough' in the toilet earlier, these kinds of statements are just a kind of self-preservation, a thing we say to stop ourselves from breaking. Finally, Don announces in a slightly choked voice that he has to turn Adele off because it's making him too sad.

These difficult openings breached, Don and I talk freely about most things. He becomes my confidant, the two of us forming a bond that lasts well beyond our return to the harbour. His son once worked on the *Filadelfia*, he tells me; he was a wild youngster for a while, and Don was the only skipper who could manage him. His daughter is a wonderful photographer and has a collection of pictures of him skippering the *Filadelfia* back to Newlyn, the setting sun right behind her proud deck. A few years ago she bought him a St Christopher which he keeps on his person while at sea. When we watch someone on the telly talk about grief, he announces gravely: 'I know those feelings. I ate my way through my dad's death.' And I think back to the boy on the bus, who sat apart from the other children talking to the driver, eating crisps from both coat pockets. A few years ago, with the help of a close friend, Don tackled his health problems; he got himself in shape, stopped getting kebabs every evening he was back on land, started taking more care of himself. I quietly tell him that I survived my own teenage unhappiness through *not* eating. He nods but asks no more. In this way, we find an equivalence between us, a meeting between sea and sky at the horizon line.

'Goodnight, sweetheart,' Don calls back to me as I turn to leave the wheelhouse. 'Sleep well.'

The brittle shape you hammer copper into is not necessarily permanent, Mikey Johnson told me as I was leaving his workshop. There is a process called annealing that alters the metal's properties, making it soft once more – like a way of rubbing out – and allows for mistakes, for changes of heart.

16

LOCAL

It is early autumn now and I have been away from Cornwall for a while, missing the summer months with its mad heat of people.

The seasons have taught me not to trust the validity of memory. Every time a season comes around again after a year of absence, the experience comes as a complete surprise to me. I never remember it right, or I never remember it enough, and this makes me think about other memories too. If I can't accurately picture what it is like in summer to lie with a friend in a park drinking beer until the light finally departs around nine, unless I am actually there in that moment, cracking open a second tinny as the shadows chase us over the grass, then how can I really say I remember what it was like to have loved a particular boyfriend, to have felt so unhappy I could not leave my room, to be afraid of the dark?

Maybe you're not supposed to trust memories. If they were so good and true that we could play the past back like a film, we'd stop facing forward, stop reaching towards new moments to transform later into imperfect, hole-ridden memories.

To return to a place that has settled in one's mind as good, solid and finished, scares me like nothing else. Since childhood I've had a tic of dividing experiences into discrete halves. Once I get through the first half of something – be it a term of university, a holiday or a single date – and nothing terrible has happened, a tension that I did not even realise I was holding passes out of my body and my shoulders relax. In this way, I am able to seal off memories and place them in glass jars. Then, at a later stage, I can hold them up to the light and see the words shine across them: '*This was a good time in your life.*' The last note I wrote in my diary heading home on the train after my first visit to Newlyn is a perfect example of this: 'Remember that you have been happier and felt more solid here than you ever did in London. Remember that this cannot and must not be the end of your time in Newlyn.'

And yet, despite my best efforts neatly to sum the place up, once home I was unable to confine my time in Newlyn into one of my glass jars. Its difficulties refused to be resolved or forgotten. Instead it continued to intrude upon my daily life, coming with me to the pub and round to friends' houses for dinner, the noise of it blocking out what people were saying. Like an image hitting a retina and being upturned, each new experience I had after leaving that first time got reformed somehow, feeding into and deepening my understanding.

When Synge returned to the Aran Islands after some time back home on the mainland, he wrote: 'This year I see a darker side of life in the islands. The sun seldom shines, and day after day a cold south-western wind blows over the cliffs, bringing up showers of hail and dense masses of cloud.' The sun still shines on my return to Newlyn – if anything, the October light is brighter and cleaner, the skies and landscape wind-rent. In the same way that once your love for someone moves beyond those first blinding sparks of obsession you are able to notice their flaws and they yours, this light also reveals to me Newlyn's fault lines. At first I don't want to see them, but to keep one thing gleaming in your field of vision would eventually damage your view of the rest of the world. This recognition forces me to confront what I had written, respond to myself with: 'No, it did not simply make you happier and more solid. It is not that easy. Think harder. Allow it to be more than that.'

Newlyn has its inconsistences like anywhere else. It is the most loving place. Every person is noticed: if you are struggling, you will not be left behind. When Cod lost his legs through septicaemia, the community grouped together to pay for his prosthetics so that he could fish once more. 'I think life is that way,' he tells me in the Star one evening after returning from a day of catching squid. 'People saw I was in trouble and they saved me.' He believes his illness has done the rest of the town good, too. 'They looked at their lives and thought he's still having a great time, what's wrong with us then?'

But it also has its demons. There is an anger and insularity here, which is mostly levelled at the land beyond the Tamar. When I tell people I'm from London, I often get responses like: 'There's too many people. It's filthy. And no one speaks to you; no one speaks English, even.' The first time I stayed in Newlyn, I would nod. London is dirty; it is too full, too broken; but it is also pretty extraordinary. On my return, I want to say more about my own place, to describe what it means to me to live somewhere filled with people from across the world, how miraculous it is that we all take the same tube together each day and breathe the same polluted air.

Before my second stay in Newlyn, I visit Lelant for a few days with my family. On a cold, still morning, Mum and I head down to the beach, as we have done a thousand times before.

Virginia Woolf could see the slim line of Lelant beach across the bay from her holiday home in St Ives, and describes it in her diary of 1905, when she was twenty-seven:

> At ebb tide in the evening the stretch of the sands here is vast & melancholy; the waves spread themselves one over lapping the other in thin fan shaped layers of water; so shallow that the break of the wave is hardly more than a ripple. The slope of the beach gleams as though laid with a film of mother o' pearl where the sea has been, & a row of sea gulls sits on the skirts of the repeating wave. The pallor of the sandhills makes the scene yet more ghostly, but the beautiful sights are often melancholy & very lonely.

There are times when Lelant beach is the exact image Woolf describes: blanched days, when the flat sea has pulled right out and the sand lies like a dust sheet over all life. Viewed from jaunty St Ives, as Woolf would have, it somehow seems the unhappiest of all the beaches in the bay. But there is joy here too, when the sea flies right up to meet the dunes, snapping at their heels, just as the first light comes pink and orange from behind the cottage-dotted cliffs at Hayle, when the sandpipers hop in and out of the foam left by departing waves, when the water is so inviting that it seems to call out: 'Come and meet me here! Come all the way out!' and you cannot help but strip off and race straight into it.

This day the beach is more like Virginia Woolf's sombre portrait. There is an exclusion of light, the sky and sea bloodless. Mum reminds me that when I was a toddler, as soon as my short pink legs touched the sand, come rain or shine, I would pull all the clothes off that she had painstakingly dressed me in, and rush towards the water, bare-skinned and free. When her mother first placed her before the sea at a similar age, Sylvia Plath 'crawled straight for the coming wave and was just through the wall of green when she caught my heels'. Plath wonders what would have happened if her mother had not stopped her: if she'd just kept going on and on, right through the skin of the water.

In Newlyn, I ask people questions about their lives, their families' lives, their work, their ancestors, their Cornwall, but as we walk side by side over the landscape of my mother's childhood, I realise that I have never thought to ask my own mother about her memories of this place. Tell me your Cornwall, I say to her.

Mum's father died when she was eleven. In the wake of his death, her mother moved the family from St Helena, a tropical island in the South Atlantic where her father had been a doctor, back to Lelant, the village she herself had grown up in. Mum describes her first memories of Lelant, staying in a now-demolished bungalow opposite St Uny's church, as an unending series of grannies – 'hundreds of grannies: Granny Ball, Granny Buchanan, Granny Frieda, I mean hundreds of grannies. Everyone was a granny.' She remembers her first time on the beach, what it felt like just to run and run with no end in sight. She remembers coming back from ballet school during holidays to eat endless pasties and saffron buns, to play folk guitar and sit reading down by the slipway.

As soon as she was old enough, Mum said goodbye to her Cornish home and moved to London to start acting in the West End. 'You can love a place more than anywhere in the whole world,' she says, 'but that doesn't mean you can stay there.' Once acting, she could not come back to Lelant as often as she would have liked, in case she missed auditions. That severance is not easy, it is not a clean break, she tells me. You feel bereaved when you know you have no choice but to leave somewhere, as you would feel leaving a loved one. When she did come home, she would go straight down onto the beach. 'I don't know how to explain it,' she says when I ask her what that return was like. 'I felt relieved, like I could breathe again. It's the stretching of the eyes; it's looking out at the horizon again.'

'The health of the eye seems to demand a horizon,' Ralph Waldo Emerson once wrote of the healing powers of nature. 'We are never tired, so long as we can see far enough.' Mum and I continue walking purposefully along the beach, feeling ourselves open up, becoming more malleable, more forgiving of one another. Now and then we break from our conversation to acknowledge the extraordinary things the sea has done since we were last here: the jagged rocks by the estuary we had seen last spring have been hidden by a layer of sand, the shell line has been replenished and a large tree branch has been blown back by the wind so it arcs back into the sand as graceful as a dancer. I ask whether her experience of Cornwall changed as she grew older. 'It got less magical,' she says. Her answer surprises me. 'Once you've got people who depend on you, you can't go out into the dark world in your head so much.'

I ask her what she means.

'It was because of my mother. Cornwall was an escape for her after my father died.'

When they first came to Lelant, my grandmother discovered that it was no longer the joyous, social village that she remembered from her youth. The people she had known had moved away or become old. Mum watched as Cornwall become more muted for my grandmother, never quite fulfilling the fantasy she needed.

My own relationship with Cornwall had never been one especially preoccupied with reality. Since I was a baby, Mum has taken me on frequent pilgrimages to the bare church of Zennor, St Senara, which has occupied the same desolate site since the sixth century AD. Zennor is a village set on a high, lonely stretch of the north coast – far rougher and less concerned of human lives than the port towns of the south. Here, under the stone arches of the church, Mum would recount to me the folk tale the Mermaid of Zennor and show me the 'Mermaid Chair', a wizened old pew thought to be six hundred years old, which has a mermaid regarding herself in a mirror carved into its end. As I got older I would spend hours standing before the sea at Lelant, waiting for a mermaid to reveal herself, never wholly able to detach myself from the story of Matthew Trewella, the best singer in Zennor, who one day, without speaking a word to his family, disappeared off the cliffs and into the sea in pursuit of the mermaid, never to return to land again. The mermaid's tale is indelibly written into my childhood – this half-woman, half-fish being, whose gravitational pull was so urgent that it pulled a man right over the edge of the world. When we visited her pew, Mum and I would crouch down to etch her outline onto paper with a piece of graphite, the same question repeating over in my head: why did you take him; why was it him you chose?

Staying in Newlyn was the first time I was forced to question the fantastical image of Cornwall I had spent my childhood constructing – to view Cornwall with an adult's eye, populating its landscape with other humans with their own lives for the first time.

When we reach the cliffs marking the end of the beach, from where a stream with a red copper line running through it trickles down into the sea, I admit something that has been worrying me. I tell Mum that, able to think more clearly about my relationship with Cornwall now, I realise I have used this place as an identity that doesn't really belong to me. It has grown into a big part of what I say I think I am, I say, even though I don't live here.

'But that's the thing about Cornwall,' she replies. 'Everybody goes from it at some point, but that doesn't mean you don't feel Cornish. I'm a great believer in "You are what you feel you are".'

I want so much for this to be true. *You are what you feel you are*. It is a statement that speaks to my mother's unremitting optimism. Her joy drove me mad as a child; I could never quite believe in it – her love for every film, TV show, play and book she has ever seen, every person too. As I get older and become, reluctantly, like every other daughter, more similar to her, I begin to understand this better. Her seemingly boundless compassion for the world is part of why I was able to fall for Newlyn. While there, I would ring Mum most days, even if only for a few caught minutes, to fill her in on my Cornish adventure: people I have met, places I have seen, boats I have been on. I show her the Cornwall I am finding for myself, the self I am starting to find amongst it.

Through this place, Mum is able to touch parts of her old life again. 'You feel family around,' she says, 'those no longer with us, knowing the dog is here, my mother, my grandmother, my brothers. They're all here.'

The day before I move back to Newlyn, my dad and I head to Stevenson's to call in on Denise and buy some fresh fish. On our way in a fisherman passes me, dragging a box of sloppy monkfish tails just purchased at the auction. Laid out on the three front counters are lemon and dover soles, fat orange salmon fillets, pink gurnards and glistening shellfish with sprigs of parsley artfully arranged between the various fish. Above is a large blackboard with the mornings' prices for crab sandwiches, whelks, cockles, prawns and mussels chalked up. I cannot see Denise, so bound over instead to Elaine, who runs the shop.

'Elaine, hello! How are you? How's the shop?' I say, breathlessly.

She looks at me, her eyes squinting. 'No, sorry,' she says at last. 'I can't place you, my love.' My arms fall to my sides and I look

177

back at my dad sheepishly. We buy our fish and head back to Lelant, dad laughing at me all the way across the coast.

We want to know places. When we begin to, we believe such knowing will be reciprocated, that our indentations on the land-scape will hold so that those in future generations will continue to see traces of us upon that land. Through Newlyn I learn there is value in being forgotten. Though the town felt a huge experience for me, I was a blip, barely even that, in the long lives of most of its residents: a kid with a smart London accent who stuck out like a sore thumb, who asked a few questions and then left again. The town went on without me. Of course it did. But, somehow, naively, I thought it might not have.

A few days later I drop my unnecessarily large suitcase off at Lofty and Denise's for the second time this year. Before joining them at the pub, I take some time to refamiliarise myself with the cottage and to greet their cats, who regard me with the utmost suspicion – yet more Newlyn residents who can't place me. I walk slowly through each downstairs room, noticing again the many shells and paintings of the sea, including one by Ben Gunn, a jar of sand on the mantelpiece, the cats that Lofty made at the Copper Works... The place hasn't changed an inch; it is as warm and welcoming as the day I first arrived. On the side of the fridge, my name and number are still written on a whiteboard with the words 'Student, might stay?' written beside it. I put on the fleece that I never took off while I was on the *Filadelfia* and head down the road to the Star.

Its windows have steamed right up, but I can just make out the shadows of innumerable bodies behind the glass and hear the roars of laughter that pass through the door and roll out towards the harbour. I draw a nervous breath in and pull open the door. I'm hit by a warm, golden light, the Beatles ringing out on the jukebox and a cry of: 'All right! Welcome back!' from the nearest wooden table, around which are sat Lofty and Denise, Jolan, and Ben Gunn and his wife Jackie (both of whom later admit they couldn't remember my name or who I was either and were just joining in with everyone else). They are all here. I didn't dream the thing up.

My friend Jolan, who works on the *Scillonian* ferry shuttling queasy tourists to and from the Isles of Scilly, gets me a drink. He tells me he is not surprised to see me again. 'People come back here,' he says. 'They always do.'

There is something about this place that draws people to it: a tangible, tactile rhythm, the tides, the patterns of life here that continue to echo through your own body long after you've left and ensure you cannot forget this place.

Isaac, who I'd spent many a drunken night with in the Swordy, or up at the Coastguard's in Mousehole on my first visit to Newlyn, has himself left Cornwall by the time I return. We vow to write letters to one another – mine from Newlyn, where he grew up, his from Manchester where he is working, a city not unlike my own. It becomes a habit. I sit in Newlyn's Duke Street Cafe and attempt to render my experiences of this place, his place, into letter form, while he tells me of the changes to his own life now he is in Manchester. When I ask him to write to me of the landscape he grew up in, he replies: 'It's hard to know where to begin. I think one of the first things I noticed about moving away was that many places in Cornwall – Newlyn, Tredavoe, Gulval – felt like ballasts for me. While I was, and in many ways still am, uncertain about almost all other aspects of my life, I've always felt so clearly my home, and my family there, to be the most essential to me.'

It makes me jealous when I read this. I hadn't realised it was possible for someone my age to have a sense of self tied in a fast knot to a particular land. Over time I come to accept it is because the relationship between people and place in Cornwall is different to that in cities. In some ways the two are in indistinguishable here: people are place. They grow out of the land and the sea, every few days re-establishing that connection, dipping their feet into the water, pressing their palms into the sand.

I meet a woman that night at the Star who grew up in Newlyn and started her own family here but a few years ago moved up to become a landlady of a pub in Manchester. She has the same wicked sense of humour, which is instantly identifiable as bred in Newlyn – where jokes are the lifeblood of all conversation, repeated and added to throughout the night as the pints stack up across the tables. She tells me that her daughter misses Newlyn terribly and has given her a long list of things to bring back with her, including her favourite pasties from Aunty May's just by Newlyn Bridge and ice cream from Jelberts.

'I'll always be from here,' she tells me. When in Manchester people ask her what her local is she tells them, the Star.

'Where's that?' they say.

'Newlyn,' she replies.

'Come again?'

'Near Penzance...'

This continues until she gets to Cornwall and they say: 'Oh! God, all the way down the bottom?'

After a few drinks, Denise, Lofty and I head home together. Lofty makes us all bacon sandwiches and I take my usual place on the sofa to watch *The X Factor* with them. We chat about our summers, things that have happened in town since I left: the raft race to raise money for the harbour lights, the annual fish festival. We crack open the bottle I bought them as a thank-you-for-having-me-again gift. They have bought an extra-large tub of peanut butter for me so I won't eat all of theirs.

I hug Denise and Lofty goodnight and head upstairs. They have done up the guest room since my last visit and it still smells slightly of paint. Lying in bed, listening to the booms from the market once more, I let the sounds wash over me. Not wash, break. All Newlyn breaks over me and I am back.

17

A FEAST OF SEABIRDS

In the same crepuscular glow in which the day-boats return to shore, the ring-netters are just preparing for their evening of fishing. Tonight I'm going out pilchard-hunting with Danny Downing and his three-man crew on the *Golden Harvest*. From the Fradgan, leading down towards the harbour, I take the blue-elvan cobbled path whose pebbles do not seem to have been laid in any sensible order, but rather, like water running through a rocky stream that finds itself constantly diverted and re-routed, shoot off in various directions.

As ever, I am nervous about meeting a new crew on one of their boats for the first time, but when I arrive there is no one about. The *Golden Harvest* PZ63 is a terracotta-coloured ring-net fishing boat moored at the end of the Mary Williams Pier. It is much smaller than the *Crystal Sea* or *Filadelfia*, and has a large wheelhouse and modified stern which opens up like a twin rig from where its nets are thrown out to capture shoals of pilchards. I check my phone to find a text from Danny saying he's running a bit late but the other lads should be there shortly. I sit on an oil drum and swing my feet over the edge of the pier, noticing how the wind strokes across the harbour like a straw being blown through paint, sending it out in fans of activity. I look out at the horizon and see a few trawlers just visible, seeming to hang above the water through a sea mist.

Sure enough, a few minutes later I see three lads sauntering down the pier, swinging plastic bags containing their dinners. Once close I realise I recognise them all. Tom often frequents the

Swordy and I've seen Ed about town. The third crew member is the son of the Star's landlady Debbie. He shares with her the same quiet manner and large grey eyes.

When Danny turns up five minutes later, the other crew immediately notice the conspicuous bag of KFC nuggets in his arms. 'You're late because you went to KFC?' 'That better be for the whole crew!'

'No bloody way!' replies Danny, leaping nimbly from the last few rungs of the ladder onto the boat, introducing himself to me and climbing up into the wheelhouse in one movement. He leans out of the one of the oblong windows around the wheelhouse. 'Well, come on then, you lazy bunch! You all just been sitting around waiting for me?'

As the men kick into action, he sticks his head out the window once more: 'We've got a girl with us tonight, so act civil and no swearing.' He winks at me. 'You fuckers!'

He turns back to check his equipment, fill in the ship's log and get the engine going, ignoring the cries from the deck of: 'You've got the filthiest mouth of the lot of us!'

With the sun just sinking, we pass Newlyn Lighthouse for our night of pilchard hunting. The last light sits above the bay in a romantic purplish haze. The clouds are wispy and unfocused, the moon hanging low, its tendrils threading through the lines of the water. An old St Ives term for the crescent moon, when the evening star seems to follow at the moon's heels, is 'the ship towing her punt'. It was believed to be a sign of good weather to come.

Just clear of the harbour, Danny gets out his still-hot KFC chicken thighs from their brown paper bag. Just as he hands one to me, Tom comes up into the wheelhouse and begins an outraged torrent of abuse at Danny for never sharing his chicken with him. 'All right, all right!' He reluctantly slings one at Tom too, warning him not to tell the others.

Tom nods and immediately yells down into the galley: 'Danny says he has loads of chicken he wants to share with us!'

Danny is immediately likeable. Though he messes about and teases the crew any opportunity he gets, he is a shrewd fisherman, retaining the absolute respect of the men with seemingly minimal effort. Before he got into ring-netting, he was apparently one of the best single-manned mackerel hand-liners fishing off St Ives, and after that he did his time on some of the bigger boats. The Downings are a respected name in fishing throughout Newlyn, and the *Golden Harvest* herself has been part of his family for over forty years, having been built in 1976, the year Danny was born. She began her life gill-netting but had almost fallen into disrepair. A couple of years ago, Danny, who is also trained as a shipwright, stripped her down and transformed her into a ring-netter, leading the return to pilchard fishing in Cornwall.

The moon slips down into the sea and it is really dark now. The men pull their oilskins up, ready for Danny's command to throw the large ring-net out into the water as soon as he has closed in around the pilchards. From a distance, I can just make out the flashing colours of the amusement arcade down on the prom at Penzance. It feels strange to fish so close to the land. I had grown accustomed to thinking of fishing as synonymous with disappearing from humanity for a while. Maintaining the land in sight makes the work feel more perfunctory – more like a job and less like an escape. There are two other ring-netters with us in the bay that night. Pilchards shoals are usually found quite close together, so the three Newlyn boats tend to follow each other round the bay and call one another up on the VHF if they get a whiff of anything. As we set off to the location where they found a huge shoal the previous night, Danny tells me that pilchard fishing is now an MSC-certified sustainable fishery. Since there are just three boats in Newlyn, only another six fishing out of Cornwall and no others at all in the rest of the UK, it is seriously good money. Ring-netting also has minimal environmental impact: there is little by-catch and the nets do not go deep enough to damage the seabed.

The pilchards' fishery was once the lifeblood of Newlyn, with the majority of the catch being exported to feed Catholic areas in northern Europe during periods that required abstinence from meat. In the eighteenth century, a typical toast in Newlyn would be: 'Long life to the Pope, death to our Best Friends, and may our streets run in Blood' – 'Best Friends' being the pilchards, and 'Blood' the juices that flowed onto the cobbles after the fish were pressed and salted in the so-called pilchard palaces, repurposed cellars in fishermen's cottages, that once littered the town. By the start of the twentieth century, pilchards had begun to be regarded as peasant food and the market for them fell into decline – compounded by several bad seasons of fishing in Newlyn. In the last few decades, however, there has been another glut of pilchards in the bay and the price of pilchards has risen once more. A lot of this present success, both in Newlyn and across the UK, is down to Nick Howell, who bought the Newlyn Pilchards Works in 1981 and got together with M&S to rebrand pilchards as 'Cornish Sardines', transforming them into a luxury item by selling them in pretty tins, and mixed with oil and lemon.

Unlike most forms of fishing, where there is no way of knowing what you will bring up in your nets, pilchard fishermen can see the target they're stalking. It is a primal kind of fishing, we become hunters chasing our prey across the seas. Danny sits up in the wheelhouse, his eyes carefully trained on the full-circle sonar screen, watching for the dark red blotches that will indicate there is a shoal nearby. Every few seconds a line through the radius of the circle wipes across the screen, illuminating the very latest activity happening below the water. It makes for hypnotic viewing; Danny and I keep our faces right up to it, jumping every time a sliver of colour materialises on the screen.

When a huge red splodge of activity suddenly appears, Danny leaps into action. He yells down to the boys to ready themselves on deck and they wrench open the heavy door in the aft of the boat. An icy tunnel of wind rushes into the galley, causing cupboard doors to slam shut and a half-eaten packet of crisps to fly from the table. Danny turns the engine down low, carefully easing the boat around the moving shoal to prevent the pilchards from scattering before the net has surrounded them. The men wait, poised over the net. And then, at last, Danny gives a great bellow, signalling them to throw the net out.

There is a silence. We wait in anticipation in the wheelhouse, but nothing happens. The silence holds. There comes a flurry of swearing from outside. Danny and I look back at the sonar: it shows an empty, black sea; the pilchards have dispersed once more. Danny slams his hands on the dashboard, muttering under his breath. After a few seconds, he calls out to the boys: 'What the hell happened there, then?'

'The first ring got caught,' one crew member shouts back across the raging wind.

'A ring got caught?' Danny repeats slowly.

The other men join in, trying to explain what happened.

'A ring got caught,' Danny says again, leaving a pause between each word, a note of threat in his voice. He turns to me. 'These goats! Things like that should never, ever happen.' He yells back at them again: 'Next time when I say I'm ready to go, you check it, you double check it and then you triple check it, all right?!' He sighs, shaking his head. 'They were lovely marks, 'n' all ...'

We abandon the spot of our near miss and Danny pushes the *Golden Harvest* onwards to seek out other shoals lurking within the shallows of the bay. Pilchard fishing can be maddening. Every time we get close to a shoal, they split and scatter, the bright marks on the sonar vanishing as quickly as they appear. At other times, just as we are chasing a huge shoal, they'll swim right into a load of rocks, where we cannot follow them without damaging the boat or ripping the net.

Danny tells me that sometimes he thinks the pilchards know exactly what they're doing. 'You can't underestimate what you're hunting,' he warns me. Now and then, I hear him whispering to them under his breath: 'You bastards.'

The more time we spend watching these smudges of activity, the more I do imagine the fish as cognizant, goading fishermen towards ever more treacherous rocky grounds at the peripheries of Mounts Bay like Sirens luring sailors.

'You lads know the territory we're in,' shouts Danny out the window to his crew, who are leaning out over the water, their faces wet and their eyes glittering from the sea spray. 'Sacrificial net, init? We got a spare...'

They nicknamed their previous net 'Frankenstein's Monster' because it suffered so many rips and tears over the years that by the end it was a patchwork of different threads and offcuts of old nets – almost beautiful in its tatterdemalion way. Each pilchard net takes three and a half months to make and costs a fortune. Their new one is worth over thirty grand and was made in Cornwall, but they have another larger that was made in Peru for £85,000. Every ring net is made of three parts: a central purse of fine, tanned webbing and two wings of coarser mesh. Each square of net is knotted together to form the almost invisible nylon blanket that hangs in the water, ensnaring the shoals within it.

In their local history, *Newlyn Before the Artists Came*, Pam Lomax and Ron Hogg write that after each new fishing vessel was built in Newlyn harbour in the 1800s, every member of the crew was obliged to contribute their own fragment of net to its overall composition. This completed net, a patchwork of threads joined in a reticular pattern, would remain part of the boat for its duration in service – a symbolic representation of the inter-weaving relations between the crew who would fish with it.

Danny tells me that the other two ring-netters have gone back in to land already, having caught a huge shoal within about an hour ('jammy bastards') but we can just about make out the other boat still, its lights blinking up behind St Michael's Mount. We wheel and flick across the harbour, seeking latent shoals hiding in the bay's dark folds, creating disorientating corkscrew patternations across the water. Anyone observing our zigzagging from the prom would surely imagine that the skipper had gone out blind drunk.

The crew get a message from their decky learner. He's recovering back home at the moment; Danny accidentally ran over his foot with a forklift a few weeks ago while they were landing the pilchards. 'Looks like you lot are going around in circles again,' the message announces gleefully, sent from his warm bed on land. He must be watching us on the AIS, Danny tells me, a habit that many fishermen fall into when they are not able to go to sea for some reason – following the snaking trails of boats they once crewed and wishing they were out there with them. Once back home, I too found myself slipping into a daily routine of looking up the boats I fished with on the AIS. Sitting in a cafe in Haringey, my mouse would trace fishermen's past voyages through the large expanse of unnatural blue that stands for the sea on the Marine Traffic website, following the faintest scents of some elusive pilchard shoal – watching the red, arrow-dotted line twist and turn back in on itself in real time, drawing conch patterns across the water. Its thread of movement remains emblazoned across the sea as a record of the trip like the trails of phosphorescence that followed Simon home on his last ever fishing trip with the *Governek of Ladram*.

After almost an hour with no luck at all, Danny opens up the window again and shouts out dejectedly to the cold night: 'Come in for a bit, boys.'

There is no response. He leans out the window further and finds only Ed on deck.

'Have they left you again? Why is it always only just you, eh? I'll have a word.' Danny jumps down to find the other two crew warming themselves up in the galley and slumped around the table. The smell of their burgers and frozen pizzas heating in the microwave passes through the room. 'You lot having a nice sit-down dinner, then?'

They grin up at him unapologetically.

As I head back to the wheelhouse with Danny, Tom shouts up behind me: 'What are you doing to the fish, Lamorna? Knew a girl on board would be bad luck!'

While we wait for the elusive shoal, Danny and I get to chatting. He and his wife have three daughters, who he says definitely won't go into fishing because they're far too smart for that. He's let the oldest steer the boat round the harbour though – 'She picked it up in seconds,' he tells me proudly. We speak more broadly of the changes that have occurred in the town during his lifetime. The Swordy's a mere shadow of its past unruly wildness, he tells me mournfully. But sometimes, very occasionally, that spark returns and the pub becomes red hot once more, as it did that first night after the Lamorna Walk. Like many of the other fishermen with young families, they live outside of town now, the connection between the community and the fishing industry becoming thinner, more threadbare. Mid-conversation, Danny freezes, his eyes widening as he stares down at the sonar. It blooms red, the colour spreading outwards with each wipe until it's covered the screen.

'Gogogogogo mother fuckers!!!!' he bellows down below.

The crew throw their down burgers mid-mouthful and rush out to the stern of the boat.

Danny is no longer sitting but hopping from foot to foot. 'Now, where did you just come from?' he addresses the bright pulsing organism before us. We readjust positions and they disappear momentarily on the sonar: 'No, come on, don't you fade away on me!'

Without realising it, I am on my feet too, shouting at the screen together with Danny as if we were watching a tense football match.

'Yes!' we yell, stamping our feet and punching the air, as the mark materialises once more. 'That's better, okay, okay, okay!'

Danny jumps over to peer out the window again: 'Is it cold out there, boys?' He laughs. 'Yeah, yeah, mate. I tell you what, Lamorna and I are feeling a bit of a draught up here ourselves, aren't we girl?'

He teases the boat forwards, deftly shifting her into the perfect position.

'That's the baby, that's the baby…' he croons. 'Come on, come on.' His voice rises to a crescendo. 'Come on!'

The first time I read Nance's *Glossary*, the collection of fishermen's words did not conjure much. That night on the *Golden Harvest*, the water below us dense with fish, the words drove back to the front of my head, providing me with a new vocabulary to express the miraculous events unfolding around our boat:

Cowl rooz! – shoot the net
clyne, a feast of seabirds, indicating a shoal below the water
scrawled or *ascrawl*, fish swarming together in a living mass.

At last Danny screams, 'Oy, oy!!!!' and I hear a much older fisherman, his voice more thickly Cornish, bellowing *Cowl rooz!!!*

This is the cry the men have been waiting for. The metal rings rattle and clang against one another as the men unravel bits of net and frantically ready themselves to shoot it out around the shoal. With the bright light of the boat behind them, they appear as silhouette cut- outs, their raised hoods rendering their shadowed outlines cartoonish, misshapen. A heavy rain pours down from unseen dark clouds, pelting the men's oilskins. When caught in the hard light of the boat it looks like a million sharp needles coming for us.

I hear the steel rings come off the boat one after another and fly into the water with a clunking noise. We draw the lasso of weighted net in a wall around the fish, which stands up vertically in the water due to the strong corks tied to the top of it.

'Halfway!' the crew cry out to Danny in the wheelhouse.

I hear the grinding of more rings slipping out behind the boat.

'Three rings left!' they yell again and then, a moment later: 'Last ring!'

The hunt is over, lasting a matter of minutes at most. I sprint out of the wheelhouse and onto to the starboard side of the deck to take a look at the top of the net floating all around us in the water. Outside I am met by a gaping black stillness, as if the air itself were letting out a large exhalation of breath to recover from the scene it has just witnessed. I stand on my tiptoes to try and catch sight of the pilchards swarming below in the water. In the gloom, I can see almost nothing, but fancy I sense the presence of a great hive-mind teeming below us.

Out of the aircraft hangar of silence comes a single screech like a crack of lightening. The sound intensifies until there blows through the night a whole chorus of screaming. It sounds like insanity, how I imagine madness would speak. And then, there appears out of the darkness a *clyne* in the form of what must be tens of hundreds of seagulls heading right for our nets like a flight of kamikaze pilots. The surging welter crash-land into the sea right beside us, sending shock waves through the water. They do not settle but rocket back up into the air to crash down upon the water from a great height again and again, their talons outstretched in an attempt to snatch at the prized silver fish wriggling just below their grasp. They repeat this performance as many times as it takes them to meet their mark. As soon as they've swallowed their prey, the hunt begins again. The sea froths. The sight of it is dizzying. Their calls sound angry and desperate, close at times to a human scream, but somehow distorted, as if played backwards.

The sky is white with gulls now, everything taking on a frightening pallor as though the world has been switched to negative. They churn the air up into a rage. The boat's floodlights illuminate their pale feathers as the birds go wheeling past. Danny sees the shocked look on my face, my pupils dilated, and reassures me that it is a good sign; you can trust the birds to know when there are a lot of fish.

They get everywhere, landing on the head of the fishermen as they tug the net back up onto the boat, on every piece of rigging and patch of sea. At one point, Ed lets out an almighty torrent of swearing and rushes back into the galley, spitting and running his hands over his tongue. Breaking from the work, the crew and I gather around him, waiting for some explanation. He spits once more, takes a swig of an energy drink. 'Seagull shat in my mouth,' he shudders, causing us all to burst into hysterics.

The ropes of the net bag are contracted right in like the strings of a purse, forcing the pilchards into a smaller area. I see them now. First, it is just their scales that appear, flaking away from their bodies and shimmering through the water like the sequins you find pressed into the cracks of the roads after a carnival. Then the fish themselves rise up to the surface of the water and boil as if being burned from below, their reflective skin catching in the lights of the boat like licking flames.

Once the fish are in a tight mass, *ascrawl* beside the boat, a hoover-like machine sucks them out of the water and down into a chute. From here, they tumble down into a large metal bath on the deck so that they can be scooped out, packed into boxes and sent off to the processors waiting back on land. I watch them cascade in a chaos down the metal slide into the metal bath on the deck. They keep coming and coming, these perfect, tiny fish, as if the entire sea were being emptied of them. The bath is alive with their dancing, slamming against its sides with a sharp, almost metallic noise that the crew call 'Snap, crackle and pop'.

I stare at the writhing tank, letting my tired eyes become unfocused so that the whole bath appears animated. Danny tells me that the numbers are unfortunately deceptive and that it was actually a pretty meagre haul – only one tonne, when usually they want three or four. This means we'll keep hunting for more shoals tonight.

'Dunno what the seagulls got so excited about,' one of the crew says, kicking the tank disappointedly.

Scattered amongst the thousands of polished, silver pilchards are a dozen or so blue-sheen-backed anchovies, which are worth much more than the boat's target species. Tom picks one out of the bath and hands it to me to keep, telling me they are delicious fresh for breakfast fried up and eaten on toast. They are elegant fish, slender, silken to the touch, and complete with miniature rows of sharp teeth. There is something mechanical about their motion and the neatness of their scales, like they have been sculpted by a great craftsman. Their eyes are perfectly spherical, with shocked black pupils right at their centre. Sebald writes that 'once the life has fled the herring, its colours change. Its back turns blue, the cheeks and gills red, suffused with blood.' Like the herrings whose colour at the moment of death is brighter than when living, the little blue anchovy in my hand is so extraordinarily bright that I cannot quite believe it will not spring back to life again.

The night has gone a deep purple. We set off once more around the bay, the blind eye of the radar feeling out for the hint of a pilchard shoal. The neon lights of the Penzance arcade still flash in the distance. Life on land continues as usual, the inhabitants of the villages along the bay oblivious to the sensory overload we have just experienced. Occasionally we spot the slightest trace of movement on the sonar, but as it gets later, the men tell me, pilchards tend to disperse into much smaller groups. Eventually, Danny decides to give up and head back to land with our small catch.

As soon as they know they're heading in, the crew's mood grows lighter once more. While Ed is fixing up equipment on deck, the other two pour half a bag of sugar into Tom's water bottle (they couldn't find salt). Meanwhile Danny grabs someone's sandwich and chucks it into the microwave, blasting it until it sinks into a soggy pulp. After Danny puts his own pizza in the microwave, he has to keep darting out of the wheelhouse to check no one has messed with it. 'Would we do that to you, Skip?' Tom asks with an evil grin. 'You're getting paranoid!'

As we near the lighthouse, Danny says to me: 'Right then, are you landing the boat?'

I laugh, assuming he is joking. 'Yep, sure.'

'Cool.' He gets up and motions for me to take his seat. I dither for a second, before clambering up into it and eyeing up the intimidating number of buttons and levers on the dashboard. But Danny stands right beside me, carefully instructing me which levers to pull and when, how to change the course of the boat by making only the slightest of turns at a time. We thread our way through the Gaps, my hands shaking slightly as I feel the million-pound boat judder beneath my control. We move along the silent channel of towering trawlers towards the market, where the buckets of pilchards are levied up and driven along in forklifts onto the waiting vans, bypassing the auction.

The last few fish are sloshed out of the bath and raised into the air. 'That's the last I see of the things, thank god,' Danny says, as the van doors slam close.

Pilchards were once emblematic of the way that fishing connected the lives of Newlyn's inhabitants to one another. Long before the *Golden Harvest's* radar technology, a man would stand on the cliffs above the bay, armed with a huge furze bush, straining his eyes while he watched and waited for the distinctive shadow sliding through the sea which would announce the arrival of the pilchards. The purse seine boats stayed anchored on their sterns from dawn to dusk, waiting for the huer's call, their crews sheltering under a makeshift tent called a tilt, where they would yarn and smoke while drinking coffee from portable stoves. At this point the huer would wave the bush frantically and shout '*Hevva!*', signalling to the fishermen below to race into their boats to capture the shoal below.

Once back on the shore, the pilchards would be loaded up in *cowal*s – woven baskets that women and children would carry on their heads – and taken back to the pilchard palaces to be salted in a process called baulking: forming large piles of pilchards on paving stones in alternate layers of fish and salt. Men, women and children would work in the candlelit palaces late into the night, before taking the outside stairs to their living quarters on the floors above. Once salted and left for three weeks to pro-cure, the pilchards were known as 'fairmaids' and packed into hogshead barrels to be sold. At the dawn of the twentieth cen-tury, women working in Newlyn's pilchard palaces were paid thruppence an hour, and a glass of brandy and a piece of bread with cheese every sixth hour. There are still traces of old pil-chard palaces around Newlyn; the stones once used for baulking are now ornaments in gardens, while the oil that ran from the pilchards has stained the cobbles that wind up the Fradgan dark brown.

After the crew has sent the pilchard vans on their way, Danny turns to me and says: 'Right, are you ready to moor her now?'

I sit back in Danny's chair and with him calmly guiding me, slowly ease the *Golden Harvest* to her usual docking space at the end of the Mary Williams Pier. A few of the crew's friends are sitting on the quayside with beers, and I think of the

seventeenth-century Newlyn fishermen lolled out about the harbour, joking and yarning, waiting for the huer's cry.

After we moor up, the men call out to us: 'Come on! Let's go
for a pint, then!' and we all head off to the Star – Danny tells
me he tends not to be able to sleep until the early hours after the
thrill of ring-netting anyway.

We settle down with a few other fishermen just in from
sea: Richard, the ex-army man from the *Joy of Ladram* gill-netter,
her skipper and an Irish fisherman I've never met before, who has
a glass eye because a crab pulled out his real one. Our table soon
grows crowded with pints, Danny triumphantly telling anyone
that will listen: 'You know what, this girl landed my boat this
evening!'

I look down and remember I haven't changed out of my
gumboots yet, realising that this is the first time I have gone
straight from the sea to the pub. I sit back in my chair content-
edly, listening to the men nestling their pints and prattling, the
whoosh of the evening wind careening down the Strand. All of
our shirts are caked in scales – or *golowillions*, another from
Nance's *Glossary*: the shining scales of herring or pilchard left on
clothing after the cleaning of fish.

Later, back in the cottage, I feel something slimy wetting the
inside of my pocket and pull out the anchovy Tom gave me earlier.
I hold it in my hand. Its scales are no longer luminous but have
faded to a matt grey.

18

ROSEBUD

The most striking image I have seen of a Newlyn fishing vessel is not of a trawler raging against a storm, but of an old lugger making its way down the River Thames, the Houses of Parliament half hidden in a smog layer behind it. If you look closely at the black and white photograph, you can just about read the boat's name painted in white on its bow: *Rosebud*, PZ87.

The *Rosebud* was a long-liner (a vessel designed to shoot from its stern a long line strung with baited hooks), built in 1919 from Cornish oak, out of Joseph Peake and Son's workshop in Tolcarne, a family-run shipwrights famed for its sleek fishing vessels. On 19 October 1937, she set off for London carrying a petition signed by 1,093 Newlyn residents hoping to save their town from demolition. As she entered the bay, 'Fight the Good Fight', a favourite hymn in Newlyn, could be heard through the crashing of the waves as the whole town gathered around the harbour to send the crew on their way.

The problems had begun in 1935 when Penzance Council sent their medical health officer, Richard Lawry, to Newlyn to determine which of the town's cottages were 'slum dwellings' with a view to them being torn down. The criteria for unfit homes included those that lacked basic structural and safety features, were unhygienic, overcrowded or badly ventilated. Crucially, the specifics of this criteria were created in reference to city slums, where such issues were more likely to lead to life-threatening conditions. Though many of the cottages in Newlyn had no running water, they drew pails from chutes around the town;

though they had no toilets, their enamel buckets were regularly emptied into soil carts (Penzance boys used to joke you could tell a Newlyn boy from the red rings around their backsides and called Newlyn girls 'ring doves'); their cottages were not well ventilated and tended to smell of fish from the pilchard palaces in their cellars, but just beyond their doors was the cleansing breath of the sea and untouched stretches of countryside.

Checking off each of these unfit conditions on his list as he entered each begrudging Newlyn resident's household, Lawry declared all of the hundred cottages he visited to be 'slum dwellings' and plans were drawn up to construct a new estate up on the hill behind the town for those whose homes would be knocked down – Gwavas Estate, named after the sunken lake below Mount's Bay. Meanwhile, Navy Inn Court, previously a pub and at the time containing at least twenty-nine inhabitants squeezed into separate flats, was the first to be condemned and torn down.

The serious threat that Lawry's report posed to the town was not truly recognised until 23 September that year when a document was circulated describing which homes were to be demolished. In these plans it was not just the few slum dwellings that were earmarked for destruction, but whole stretches of streets along the Fradgan, right down into Tolcarne. The council announced that since so many of the buildings were structurally dependent on one another, there was no other option but to bring down all homes adjacent to those condemned. Worse still, while the owners of these non-slum cottages would be offered some small remittance for their destruction, the tenants living in them were to be given nothing at all.

In an emergency service held at Newlyn's Methodist Chapel a sermon reflected the sense of impending doom: 'Our little world seems falling about us. We are bewildered and in severe distress. We beseech thee in thy infinite mercy that some means may be found to save these homes and preserve the villages of Newlyn and Mousehole.' There was a shared belief that the new, neatly divided, private homes up at Gwavas would signal the end of the communal way of living that the families of Newlyn had enjoyed for so many generations.

News of the crisis soon found its way into the national press, with various figures from London turning up to see the slums of Newlyn for themselves. A journalist from *The Times* was surprised to observe: 'A visit to more than a dozen of the condemned cottages revealed them all as spotlessly clean and attractive as hard-working women with limited means can make them,' and cited one resident who stated: 'People don't die here; after a certain age, we have to shoot them.' Elsewhere, Newlyn resident Mrs Bessie Strick was quoted as saying that the last person to die in her home on Lower Green Street had lived to the age of 101 – a far cry from poverty and disease-ridden homes that the nomenclature 'slum' suggested.

This all seemed to bode well for the village's fight, but there were greater complexities to come. Though many loudly protested the loss of the rustic and shambolic charm of the village, some younger residents welcomed the move to newly furnished and well-heated homes up in Gwavas. A petition from the 'Younger Residents' stated: 'We the young people of Newlyn are no longer going to endure the filthy and insanitary conditions in which we live ... We say that Newlyn is no longer a fishing village – granted a few elderly men and a few out-of-date boats ... They will soon disappear. The sons of these men are not going-fishing.' There was similar division amongst men and women, with fishermen wanting the stability of remaining in those places they knew and loved once they came in from sea, while many of their wives longed for better living conditions.

The *Rosebud* mission in 1937 to deliver Newlyn's petition to Parliament continued a long tradition of popular protest in Cornwall. In 1497, a rebel army had marched on London with picks and crowbars to protest against Henry VII's suspension of Cornish Stannary privileges (legislation brought in by King John in 1201 to protect miners and mining towns, many of which were in Cornwall). There would be four further revolts in the county before the end of the seventeenth century – each time Cornishmen crossed the Tamar to protest against their mistreatment. During the English Civil War, the Cornish played an especially active role as a royalist enclave after the few Cornish Parliamentarians were defeated in Launceston in 1642.

The early modern historian Mark Stoyle regards these rebellions not as isolated events but part of a determination to protect the Cornish identity from assimilation into Britain. In his *Survey of Cornwall*, published in 1602, the Cornish translator and historian Richard Carew expressed his frustration that though some West Cornish inhabitants understood English, when he tried to speak to them they would answer uncooperatively: *Meea navidna Cowzasawzneck* (I can speak no Saxonage; Stoyle corrects Carew's translation; it is closer to: 'I will speak no Saxonage'). Indeed, a specific Cornish identity can be traced all the way back to the founding myth of Britain. The aspect of it most recalled today is that of Brutus arriving with refugees from Troy to colonise Albion, naming his new land the kingdom of Britain and splitting England, Scotland and Wales between his sons. But there is another, often forgotten, branch of this legend. A second group of Trojans, led by Corineus, a legendary fighter of giants contemporaneous with Brutus, landed in another region, part of the same landmass as Albion, which he named Cornwall.

This divergent creation myth has coloured how many Cornish perceive their nation up to the modern period, choosing to look to a mythical origin story as their county increasingly found itself suppressed and absorbed into a purely English narrative of the past. In fact, the West Britons in Cornwall fiercely defended their land against the Saxons and were not brought under British rule until ADE 838. And even after this period, the Cornish both considered themselves and were regarded as distinct from the English. The Italian scholar Polydore Vergil wrote in his 1535 *Anglica Historia* that Britain was divided into four parts: the English, Scottish, Welsh and 'the fowerthe of Cornishe people, which all differ emonge themselves, either in tongue, either in manners, or ells in lawes and ordinaunces'.

The year 1648 in the English Civil War marked the last and most hopeless revolt of the West Cornish. A force of men from Land's End rose up in the name of the king and occupied Penzance, where seventy Cornish royalists had already been killed, calling upon men from the Lizard to support them. But, by the time the men from the Lizard arrived in Penzance, the Land's End men had already been defeated. It is recorded that the rebels did not simply give up after this revolt, but 'joyned-in-hands' threw themselves into the sea, 'a desperate expedient on that rocky coast'.

Such determined resistance reflected a larger sense of loss in Cornwall – that of its language. By 1660, traditional Cornish was already in decline; by 1750, Dolly Pentreath of Mousehole, said to have been the last Cornish speaker in Cornwall, was dead and interred. With their private language forgotten, the fierce lines drawn between Cornwall and England started to fade. What must it mean to know, if you met them somewhere after this life, that you would not be able to commune with your ancestors – to know that the words you have learned for each part of the landscape, were not the original names given to it, not the first words the land had heard to name itself? And yet, across Cornwall today the old language is gradually being rediscovered and reintroduced.

To me, Cornwall has always felt like another country, more certain in its perimeters than other parts of England. This has something to do with its shape: the tapering foot of the UK, which in maps seems longing to wrench itself away from the body of England and step out into the water. There are high places in West Penwith such as Trencrom, a Neolithic tor that was re-appropriated as a hillfort in the Iron Age, from where you can see the sea pressing against both coastlines at once. This must mean something – to have one's land so determined by its encounters with the sea. In 2014 the Cornish were granted minority status, a promise to recognise and protect a distinct Cornish identity. Some of the friends I made in Newlyn tell me when they have to fill out nationality forms, they add their own box 'Cornish!' It is something of a joke, but there is also a seriousness to their actions, a desire for their home to be acknowledged, its past autonomy remembered.

Back in 1937, the beginnings of an idea for a bold stunt that might save their town spread around Newlyn, inspired by the history of the Cornish revolts, this time in the form of a protest to London – not across land, but over the seas. A crew of nine upstanding Newlyn men came forward ready to set sail for Westminster: Cecil Richards, W. (Swell) Richards, skipper, J. S. (Jimmy Strick) Matthews, Ben Batten, J. P. (Sailor Joe) Harvey; W. (Billy Bosun) Roberts (a preacher), J. (Jim) Simons, J. H. (Jan Enny) Tonkin and W.H. (Skinny) Williams. The *Rosebud*, owned by the Richards' brothers, was to be the chosen vessel.

Three days later the *Rosebud* was steaming down the Thames carrying a vial of water from the sacred Madron Well in West Cornwall and a petition declaring: 'We the undersigned inhabitants of Newlyn and district wish to protest respectfully and strongly against the wholesale destruction of our village. This ruthless appropriation of private property involves, in most cases, the loss of a lifetime's savings and the means of a lifetime.'

On their arrival in London the men were amazed to find throngs of supporters and press packed along the banks of the Thames. As the lugger moored up, Penzance MP Alex Beecham made a mealy-mouthed speech to the crowds at Westminster Bridge: 'I am delighted to welcome the fishermen of Newlyn who are arriving in such a romantic manner, because it is well that the citizens of London should be conscious of the existence of these fishermen who, I am sorry to say, are encountering very great difficulties in making a livelihood.' Frustrated by the MP's evasiveness, Newlyn preacher Billy Bosun bellowed back: 'The Cornish boys are here to fight for their homes!'

The crew of the *Rosebud* were quickly ushered into the offices of the Ministry of Health to meet with Conservative minister

Sir Howard Kingsley Wood, who had laid on the sweetener of a proper Cornish tea, sent all the way from Looe, comprising pasties, clotted cream, splits, and saffron cake. Sitting in the smart wooden-panelled room, the creams teas before them, the fishermen laid out their demands. 'When I put my hand into that of Sir Kingsley Wood,' wrote Billy Roberts, optimistically, 'I knew this was the hand of a friend and a strong man. Sir Kingsley would have made a great fisherman.'

The next day, the headline on the front page of *Cornish Evening Tidings* was 'Newlyn Saved', while the *Daily Mail* declared: 'Newlyn gets respite, revels all night, boat pilgrims saved 94 homes'. Such pronouncements were, however, premature. Over the coming days news emerged that, despite their very best efforts, over half of the Newlyn cottages earmarked for demolition were to be pulled down – Cecil Richards's home amongst them. When informed of this, he told the *Western Morning News*: 'As a fisherman I know there is a big difference between seeing a shoal of fish and actually getting it into the nets.' The battle for their homes lost, the people of Newlyn began the process of carrying their possessions up the road to the new estates.

The *Rosebud* resumed her daily duties as a fishing boat, before ending her days as the *Cynthia Yvonne*, abandoned in the muddied estuary between Lelant and Hayle. A few years ago, a note in the *Cornishman* announced that the lugger was finally set to be broken up and that those who wanted a piece of her and her history should go down to Lelant Saltings as soon as possible. Many members of the community have fragments of her in their homes today, hanging above doors and on mantelpieces, reminding the people of Newlyn of the message the *Rosebud* fishing boat carried up to London: 'Fight the Good Fight'.

19

DROPPED THINGS

By Friday morning on the *Filadelfia*, my ties to home have begun to unloosen, and I let the boat be the only place left in the world. From here on in, I learn not to count the days, not to think of my bed or my parents or my unbounded cross-coastal walks, or the reassuring sound of the surf coming into contact with the land. Instead, I start to think of our fishing boat as the centre of the universe, all life reduced to the single disc of sea surrounding us, like she is the attraction trapped in a snow globe. I imagine each boat in this way, solitary baubles floating over the seas, thirty miles out from the land.

I wake early and tear myself straight away out of my sleeping bag. My dreams have been coloured with yesterday's grey and I am keen to greet this new morning with as much energy as I can muster, casting from my mind the anxious thoughts I wake with: *I cannot believe we still have three more days of fishing left... I wonder if mum knew I would be gone this long... How long would it take me to find out if something had happened back on the land?*

It is still dark enough to make out the stars through the bathroom porthole. Each time I find myself out at sea overnight, my eyes are always drawn to a small, faint constellation low in the sky. The dim points of its stars draw out the two loops of an eight, but the lines do not quite cross over to finish the number and the upper loop is slightly distended. Perhaps it is because of light pollution, but I don't think I've ever seen this lasso-shaped cluster of stars from the land. I begin to associate it with the sea: a guiding constellation for fishermen. Back home, I scour endless star charts of the Northern hemisphere on the internet to find my fisherman's constellation, but none of them seem quite to resemble it. Perhaps it was the Pleiades or Seven Sisters to the south, or was it Cassiopia or Cepheus or even Ursa Minor to the north? I am almost glad not to find it. That way it remains a secret of the sea, one that is inaccessible to those on land.

I head out onto the wheelhouse balcony. Where we were alone at sea for the first few days, there has joined us now the dotted lights of Cornish trawlers at every compass point along the horizon line, adding grammar to its otherwise uninterrupted perimeter. Every skipper I have ever spoken to, including both Don and David, is perennially convinced that all the other boats nearby are stalking them. They tell me that since they themselves are one of the best skippers in Cornwall and know where the big shoals of money-making fish are (which, in truth, no one can absolutely know), the other boats follow them. Whenever they set off, the area will inevitably be congested with local fishing vessels a few days later.

The wind is not as harsh as it usually is this morning. There is a touch of warmth, an almost balminess to its breath. I look up. The figure of eight and all other traces of stars have already fled in preparation for the unfurling of the day. A pink haze, emanating from the east, spreads out in both directions until it has stained the canopy of the sky. Then, the lowest streaks of cloud begin to glow from below. The clouds grow hotter until they appear gilded all over like burnished metal. At last, from under the sea, there comes a sliver of blazing light. And then the round ball of the sun appears in a way I have never seen before. It is not yellow or gold, but arrives in a bright, lime-green instant.

A few days earlier, the crew had told me about the elusive green flash. They occur when sunlight separates out into different colours as it meets the atmosphere, working like a natural prism. As the sun slips into or out of the sea, the spectrum of colours that make up its light disappear or appear one at a time; at sunrise, green is the first colour to materialise, at sunset, the last.

On a perfectly clear afternoon, the ideal conditions for a green flash, Kyle stood with the crew of the *Joy of Ladram* waiting in anticipation for the sun to turn green as it hit the horizon. But it never happened, the sun disappearing behind the world without so much as a glimmer of colour. After that, Kyle lost faith in the validity of the story, relegating the green flash to mythical status. Don says he has seen it just once in over thirty years of fishing.

In that second, however, alone outside the wheelhouse, I witness the green flash. I raise my camera up to capture it and in the second between my seeing the flash and placing the viewfinder up to my eye, the sun is its ordinary white-yellow. I continue to stare right at the sun until it gets too bright and I must look away, the dark spot it leaves on my retina sliding across my sightline like a fly.

While en route to the Brazilian port of Santos in 1943, anthropologist Claude Lévi-Strauss reflected on the difficulties of producing the rising and setting of the sun, as seen from a ship, into adequate expression. 'If I could find a language in which to perpetuate those appearances, at once so unstable and so resistant to description, if it were granted to me to be able to communicate to others the phrases and sequences of a unique event which would never recur in the same terms, then – so it seemed to me – I should in one go have discovered the deepest secrets of my profession,' he wrote.

There are rarely words good enough to describe the very best things, as there are few appropriate for the very worst. It is not impossible to describe a green flash at sunrise, as it is not impossible to articulate a tragedy at sea. But our words miss something. Language can only ever be a metonym for the universe, evading our absolute description of it, as the sea evades absolute containment by man.

The new sun sends a beam of light across the water towards our boat, a bright line connecting it to us. An hour later and the sky is a clean November blue: a paradise of light unobstructed by a single cloud. During the first gut, this brilliant light seems to surge through all of us, an electric static that makes the work faster and more thrilling.

As they empty out the insides of fish with sharp, fluid strokes, the men get to talking about what they'll make for breakfast today. For Kyle this is usually some form of Pot Noodle, of which he has a stash of next to his sleeping bag. For Andrew it is a sausage sandwich or fresh fish. This morning, Stevie says he fancies cheese on toast.

Pleased to find an opportunity to be useful on the boat, I race through my monkfish-packing and head up to the galley to make Stevie his cheese on toast before he finishes checking the engine. I put two pieces of buttered toast on the hot plate and cover them with slices of weak-looking processed cheese. After five minutes, it looks nothing like the advertisement image of a glorious melting toastie with bubbles of oozing cheese I had envisaged. The bottom of the bread is black and charred, while the anaemic rectangle of cheese is still cold. While dithering over how I might save the situation, the engine-room door bangs open and Stevie emerges, rubbing his oily hands down his tracksuit bottoms. I present the cold cheese on burnt bread to him with a deflated 'Tadah!'

'You haven't made cheese on toast before, have you?' Stevie says with a grin, accepting the plate and concealing my failure under an equalising sea of HP Sauce.

I join Kyle in the wheelhouse for our usual morning yarn. The windows and doors of the wheelhouse stand open, disturbing the usual layer of fog so it swirls and dances about the room. As soon as he hears me climb up the stairs Kyle, holding a thick length of nylon rope out to me, announces: 'Right, its knot lessons day.'

We begin with the bowline knot – used for mooring since it never binds or slips. I watch Kyle bend the rope into a loop, take one strand and pass it through, then thread it through another loop created by the twist of the first and pull the knot to. The movements seem logical. I could do that, I think. But when he passes the rope back to me, I gaze blankly at the long piece of rope, with no sense at all of how to transform its long extent into a single knot. He takes the rope back and patiently shows me again. As he twists and contorts the rope, he tells me how long it took him to learn to tie knots back when he was a decky learner. He'd spend hours in the wheelhouse practising, his fingers growing raw and shiny from the friction of the rope's rough edges. After about four attempts with Kyle's careful supervision, I make a messy version of the original knot he showed me.

'Great. Untie it and start again,' Kyle instructs me. The rope holds none of its former shape and once more I stare at it dumbly, urging my muscles to remember the motions they had just made. Slowly, I start to get the feel for how the rope should bend and twist in my hands during each complication of its parts. I tie it and undo it, tie it and undo it, recreating the shape of it until my hands act without my brain.

Next, Kyle shows me the double sheet bend. Two separate pieces of rope are knotted together in such a way that they should never come undone, if tied correctly. I watch Kyle lace two ropes together, drawing them together into a tight embrace. I try to copy the movement, but somehow miss the loop so that when I endeavour to pull the knot through, one piece of rope falls slack to the floor. After multiple attempts, I hold in my hands a single, intertwined length of rope; I try to unravel it, but the knot holds fast.

In maps of the stars, the sharp points of the Pisces constellation, visible from the northern hemisphere and seen most clearly in autumn, trace out two fish swimming in opposite directions tied together by a single star where their tails meet, creating a V shape in the sky. This star was first given the Arabic name Al Risha, meaning the knot or cord. In Greek mythology, the Pisces constellation is aligned with the story of Aphrodite and Eros, who transformed themselves into sleek-scaled fish in order to escape the serpentine monster Typhon and attached their tails together in a knot so they would not become separated from one another. Observed with the naked eye, Al Risha appears as a single star, one of the dimmest in its constellation, but it has recently been discovered that Al Risha is in fact a double star. While from earth these stars merge into a single point, in truth they are as far away from one another as our sun is from Pluto.

Looking up at the dark blue silence of the night sky from another boat, in another world, our solar system, too, would fold in to become nothing more than a blot of light, each planet barely distinguishable from the rest. I imagine these two fish swimming in alternate directions when I think of Newlyn: the fishermen who face the sea each week and those back on land, who try to hold on tightly to their men, even as they disappear, amphibian-like, behind the horizon. They are two ways of facing the sea, two stars orbiting the same centre of gravity that is the projected centre of the town, two knots tying together two fish.

We move on to the cod-end knot, which I see the men undo on nets at the start of every haul to release the fish bulging within them, before refastening to send back down to the seabed. Kyle tells me that there's always huge pressure resting on getting this knot right; if you mess it up and the cod-end comes loose while you're towing the nets, you could lose a whole haul worth of fish, which could be worth in excess of several thousand pounds. 'When you get good enough, I could let you tie it!' Kyle grins, just as I find once more that the flimsy knot I have just tied falls apart in my fingers as soon as I tug it. I refuse flat out, imagining Don making me walk the plank if we lost that much money in a single haul.

Finally, Kyle teaches me to eye-splice rope. You fray out the three twisted threads intertwined together in a piece of rope and turn them back in on themselves to plait into the main body of the rope, making a hoop shape at the rope's end. Kyle unravels the end of the rope part the way down and tapes the ends up. Then he weaves the middle strand back into the rope, before repeating the action with the strand to its left, and then to its right, until all of the strands are plaited back into the body of the rope. I find splicing easier than the other types of knots; it reminds me of all the plaits that friends and I used to do on each other as children.

Kyle agrees, saying that he is great at plaiting hair now: you just have to pretend it's rope. I start to get the knack of it, feeling how knots are not single, finished objects, but processes. Like any art, their craft takes time to learn and disappears if you do not practise it often.

The sunshine comes streaming in through the windows. Splicing puts you into that particular state of detached concentration that becomes the perfect condition for conversation. Walter Benjamin attributes the lack of repetitive, monotonous work in the modern age to the decline in oral storytelling. 'It is lost because there is no more weaving and spinning to go on while they are being listened to,' he writes. When such rhythms of work used to be carried out, the weaver 'listens to the tales in such a way that the gift of retelling them comes to him all by itself'. Together with the degeneration of craftsmanship, Benjamin predicted storytelling would also unravel.

And yet, here we are: Kyle and I taking turns to tell each other stories about our lives as we rhythmically plait one strand after another back into the cord of rope from which the strands first came. We start to speak of our origins, discussing what it is we think we are. In many ways, Kyle's 'whats' are more fixed and definable than mine: he is a fisherman; he is Newlyn; but he is also about to become a father, which will bring with it countless new strands of identity that will complicate his simple relationship with the sea. My own terms sound more nebulous when voiced, the outline that rounds me less solid: I am London, which is vast and forever shifting, but some of me is here too. I am a writer; I don't plan to settle, or even meet the person I might settle with, until I am at least thirty. No, none of it is graspable like being a fisherman in Newlyn, I think.

'It doesn't feel enough to say I'm a posh girl living in London and spending a lot of time on my own writing. That description doesn't sound like a whole person to me,' I say to Kyle, looking down at my piece of rope to hide the embarrassment of articulating these fears.

'Hang on,' Kyle says, 'you know you're posh?'

I snort.

'Oh! I thought I was going to have to tell you!' He grins. 'You're the first actual posh person I've met.'

'How am I doing, then, for a posh person?' I ask him.

'Yeah, you're all right. Very slow at splicing.'

The sky is prismatic now, a full palette of pastels carved into it. I head back up to the wheelhouse, where Don is listening to Ed Sheeran. He watches me grinning into the sunshine and remarks, sagely: 'I wouldn't enjoy it too much. We'll pay for this.' He regards the sky sceptically. 'A day of good weather like this always tells you there'll be storms coming soon.'

From the wheelhouse, I see Andrew leaning against the bulwarks on deck. He is topless, showing off his bronzed chest and dark blue tattoos, and holds a knife between his teeth as he works lines of rope through a ripped piece net to mend it. The sun is hot, reflected off the sea and onto the deck, but I am still not certain it's take-your-top-off weather. There is a self-awareness about Andrew: a practised, film-star coolness that the other men lack. Over the week he narrates countless stories of girlfriends and wild parties in Newlyn, his life on land apparently a perpetual, almost teenage, haze of pleasure. A past girlfriend once told him that 'dating a fisherman is like dating a new man each week. You're always a bit different,' Andrew remembers fondly. 'They find it sexy too,' he says. 'When you're making them breakfast and you tell them "I caught this fish, and now I'm cooking it for you".' I think back to the cooked fish breakfast Andrew made for me several days ago and smile.

And yet, I get the sense that fishing matters to Andrew beyond all else. Unlike some fishermen, who express anguish at the separation they must endure each week, it is part of the appeal for Andrew. He could easily have taken a break while the *Twilight* was being fixed up, but he tells me he soon gets bored on land and so jumped at the opportunity when Don offered him a berth.

In *Moby Dick*, Herman Melville devotes a chapter to a mariner on the *Pequod* called Bulkington. Though only just returned from a four-year treacherous voyage, he immediately leaps at the opportunity of returning to sea once more to join Captain Ahab in his quest to hunt down the white whale. 'The land seemed scorching to his feet,' Ishmael explains. Like the 'storm-tossed ship', the comfort of the port is more grief for men like Bulkington. 'But as in landlessness alone resides the highest truth, shoreless, indefinite as God –, so better is it to perish in that howling infinite, than be ingloriously dashed upon the lee, even if that were safety!' The leeward side, the part of the ship that is sheltered and turned from the wind, provides him no solace, when on the other side lies the wide, open territory of the ocean.

His head in profile, Andrew squints into the far reaches of the sea. Its gentle undulations draw stripes across his face so that he looks like some great watery cat. Lopez writes of a particular day he spent on one of his Arctic trips, just sitting 'high on a sea cliff in sunny, blustery weather in late June', watching seals and birds crossing the landscape. He describes how the rush of joy and exhilaration he experiences at the sight of creatures in their natural habitat is summed up in a single Eskimo word: '*quizannickumut*, to feel deeply happy'. Andrew is more at ease out at sea, more deeply content in his own relationship with the water than any other fisherman I have met.

I follow him out onto the deck, proudly informing him that I can splice now if he needs any help. 'Sure,' he grins, and gives me a few ends of rope to splice, which he can then work into the net. 'It's just knitting, really,' Andrew tells me. When he was a decky learner, the older fishermen all made thick-knit jumpers to pass the time while they were on watch. We stand together for a good few hours, warmed by the sun, listening to Don's music blasting from the wheelhouse above, until the rough rope has turned my hands bright red.

Still thinking about Don's Cassandra-like weather forecast, I ask Andrew if there are many fishing superstitions left. 'I'm looking at one,' he replies with a wicked grin – the 'aren't women bad luck on boats?' refrain dogs my time in Newlyn. 'Oh, and this one,' he says bringing his hands up to his head and waggling them while sticking his front teeth in front of his lips. I am momentarily

211

dumbfounded by this, before realising he's imitating a rabbit, a word you cannot say on board a boat unless you want to be met with terrible fate. If it so happens that you really do need to mention rabbits during a voyage, the men call them 'underground greyhounds'. There are countless other creative substitutes for taboo words. It is bad luck to run into a pastor before going to sea; Nance writes in his *Glossary* that the fishermen call men of the church 'fore-and-afters' or 'white-chokers'.

Light dapples the waves as we look out at the blued world below and beyond the *Filadelfia*, the endless depth of which is suggested by the intensity of its colour. My mind breaks the surface and dives down to observe the fish spiralling and ricocheting around the sea like a chaos of unconnected atoms. 'Yeah, it's the same thing all day, every day,' Andrew says into the wind, 'but there hasn't been a single week I've been out here where something extraordinary, something you've never seen before, has not happened.'

He starts to catalogue the unbelievable things the nets have pulled up during his time as a fisherman – the trinkets the sea has chosen for itself, which the contraptions of man have brought up again, sometimes many years later. Fishermen often discover, amongst the congeries of fish brought up during hauls, whales' skulls and cavernous rib cages, curved like a vaulted ceiling, their thick bones bleached white by salt. Kyle keeps these to give to his uncle, who now has a whole whale burial ground in his garden. On the last day of our trip, Kyle gives me a dark lump of honey-coloured amber, larger than my balled fist, containing a petrified insect, which came up in a haul. One day we pick up a grizzled and barnacled anchor so large that it unsteadies the boat's ballasts. Since there is not enough space on board, Don drops it to rest once more amongst the other lost things, warning other fishing boats nearby of its whereabouts on the VHF.

The sea marks used to indicate the location of underwater hazards are called cardinal marks. Each cardinal mark around a hazard, such as a shipwreck, indicates a distinct compass direction, which allows the fishermen to navigate away from the looming danger. In the day you can tell which direction the hazard is from the cardinal mark by the four distinctive warning stripes, like a wasp, which show whether it is to the east, west, north or south of the hazard. At night, cardinal marks north of the hazard show a continuous flashing, to the south six quick flashes and one long flash, east three flashes and west nine flashes. These human marks are strung up across the breadth of the ocean, letting vessels know how to move safely through the borderless waters.

Another time, Kyle got a message on the VHF warning nearby fishermen of a large tree floating across the sea. He thought it must be someone taking the piss until he saw it, an oak tree silently drifting past the *Filadelfia* while he was on watch. And each man on the *Filadelfia* tells me of humpback whales that dwarf their boat, of schools of a hundred or so dolphins right beside them, and of turtles and pancake-shaped sunfish waving their fins out of the water.

On the *Crystal Sea*, we once lugged up a mess of thick, coiling wires covered in seaweed and barnacles, which I initially imagined were the tentacles of some ancient octopus. The crew informed me that they were in fact old, obsolete communication cables: long stretches of twisted copper wires that extend between continents across the ocean floor. The first transatlantic telegraph cables were laid in the mid-nineteenth century. I hear a story of one Cornish fisherman who pulled a stretch of cables up in those early days of transatlantic communication and was convinced he had discovered a type of seaweed that contained copper. He travelled most of the way along the line of cable up towards Ireland, pulling up the copper seaweed as he went, certain he would be rich for his discovery. Instead, the ships that laid the cables along the ocean bed had to begin their work all over again.

With the coming of telegraphy, Porthcurno, near Land's End, suddenly became a thriving cosmopolitan area. Skilled men and women from cities around the UK were sent down there to work at the telegraph station, where many of the world's submarine cables came ashore. The Cornish were somewhat suspicious of these telegraph stations that cropped up around the coast, attracting hordes of foreigners. In 1904, *Cornish Evening Tidings* reported a belief circulating amongst those living on the Lizard that the reason they had been suffering such awful weather recently was because of Marconi's telegraph station in Mullion, declaring the high level of electricity coursing through their villages was 'plainly an uncanny presence and capable of the worst, in the eyes of all good fishermen, who do not believe in upsetting the laws of nature'.

As the heavy copper transatlantic cables began to be replaced with fibre-optic cables, the Porthcurno telegraph station became less necessary. In 1970 the station was finally closed, the staff moved on and Porthcurno once more became an unassuming, seaside village. All these years later, trawlers are still ripping cables up from the sea floor – past technologies a museum left below the sea.

You hear stories, too, of trawlers bringing up enormous bags of cocaine and marijuana thrown overboard by smugglers when navy ships approach to search their boats. Now and then mannequins with half-eaten arms and seaweed tangled through their nylon hair are found caught in the nets, brought on board and dressed up to make the other crew mates jump out their skins. In Marianne Moore's poem 'A Graveyard', the speaker observes how, from its surface, the advancing motion of the sea 'under the pulsation of light-houses and noise of bell-buoys' looks as if 'it were not that ocean in which dropped things are bound to sink/ In which if they twist or turn, it is neither with volition or consciousness'. If a body brought up from the water breathes or gasps, it is neither with volition nor consciousness either, but that does not stop man from believing there is some mystery, some regenerative power of the seas that might bring lost things back to life for us.

Andrew tells me of the time when they could make out between the flapping bodies of fish in the cod-end a thing so white it was almost blue, parts of it flaking off to reveal pale bones. Without warning this form took a huge, noisy breath, scattering fish left and right to reveal, caught there within the net, the body of a grown man. Andrew explains that sometimes when a body is brought up from the seabed, the gases in it expand and cause a sudden expulsion, as if the person is taking one last heaving breath – 'Scared the living daylights out of us'. No one knew what to do with this ghost from the depths, his bare ribcage stuffed full of small fish like an aquarium. They wondered who he might be, whether his family were out there somewhere, waiting for their husband or father to come home, and so kept the body in the fish room, handing him over to the authorities once back on land to see if they could identify the lost man.

The thing we see this week that Andrew has never seen before appears on that Friday evening. Midway through pulling up the gear, Andrew shouts to the wheelhouse for us to go and look over the portside of the boat. Down in the water, right up by the nets, there is a lone leopard seal pup. It's pale grey with dark spots, smaller than any of the fat seals I have seen lolling around Newlyn harbour, whom the fishermen curse and swear at because they dare to nick fish from their nets. ('If they took the whole fish, I wouldn't mind so much,' one fisherman tells me, 'but they take little bites of every single fish, so when it comes up in the cod-end the haul is ruined – thousands of pounds lost, just from that one bleeding seal.') Any fish-hunting competitor, be they French, Cornish, Spanish – or seal, is begrudged equally.

'I've never seen a seal cub this far out to sea before,' Andrew yells up to me. I try to capture a photograph of the pup, but the image blurs in the dark so that it just looks like a patch of shadow across the frame. Still, it is not the seal's appearance that has struck the men as extraordinary; it is the fact that a young seal has come this far out on its own, that space has somehow shrunk and brought this young creature right out to our boat in the middle of the sea. 'We're not your mum, lad,' one of the crew cries down at him.

While on a boat in the Arctic, Lopez makes eye contact with a seal on an ice floe. In that silent moment of recognition, he realises that 'to contemplate what people are doing out here and ignore the universe of the seal, to consider human quest and plight and not know the land, I thought, to not listen to it, seemed fatal'. As we witness our baby seal's encounter with this strange, manmade hulk of metal roaring through and disturbing its natural environment, none of us can help but listen to its universe. The very tangibility of fishing makes it impossible to ignore the non-human lives intermeshed with our own. When fishermen suddenly find swarms of cuttlefish and yellow fin tuna– which are usually found in warmer waters – off the UK coast, they cannot but notice the changing of the climate. When in a single year – 1980 – the population of mackerel dropped to almost nothing, they cannot but recognise what sustained overfishing might do the oceans, what we will do to the liveability of the planet if we continue to pretend we cannot hear it.

There is a clear sense of guilt when fishermen tell me of the overfishing in the 1970s and '80s; how the drive for wealth fuelled by competition and rapidly advancing technology on boats damaged the populations of certain species, especially mackerel. But attitudes have changed. Fishermen realise that the supply of the sea is not illimitable. They talk about sustainability with utter seriousness now; it is a continual process of learning about the invisible world below you so that you can continue to support it while it supports you. We cannot hide from our impact on the sea, and we must endeavour to work harder at improving our relationship with it. As has been seen in the improvements in fish stocks in the last few years, oceans can be replenished.

Besides the wondrous, strange things the nets bring up, in every haul we find a large amount of plastic. There are tiny plastic beads drifting through the waters from our face washes, plastic bottles and plastic six-pack rings that sea creatures become trapped in, and plastic islands in the middle of the sea, such as the Great Pacific Garbage Patch, where floating waste is brought together by ocean currents. There is not a place left untouched by what we have done to the planet.

Coastal communities are often both the most vulnerable to and conscious of these changes we cannot feel in the metropolis. When sea water rises, it is their homes that are flooded; when the seas are contaminated, it is their jobs that are lost first. In Newlyn, they see the exotic warm-water fish that now turn up in Mount's Bay, they see the plastic washing up on the shore, intermingling with the line of shells. Perhaps this is why Penzance Council has taken one of the most active responses to the problem of plastic that is at last making it into the news headlines, becoming the first community in the UK to be awarded 'Plastic Free' status after large numbers of the community have taken part in whole-beach cleans and shops have reduced single-use plastics. The Ellen MacArthur Foundation predicts that by 2050, the sea will contain, by weight, more plastic than fish. David of the *Crystal Sea* keeps the plastic and throws it away later back on land – 'It's a small thing, but at least you're helping somehow,' he tells me.

After a dinner of sauce-drenched meatballs, I go outside to watch the last of the day. Colours fan out from the sun in concentric circles. The furthest regions of the sky are a milky lilac, while closer to the sun the colour shifts into a warm orange, the halo around the ball of the sun itself a dark crimson. It is exactly the same hue as a megrim sole's heart I say out loud to myself – and realise, as I do, how days spent contemplating one thing can alter your psyche, changing the way the outside world filters through your consciousness.

The gulls weave through the sky unhurriedly, reflecting the sea's calm. Their bodies transform from white to black as they pass in front of the sun and are reformed as shadows. A cargo ship cast in absolute darkness slips gently across the dusky horizon until it is right in front of the declining sun, creating a small ship-shaped eclipse in front of it.

All grows quiet and slow. Gentle colours sweep across the old empty world, readying it for black night and the renewal it will bring. The sun sinks down and is gone without a final encore. It is a firework display in reverse, every colour and flash and swirl flying back inwards to a single point before disappearing below the horizon. I stay watching the sky until there is one last streak of colour left across it: a pink haze, just as the day began.

20

SOME OLD RESIDENTS

I often spend my mornings in Newlyn leafing through old photographs and copies of Cornish newspapers in the newly renovated Newlyn Archive, once the old post office, at the harbour's edge. The archive is loyally maintained by a team of volunteers who add to its contents daily; while in there you can almost feel the past encroaching on the present, each moment bagged and filed for posterity. In a ring binder of newspaper snippings, I come across a letter from 1926 which is signed by 'Some old residents of Newlyn'. The letter proudly declares: 'For twenty years, rain or shine, wagonettes have run between Newlyn and Penzance and the public has been glad to use them,' before going on to decry the advent of motor buses, which were rapidly taking away business from the wagonette men. The letter flares out into a broader lament: 'There is a sentence which one hears very often in these times; it is used to shelve many inconvenient and distressing subjects: "we cannot stop progress". But we ask: is it progress to throw a number of hard-working respectable men out of employment and so make them and their families a charge on the community, when it can easily be prevented by protecting one mile of road?'

There is sense of hopelessness to the letter; its plaintive question seems to include within it the recognition that progress will continue and, whether they like it or not, the Newlyn these residents grew up in will slip away, sand-like, into the gaps between the cobbles.

The wagonettes may have gone from the town, but there always remain 'some old residents of Newlyn', those who look on mournfully as the places and people they remember from their youths disappear one by one. The passage of time blows these figures through the town each day, like lone leaves picked up and scattered by the wind. In the mornings, groups of elderly men and women sit on benches above the harbour, wrapped up in coats and scarves, as they discuss the things the sea has brought to them over the years. At the close of each day they are wafted home once more, as the first lamp lights in the town flicker on, to make tea on ancient stoves and tell stories of the past.

There is a sense amongst these older members of the community that the town was once joined by a single time, from which no one could fall behind or get lost outside of its passage. In his miscellany of Cornish folklore, *Rustic Jottings*, Edwin Chirgwin, born in Newlyn in 1892, writes of his childhood when the same routines governed all households. 'At 9'o'clock every night all the village clocks were wound and soon the dim candlelight in the bedrooms faded and silence settled down upon the entire village.' Throughout his adult life, first as a teacher in West Penwith, then with the Duke of Cornwall's Light Infantry during the Great War, before returning to Cornwall to become a headmaster at St Cleer, Chirgwin studied the Cornish language, learning much about the old ways from his great-grandmother. Of his early life he remembers, 'everything seemed to be beautifully planned and there was a timing set for everything'. Mondays were wash days, Tuesdays the dried clothes were ironed. Particular months had their order too: 'In September, all the jam for the winter had to be made, butter salted away in galley pots and the pilchards laid down in salt in "bussas".' This framework has all but gone now and time hangs loosely off the town.

Pat lives in a white house with blue window frames on the lip of land above the harbour, next to the Fisherman's Arms. When I call her to arrange a time to visit, she does not say hello at first, but forcefully shouts her number down the phone at me. 'Is that Pat?' I reply uncertainly.

She lets me know it is and that she was in fact waiting for a call from the London girl who is friends with Denise, adding: 'I hear you want to learn about the history of the town from the Duchess.'

'The Duchess?'

'The Duchess of Newlyn,' Pat tells me proudly, explaining that she is known as the Duchess about town because she knows everyone and everything there is to know about Newlyn. As such, her schedule is very full, but she agrees to meet me the following morning. 'At coffee time,' she says. 'Well, okay, goodbye—'

'Wait!' I cry. 'When's coffee time?'

'Ten-thirty, of course!' The receiver snaps back down.

The inside of Pat's house follows the same white and pastel-blue colour scheme of the front. On most surfaces sit china teapots – 'I collect them, aren't they lovely?' – and every table shines, every carpet kept immaculately. Pat looks perfect, too, positioned on a plump blue armchair in the centre of her living room, facing large bay windows from which she can see the whole of Newlyn harbour. Her lips are painted a bright shade of fuchsia that matches her long fuchsia nails. She wears a hot-pink woolly cardigan with gold buttons and a light pink neck scarf with threads of gold woven through it that is tied fashionably at the side. She also wears a thick, slightly orange layer of foundation that fills up her wrinkles like tributaries. Pat pours me out a milky coffee and reveals a selection of tarts and chocolate-honeycomb biscuits from under a napkin with a flourish. Then she spreads her arms out like jazz hands: 'Shall we begin?'

In another part of town, on another morning, just as I am leaving Denise and Lofty's, I nearly walk straight into a whiteish car pulling out from a parking space. The elderly man inside waves frantically at me and I begin a rushed string of mouthed apologies, all the while trying to sidestep his vehicle. It is not until the man winds the window down that I realise he is not gesticulating angrily at all but beckoning me over.

'All right, you're Lamorna?' He says in a thick Newlyn accent as I approach the car. 'Get in.'

When this kind of thing happens in Newlyn, as it often does, you don't question it. I get in the battered white car, noticing how layers of dust and moss climb up the inside of the windows like forests.

'Lofty says you want to find out about the past.'

It clicks into place. This must be Freddie Matthews, the neighbour Lofty has been telling me about, who has lived in the same house here in the Fradgan since he was born.

'It begins at the Ice Works!' he announces, dramatically.

We reverse about four metres down the road and come to a halt with the sound of a loud crunch. Freddie and I turn in our seats to watch a wheelie bin teeter and then fall in slow motion behind his car.

'I forgot that was there,' Freddie mutters to himself. He gets out, moves the bin a fraction of an inch, gets back in, reverses a tiny bit more, just grazing the bin this time, turns off the engine and gets out without a word. I stare out of the window at Freddie, who is already unlocking the door to his cottage. He turns to me and mouths: 'Come on, then!'

Once out of the car, I look down to the road at where our journey started – about seven metres up the road outside Denise and Lofty's house – then follow Freddie into his childhood home.

Freddie's cottage has not been maintained quite as immaculately as Pat's. It has that slightly frowzy mustiness, common to the homes of many older people, which is not unpleasant but suggests that the scents have, over the years, settled deeply into the furniture. Everything in the kitchen is a scale of beige, the same colour that creeps into the hedgerows along the cliffs above Newlyn come autumn. On the table are stacks of old *Cornishman*s and a mug of half-drunk tea with a fly sitting on its rim.

Now settled at the table, Freddie tries once more. 'It begins at the Ice Works!' he declares, slamming his hand down on the table and causing the fly to jump into the air.

Both of these long-standing Newlyn residents, Freddie and Pat, launch themselves into their tales with a similar degree of urgency, as if aware that they are the last keepers of the keys to the town's past. Neither has ever thought of moving anywhere else, neither are married or have children. For the two of them, Newlyn is the only world there is and their sense of its past can no longer be extricated from their own memories.

Pat and her family moved to Newlyn when she was just a girl, taking up residency in the rooms above the Fisherman's Arms where her father (Pat pronounces father with a long open 'a', as in 'faaahther') was due to be the new landlord. He was the first person to bring dartboards to pubs in Cornwall, she tells me proudly, replacing the skittles mat that had taken up half of the bar. Fishermen had never seen darts before and chucked them 'like spears', which was terrifying if you were standing anywhere near the board, Pat remembers, or in fact really quite far away from the board too.

Pat grew up knowing all the fishermen of the town through the pub. 'They were good,' she tells me. 'And I know they all get drunk and that. But they deserve it. It's a very hazardous way of life. And I tell you what,' she says, 'they may be rough, but they're gentle in their manner to women. Want a tart?' She breaks from her chain of thought abruptly, 'or a chocolate thing?'

Before moving to Cornwall, Pat attended a private school in Kent and when she arrived in Newlyn found herself miles ahead of the other children at the board school up the top of Old Paul Hill. They didn't take to her for a while either – 'being an *emmet* and all'. Though I find it hard to believe the self-titled Duchess of Newlyn was ever regarded as an *emmet*. She won the scholarship to the county school, but her father had to ask her to leave after only a year because they could no longer afford the bus fare or the books. At fourteen Pat set off around the villages on her bike to find a job. The first place she went to was Newlyn's Gaiety cinema – now the Meadery restaurant, where vast plates of chicken and tumblers of Cornish mead are served by 'authentically dressed' barmaids in a space that sits somewhere between a school dining room and an impressive medieval banquet hall. Back in the 1920s, the Gaiety's black and white features amassed large crowds of children and adults alike. Every day but Sunday there were queues reaching right across Newlyn Bridge, waiting for this new-fangled form of entertainment that came from the other side of the Atlantic Ocean.

The biggest change to Pat's young life was the coming of the war. I always imagined that Newlyn did not really feel the wars, but Pat describes the chaos of people and activity it brought with it. There was constant booming from Penlee Quarry, just up from where Pat lived, as stones were loaded on ships and taken off to Deptford and other parts of London to rebuild areas bombed in the Blitz. Pat remembers barrage balloons floating over the harbour – though a few stray bombs did land in Newlyn regardless. In the war's latter stages hordes of GIs turned up in their shiny jeeps and took over the quarry, turning it into a weather station to find the best winds for the D-day landings. The wars brought Newlyn into contact with the rest of the world, with droves of strangers from across Europe arriving at Penzance station or mooring in the harbour. 'Oh, it was seething with people down here!' Pat tells me. As well as taking in many British evacuees and French refugees, multiple Belgian trawlers moored up in Newlyn harbour, bringing whole families to stay with them.

Freddie Matthews was just a boy during the Second World War. 'We never had nothing like, know what I mean?' he tells me. (*Like, know what I mean?* is added at the end of almost everything Freddie says.) Still, the war was not a bad time to be a child in Newlyn: they spent their days playing hopscotch and marbles in the street, having fights with the Penzance boys and messing about with the evacuee children on the boats down Keel Alley, which was once part of the harbour and has since been filled in. Two evacuee children from London were moved into the cottage opposite Freddie: Lenny and Peggy Marsh. Freddie tells me that he and Lenny have stayed in touch ever since. Five years ago Lenny finally came back to Newlyn on holiday and they got a photo together outside the home he lived in when he was an evacuee.

During the war, the Fisherman's Arms was only open three days a week. It was on one of these days, just after blackout was called, that the most personal tragedy of the war befell Pat. Every night at ten, 'the military men' would come over and get all the men out the pub. But on this particular evening there was one local man left sitting at the bar. He seemed not to hear the door slam as the other men left or notice the blackout shutters drop down, his back to the door as he slowly sipped his pint. Pat watched her father, six feet tall and always quick to sense trouble, take his glasses off, put them on the counter and walk over to the man.

'Look, I shall lose my licence if you don't drink up this pint,' Pat remembers her father saying. 'Then the chap stood up, swaying, took a swipe at my father and, the way he landed, it snapped his spinal cord.' Her brow furrows, creating sediment lines of foundation across her forehead. 'He dropped dead right in front of us.' She rushes over these last words, ending her story abruptly, as if skipping forward a few pages. 'Oh, it was terrible. It was terrible. It was 18 July 1944. I shall never forget it.'

The man who hit her father was never charged because the attack wasn't deemed premeditated. Pat and her mother suddenly found themselves the sole owners of the Fisherman's Arms. The trouble was, Pat tells me, women weren't allowed to own liquor licences in those days. 'I was only seventeen,' she says. 'Very young, very young. I hadn't really seen any life at all. We were sat at the bar and mum says: "What are we going to do now, Patsy?"'

It turns out Pat's mother was too devastated to do anything much for a while. And so Pat went off alone to the licensing magistrates in court to explain what had happened and ask for a licence. After much deliberation the court agreed, making Pat's mother the first woman in the whole country with a liquor licence, Pat tells me. And that was that – two women in charge of a fisherman's pub at the end of the land in the midst of the war. As soon as word got out around the town that there were women running the Fisherman's Arms, business picked right up. Many wives were left running their homes alone while their husbands were off fighting in the war and each evening they would head up the hill to see Pat and her mother in the pub, where they knew they could have a drink and feel safe amongst female company. These women sat together in the warm, wooden interior of the Fisherman's Arms, smoking and playing darts together, whiling away the war. After closing time every night, Pat and her mother would allow themselves a healthy-sized gin and tonic each to make the cleaning up before bed go faster.

The phone rings and Pat comes out of the memory. She picks up the receiver and bellows her number at great speed down the phone. 'Wrong number!' she tells the phone. 'You want Ted in Chester. He's an old friend. Do you want the number? Good. Have you got a pen?' Pat confidently recalls Ted in Chester's number by heart to the person at the end of line. She hangs up and, seeing me look impressed, says: 'I've got a good head for numbers, I told you.'

The phone number for Sylvia Plath's grandmother's house on the coast was 'Ocean 1212–W', the title of an essay she wrote about her sea-centred childhood. She describes how she would often 'repeat it to the operator, an incantation, a fine rhyme, half-expecting the black earpiece to give me back, like a conch, the susurrus of the sea as there as well as my grandmother's "hello"'. I wonder if the particular static transmitted through a phone tells you something of its answerer's environment, whether, when I call home, the sea's voice ascends up into space and races back down to my parent's home in London, carrying with it something of its mastery.

Each person I speak to about Newlyn's past condenses it into its simplest, cheeriest moments. 'Everybody knew everybody and you never had to lock your doors,' they say of the 1940s and '50s. Even Lofty tells me the summers were longer and warmer in Newlyn when he was young. I sometimes get the uncanny sense that there is a film playing a little way behind my head where their focus lies – a black and white picture showing at the old Gaiety Cinema that every one of them has watched and rewatched a hundred times. I hear the same phrases over and again: *'They were good days'*, *'Oh it was wonderful'*, *'Everybody knew everybody'*, *'It was simpler then, it was happier...'*

Freddie started working at the Ice Works, an intimidating-looking building in front of Keel Alley, when he was twenty, the vacancy arising after an employee was found dead in the building's toilets one morning. Before 'R. R. Bath and Newlyn Ice Company' was established in 1903, the ice used by the local fishermen used to come all the way from Norway in boats, hacked from frozen lakes. Once up and running, the Ice Works could create 30 tonnes of ice a day and hold 900 tonnes of ice a year. Freddie draws out multiple diagrams for me as he speaks: how the water was pumped to the factory from a nearby reservoir; a steam-powered compressor would then puff and whirr as it converted the water into ice, which after setting in blocks was crushed and hauled off onto fishing boats waiting in the harbour. Freddie knew every fisherman through working there. It was a good place to work, he tells me: you were in the midst of it all in the Ice Works.

The works was eventually abandoned for a newer, more efficient factory built down by the harbour. The old works has stood empty for fifteen years, a haunting, salt-grey building casting a shadow over the Fradgan and Freddie's cottage with it. The wind through its walls is the only movement in the place, invisible hands raking through industrial equipment, long untouched. Ropes of moss run up its sides, blurring its architecture. Most of its windows are cracked and, inside, piles of rubbish grow towards the roof. 'When I was in there working you wouldn't even see a matchstick on the floor,' Freddie says. 'No one would smoke in there or nothing.' He looks out of his window. 'It's all bloody changed now,' he says. 'I don't know most of the people living here anymore.' He points out a number of houses where his friends once lived that are now owned by strangers who never stop to say hello.

In the 1970s and '80s shopkeepers in Newlyn such as David Barron, who for forty-five years worked in the newsagents J. Barron & Son, which had been started by his grandfather in 1920, noticed changes in the town. David said he could no longer trust the fishermen to pay him back for the cigarettes they took when they came back from sea, so he had to get rid of the borrowing book he had kept by the till for years and ask them to pay there and then. It was around this time, too, that his shop was burgled for the first time and he had to install a security system. The way of life in the town was changing – a new breed of young people appeared whose angry, impatient mode of existence David's generation could not comprehend. Everything got noisier. Enormous fishing boats came down from Grimsby and Scotland to catch mackerel, and Russian, Romanian and Bulgarian factory ships started hoovering up the seabed. Shops grew larger, stocking strange and exotic things from around the world at such low prices that Barrons could no longer compete.

'It was a marvellous shop,' he sighs. I hear of its treasures from other Newlyners – how they would persuade their parents to take them there to buy individually wrapped sweets from big glass jars and collectable cards and toys. (When I tell Isaac I am meeting David Barron, he replies to my text saying: 'I can almost smell the place now. I always used to drag mum in there with me to buy sweets. There was a delicious cocktail of smells: the smell of freshly pressed broadsheets and *Fishing News* mingled irresistibly with the smell of pick 'n' mix.') David tells me that his last week there was incredibly emotional. He had a goodbye party in the Yacht Inn and 240 of his former customers showed up. 'No. I didn't have *customers*,' he corrects himself. 'I had *friends*.'

Once the Co-op arrived in Newlyn, it mopped up most of the business enjoyed by the independent shops – all those butchers and bakers and greengrocers shutting their doors for the last time one by one, it was a tragedy, David tells me. The details he provides me with of his own life outside of the changes to shops are sparse, as if the two cannot be disentangled from one another: the shop's success, his happiness; its demise, his tragedy.

'Right,' Pat springs up like a teenager, clasping her hands together, 'shall we do the house tour now?'

Pat and her mother moved from the upstairs of the Fisherman's Arms to the next-door cottage in October 1964, asking all the local chaps from the pub to come over at five in the morning to help shift all their possessions with a few free morning beers as an incentive. 'It was a state when we first arrived, you should have seen it,' she says. 'It was all chocolate brown and dark green – like a rotting boat.' But, Pat being Pat, she rolled up her sleeves, said, 'Don't you worry, mother', and set about painting and wallpapering the entire cottage on her own. It took her five months because she'd constantly have to run back to help her mother in the pub. Her house-pride radiates out. In each room we go into, before I can say anything, she cries out: 'In'it nice? It's nice, isn't it?'

Pat takes me through a side door and sits down at a piano that takes up three-quarters of the space. 'This room makes me very happy,' she says. Covering every wall are photos upon photos of Pat posing in a variety of colourful, sparkly evening dresses, surrounded by a satin suit-wearing band on a gleaming stage. 'Of course, all my life I'd wanted and waited to go on cruises.' In 1977 Pat saw a cruise advertised a bit cheaper than usual and with the encouragement of her friends in the village packed all her things and went off to Lisbon. Since then she has gone on a cruise almost every year – 'twenty cruises all on my own'. She straightens her neck scarf and leaps to her feet in front of me. 'It was wonderful, wonderful on the cruises. Wonderful! The number of friends I've made, the places I've seen, the entertainment, the bands.' She points to a photograph of a smiling elderly man at a piano. 'And that was my pianist. We were together and I adored him. But we could never live together because he was a dreamer and I'm a doer.'

Less than a minute after I have left Freddie there is a knock at Denise and Lofty's door. Freddie is already saying – 'And another thing that I forgot!' while I am letting him in, arms clutching photographs, a diary belonging to his boss at the Ice Works, and some cuttings from the *Cornishman* – all relics he has been keeping over the years. Still in the doorway, he starts telling me more about the Ice Works, speaking with a sense of urgency now. 'So, the water for the ice comes from a reservoir up near Paul, course it's disused now'– and then his eyes light up – 'Do you want to see it?'

Back in Freddie's car before I have had the chance to say yes, we reverse, narrowly missing the bin once more, and start careening at great speed up Paul Hill. Freddie parks down a lane and leads me through a hole in the hedge that surrounds the reservoir.

There is no one else about to observe our pilgrimage. Freddie stands before the reservoir and enthusiastically re-enacts the various processes involved in checking on the water, while I, his single audience member, try to keep up. The building, made of old stone blocks and covered in weeds, resembles a dead thing whose internal organs are missing: wind whistles through its empty chambers making the same hollow sound as it does through the Ice Works. It is another leftover scar on the landscape. Once the performance is over, Freddie sighs, shrinking back into himself, and turns to look out towards Mount's Bay far below us. Then, without warning, he pelts back towards his car with me following at a run.

Nearing the Fradgan we almost bump into another old man crossing the road. Freddie waves, echoing the gesture he made to me several hours earlier, and, with no hesitation at all, the man gets in the back. 'All right,' he says, once to Freddie and once to me. I introduce myself and find out that this is Lesley, whom Freddie has picked up at 11.30 every Friday morning for the past fifteen years and driven to St Just to get hot pasties that come out of the oven at twelve at McFadden K & D Butchers. 'Best pasties in Cornwall,' they add.

Freddie turns to me: 'D'you want to come?'

I nod enthusiastically.

We travel cross-country, Freddie speeding along the sinuous roads up to north Cornwall. He tells me he makes at least three trips a day, driving to and fro around the town, ferrying fishermen friends to the sea, dropping off·baccy and supplies with them and picking up old friends to take them off to buy their groceries. I lean my head against the window, listening to the men chat weather, old times in Newlyn, and how Freddie used to be part of the now-disbanded Newlyn Pigeon Racing Club. One of his pigeons got all the way up to Leeds once, he remembers. Each time Freddie talks about a shop that was once in Newlyn, he shouts back to Les: 'Wasn't it, Les?' To which Les gives either a simple yep or nope.

''Member them five bakeries, Les?'

'Yep.'

''Member that daughter of the butcher on New Road, 'ey Les?'

'Oh, yep.'

''Member that boy Warren, Les?'

'Nope.'

A pause. 'He's dead now, anyway,' says Freddie.

Penwith, bookended closely as it is by the two coasts, has always felt mysterious to me: at a remove from the sea, which facilitates industrial development and along whose shorelines have sprouted numerous working villages, the dense green patches of wood remain protected, untouched. We see almost no one on the roads as we travel through, save for one farmer walking muddily through a field, who blinks up at us as we accelerate past.

I had assumed that once we'd got our pasties we would find somewhere in the prettily bunting-decorated St Just, but as soon as Les has picked them up it is straight back in the car once more. The delicious aroma of pasties mixes with the slight damp smell of the car's interior, as the men take up their remembering game once again. We arrive back outside Freddie's house, give the bin one last friendly bump, and then Lesley gets out, handing Freddie and me our pasties. 'All right, see you next week,' he says, vanishing as quickly as he arrived in front of Freddie's car barely half an hour ago.

'Don't you eat your pasties together—' I ask.

'Nice meeting you. If you've got any more questions about the Ice Works, you know where I am, like – know what I mean?' He goes back into his house, leaving me standing in the road with my pasty, feeling completely bewildered by my morning.

'I don't go to the doctors,' Pat tells me as I finish my coffee. 'They always find something wrong with you. The one time I did go to get my blood taken, the blood shot right out because I drink whiskey.' They told her she had high cholesterol, and she said: 'I knew this would happen! You were bound to find something wrong!' Are you really ninety-one? the doctor asked her. And after she had proudly told him that yes she was, he asked what she did to keep herself so young.

'"Sex and booze, doctor!" I told him,' Pat cackles. 'To which the doctor replied: "Well, keep at it!"'

She throws her head back and lets out a stream of laughter, even more wrinkles appearing in her bright foundation. 'I'm terrible sometimes, I really am!' she says.

Pat has been all the way around the world on her cruises, but she always comes back to Newlyn in the end, to the cottage where her mother died, next door to the pub she grew up in. I ask her if she's ever thought about moving, about living somewhere else for a while, maybe where her parents came from?

'You tell me,' she says. 'What more could you want than this place?' The Duchess of Newlyn looks out over the harbour. 'I see the sun come up over there and then the moon climbs out from the sea there each night. I see the men head out through there and then steam back in with their fish each evening. What more could I want?'

21

GRAVEYARD

As the days move winterwards, Denise's battle against the seagulls staining her washing transforms into a war against the weather. While the roast lunch to commemorate my last day living with them cooks inside, we cautiously pin her laundry up on the line, keeping one eye on the ominous sky. It becomes a game. For every pair of trousers or sheet hung, the clouds provide us with a spit more of rain, daring us to continue. We freeze, share a worried look and then, as soon as it stops, resume the pinning with greater urgency.

'Are you going to be all right all on your own?' Denise asks me as we each take one end of a bed sheet to pin. I will be moving out into my own rental cottage until Christmas: for a reason I still can't articulate, it feels important for me to be on my own for at least some of my time in Newlyn. I tell her I will be, but I'll miss staying with them. Lofty helps lift my heavy bags up the Fradgan and I hug them goodbye at the door.

I miss them almost as soon as I have shut the rental cottage door behind me, though they live barely minutes away. The sensation is similar to that of moving out of my parents' home for the first time – a sense of oneself coming of age in some way.

I take my shoes off and pad around my new home, opening cupboards and flicking through books. Everywhere there are small painted boats and stock photographs of the sea; in the fridge I find a pack of splits – closer to white bread rolls than scones – and travel-sized jars of jam and clotted cream. The cottage is a one-up, one-down affair, its wooden floors white-washed, light blue shutters across its two windows looking out on a narrow street with even smaller, more chaotic alleyways of cottages branching off it.

I barely sleep the first night in Orchard Cottage. It is, I think, a hangover from childhood: a mixture of trepidation and excitement in a place not yet known, even one as gentle and unassuming as the last cottage on the cobbled street with its turquoise door and matching bench that leads up from the harbour. The rows of slanted cottages that make up the Fradgan always put me in mind of ancient couples, hunched and leaning against one another for support. I imagine the yarns and long-held secrets kept within their rafters, which once housed so many of the town's fishing families. I check my phone to find a message from Denise saying, 'Good morning hope you slept well xx have a great day xx' – and almost burst into tears.

I often embark on solitary adventures after sleepless nights. The indoors feels oppressive and my mind, like a splinter of wood on a doorframe, catches on things and is unable to let them go. When I am outside, the world feels anew. My somnambulist state changes the way in which I see things; the notes in my diary and saved on my phone take on wild, unexpected turns. Returning to them weeks later, I cannot quite recognise the person who wrote them.

This morning, I decide to take the bus over to Marazion, from where one can board a motorboat to St Michael's Mount. I have taken long walks across the whole perimeter of Mount's Bay and looked back at Newlyn from every point along its crescent-moon curve, but I have never taken the punt or walked across the twice-daily sea-drenched causeway that leads onto to the Mount itself. When I tell friends who have lived in Newlyn their whole lives that I am finally going up the Mount, many of them admit they've never made the trip themselves. It reminds me of the relationships of Londoners with Big Ben or the London Eye. Their permanence on the skyline ensures that no local feels any pressing desire to visit them. It is only the tourists with their rapacious desire to *know* a place, to drink in every aspect of it in only a week or two, who tend to frequent these places.

And yet, for all those who live in Mount's Bay, the Mount, whether consciously or not, is a sea mark that binds together the disparate villages lined up along the coast. It provides them with a common name, regardless of the feuds and long-held bitternesses between ports. According to folklore, the Mount (its old Cornish name is Cara Clowse in Cowse – the Hoar Rock in the Wood) was built by a giant called Cormoran with the help of his wife Cormelian. Together they carried chunks of white granite from the cliffs along the Cornish coast across into the bay at low tide. While her husband was sleeping, Cormelian substituted granite with greenstone (another kind of igneous rock) in her apron because it was easier to transport. Waking to see his wife ferrying the wrong kind of stone to his new Mount, Cormoran boiled up into a great rage. He lunged at his wife, dragging her under the waves and causing the rocks to fall from her apron. Cormelian's body sank into the sea and was feasted on by fish, while the fallen rocks formed Chapel Rock, which rises from the sea midway between Marazion and the Mount.

The afternoon I arrive in Marazion it is cool and pale enough almost to be mistaken for a moonlit night. A few tourists and I wait at the water's edge for a boat to take us across the glassy water to the Mount. Over time, Cormoran's tale has grown foggy. Elements are displaced or condensed, re-emerging in stories written many years later. Leaving from his lonely, new mount, Cormoran was said to have spent his nights sneaking onto the mainland to rustle the Cornish folk's cattle. It is here that the tale merges with another – Jack the Giant Killer. In early chapbook versions of the story, the giant is at last slain by a farmer's boy from Penzance: 'I am the valiant Cornishman/ who slew the giant Cormoran.' Another story asserts that Cormoran is in fact a bastardisation of Corineus, the founder of Cornwall. According to Geoffery of Monmouth's *Historia Regum Britanniae*, Corineus destroyed a giant called Gogmagog. Finally, the legend has entered the realm of history. Folklorist Mary Williams wrote in the 1960s: 'When visiting the Mount some years ago, I was told that when excavations were being undertaken there, the skeleton of a man well over seven feet tall had been unearthed.' This giant man was allegedly found in a deep vault below the chapel, dug into the granite rock. The Chinese-whispers element intrinsic to folk tales allow figures to slip under the fabric of yarns, appearing entirely reformed: slayer becoming slayed; giant metamorphosed into man.

The day I choose to visit the Mount turns out to be the last day of the tourist season. Tomorrow, the castle and grounds will be shut off to the public for the winter and the St Aubyn family, who have owned the Mount since the seventeenth century (though they now share ownership with the National Trust) will return for Christmas. As such, there is a note of sadness amongst those working on the Mount, which diffuses through its many rooms and leaves each visitor with a somewhat sombre impression of the place. There seem to be many of us exploring the castle alone today, quietly following the designated tourist route. We take it in turns to linger at each impressive window that either looks back towards Newlyn, where the largest trawlers are just visible in the harbour, or out at the white sea and sky – a view that paradoxically feels unfinished without the Mount itself in it.

A mahogany grandfather clock in a small, wooden-floored study particularly attracts my attention. The clock's face has a swirled design painted onto it and its intricate hands are slender and bronze. Above the clock face is another measure of time: a tidal clock, whose fat-cheeked moon with drooping eyes displays the time of high and low tide in Mount's Bay. It was built in 1785 by Roger Wearne, a clockmaker who lived and worked in St Erth. The clock was not brought to the Mount for its ornamental value but as a necessary instrument for those living in a place whose route to the land is so often swallowed by sea. The measure of the tide is a much simpler form of time than hours and minutes: a high or low note, scrupulously observed by fishermen, who wait each morning for it to reach its greatest height before leaving the harbour, and once more for their return. It is a tangible sort of time too, changing the whole face of the coast, revealing at its lowest ebb hidden things like the top of the sunken Wherry Mine where Thomas Curtis made and lost his fortune in the eighteenth century. In London, I can go months without remembering that tidal time even exists – unless I take a slower route into town and walk along the Thames, which at low tide reveals a muddy flat land of dystopic, upended shopping trolleys.

I continue in a daze through various bedrooms, studies and kitchen until I get to the map room, where I pause for a long while. Each wall displays an exquisitely drawn map of Cornwall. The one that intrigues me most is an illustration of Michael Drayton's 1612 epic poem *Poly-Olbion*, which traces an imaginative journey through every county in England and Wales. In the map, a man with a shepherd's crook is seated atop the Mount. The sea around the county teems with vast sail boats and sea monsters ridden by half-naked gods. From each tributary that snakes from the land to the sea, a Melusine rises with her arms held aloft. Melusines are spirits that physically resemble mermaids but are found in freshwater rivers and spring from a distinct folkloric tradition around France and the Low Countries. In one of her origin stories, Melusine is recorded as the daughter of the fairy Pressyne and King Elinas of Albany. Her tale unravels in a series of failed marriages. Each time she promises to marry her suitor only on the condition that he will not look upon her in the bath. But, predictably, each new husband disobeys her request, peeping into her bathroom to find his wife transformed into half-woman, half-fish. Elsewhere, Melusine is recorded as the descendent of the whale that swallowed Jonah. Strangely, too, the Melusine also crops up in contemporary consumerism as the split-tailed image on the Starbucks logo. I follow the imagined space of the map. The fantastical image of Cornwall first envisaged in the *Poly-olbion* does not feel improbable to me. It echoes the way in which the sea that surrounds the land draws oral myths and adventures to it, while the wild landscape itself is infused with ancient folk tales.

After a morning spent wandering through the many rooms of the Mount's castle, I decide to wait for low tide to walk back along the causeway. I check how soon it will be on the tidal clock, imagining the fishermen at sea running their fingers down the tidal calendars, which they each keep in the wheelhouse, to learn when they will be able to come home again. I watch from the high gardens of the Mount as the sea slowly reveals the path, like a curtain pulling back.

As soon as it is exposed enough to cross, the causeway swarms with people. Around me families and couples incessantly snap photos, thrilled at the novelty of standing on something that only moments ago was submerged under the sea. I stand for a while in the middle of the seaweed-encrusted causeway while the crowds throng past me. Since I have no other plans and time seems to be dragging especially slowly, once across I pass the bus stop and head down onto the beach to make the long walk back to Newlyn.

Everything is muted this afternoon. Even the train to London slips past without breaking the air. The usual crash of waves softens to a gentle hush. It begins to rain lightly. The sea, drawn out to its lowest ebb, leaves a mirror glaze across the sand, reflecting the clouds so clearly that it feels as though I am walking among them. In an essay penned when she was just nineteen, Elizabeth Bishop wrote: 'In being alone, the mind finds its sea, the wide, quiet plane with different lights in the sky and different, more secret sounds.' It is not, I don't think, that this sea disappears while you are amongst others. Rather the colours and noises of the shore hold your attention, allowing you to forget for a while that this great, silent thing is behind.

Today I face the sea. Occasionally the sun cuts through and highlights the lines of activity upon the distant waves. These lines appear like the letters from an unknown alphabet or, as I discover later when re-examining my rough, looped sketches of these shapes upon the water, like Lissajous curves – the mathematical figures of eight Alfred Hitchcock uses for the opening sequence of *Vertigo*, spiralling out of a woman's dyed-red pupil – and

I remember the elderly woman with the recorder those months ago, conjuring words out of the sea with her solemn music.

As I walk down Long Rock beach, its large rusting pipes leaking out into the sea like gape-mouthed seaworms, I think of a newspaper report I read in the Newlyn Archive about a sperm whale that was found washed up upon this beach in February 1990. Grainy, indistinct pictures of the whale accompanied the article in the *Cornishman.* From these unhappy images, it is hard to believe that the whale had ever been alive – that this slab of rotting flesh, this dark, beached blot, had once moved with tremendous power and grace through the deepest parts of the sea. The whale, the report noted, was 47 feet long and weighed 30 tonnes. Fascinated tourists came from miles around on a similarly wet, colourless day to take pictures of this thing that should never have been wrenched from the water. We are drawn to the images that horrify us, as if they were magnetic.

Sperm whales can live up to seventy years. These days more of them are dying earlier from manmade activity than ever before. Several were found dead recently on the Californian coast; their stomachs were opened up to reveal over a hundred kilos of net fragments, lines and plastic bags twisted around their insides. It is not known how the Long Rock beach whale died, but the article notes that experts assumed it had happened years ago, its long-deceased body washed up by gales. Torn from the depths and beached upon the sand, this is what death looks like in its plainest form, shown in the bodies of magisterial creatures from the seas, beings which ought not to be seen in death, and which even to see in life seems an otherworldly event as if we have slipped into myth. I learn later that the undignified term 'beached' is also used for retired fishermen. I picture them laid out upon the sand beside the whale, their hair dripping wet, their eyes wide, their hands still working through imagined lines of nets, as people gawp and take photos of them.

The article goes on to pose a question faced by the council. What is one meant to do with something so vast and lifeless? In a place that must remain beautiful and untouched to ensure the tourists keep coming, the council could not let a huge creature from the sea just fester there to be pecked at by seagulls until its cathedral-arched ribcage shone white on the sand. Worse still, as the gases in dead whales' bodies build up, they have on occasion, been known to explode. Dead and stranded whales have turned up before at Long Rock: in 1911 eight or so whales washed up on the shore, many of whom were still alive. Onlookers tried in vain to stop them from dying, pouring water over their backs and attempting to pull them back out to sea. A group of young men though, the *Cornish Telegraph* noted, were caught hacking at the tails of the trapped whales and carving initials into their thick skins, as if they were the latest beach attraction and not sentient, intelligent beings.

This time around the council's first idea was to bury the dead sperm whale right there on the beach, twenty feet under the sand. I imagine the hundreds of bare feet crossing the sand each day, not knowing what lies underneath but for the occasional smell of rot mixing in with the sea salt. In the end, the sand burial fell through. Instead, a lorry came to transport the whale to a land-fill site, to dump it amongst other detritus and unwanted things. When the council workers arrived, they realised that the whale was too large to fit in their vehicle. In a final act of undignified violence, the men had no choice but to chainsaw the whale's body in half.

During my first stay in Newlyn I watched the controlled explosion of the *Excellence*, an old trawler that had been slowly sinking under the scummy harbour waters, damp stains blossoming around her body. Often if a boat is no longer seaworthy, owners will just abandon her in a harbour or sell her on to another owner for a penny so that they do not have to bother with the effort and expense of having her broken up and extracted from her watery grave. Unlike the other great beasts of the sea, these boats cannot quietly sink down to the seabed to decompose gracefully. Man cannot just vanish away the things he has brought into the world. A crowd gathered along Newlyn's harbour walls to watch the vessel's execution. I looked down at her, noticing the way the parts of her now submerged had grown flabby and amorphous through contact with the waters. The explosion came with a crack of thunder, splitting her into hundreds of splintered pieces. The audience let out a collective gasp as she broke. We did not stay to watch the crane lift her into the truck that would take her to the dump, crushing her until every vestige and sign left by her past crew would be lost forever.

'It is human nature to stand in the middle of a thing,' begins 'A Graveyard' by Marianne Moore. 'But you cannot stand in the middle of this:/ The sea has nothing to give but a well excavated grave.' The speaker's vantage point must be the very edge of the land, looking out at the black hole of the sea like a mourner before the cut-out oblong of a grave. The day the whale washed up on the beach that grave was violated: 'You cannot stand in the middle of this' – and yet, that is exactly where fishermen go each day. It shifts the way I think about the water when I am next at sea, picturing our boat suspended above a grave within a place of mourning. 'That ocean in which dropped things are bound to sink–/ In which if they turn and twist, it is neither with volition nor consciousness,' the poem goes. Though sunk, the sea did dig this one dropped thing back up.

I continue my walk back home towards Newlyn, imagining the body of a great whale buried deep below my feet, landlocked for the rest of time. The palette today is so unlike that of my very first visit to Newlyn in spring – a washed-out watercolour, where before it was painted in thick oils. There is barely anyone else out walking: the day is too without substance to attract the casual walker; only a few dogs' noses investigate the shoreline, their owners pressed close to the side of the beach nearest the road. And in the distance I can just see a group of rain-coated figures, their backs curved as they gaze down at the sea-slicked sand so that from afar they look like small, grey crowbars sticking out of the beach.

I reach Penzance promenade. With the tide this far out, the backbone of the old harbour wall that once ran along from Penzance to Newlyn, that for generations protected homes from being swept away by sea storms, is just visible. I pass the bronze fisherman's statue, staring out across the bay. There he stands before the graveyard of the sea, waiting for his fishermen to come home, and silently remembering those who never will.

22

STORMS DO COME

If you trace the curve of the bay past St Michael's Mount, past the almost-grave of the Long Rock sperm whale, forever newspaper-print coloured in my mind, past the fisherman's statue, past Newlyn town, the rows of houses start to thin out, the hedges thicken and eventually you will come to the old Penlee lifeboat station. The negative space of the station marks Mount's Bay as powerfully as the Mount itself, a lacuna in the coastline. It comes up in almost every conversation I have while I am in Newlyn, a fissure in the town's communal history. I think of the life class teacher who told us bodies emerge on paper not by our sketching out limbs and skin, but by attending to the parts of the frame empty of the human form. So too can a place's present shape be better understood by discovering what has been lost from it.

I pass the old lifeboat house most mornings on my sunrise runs along the coastal path towards Mousehole, which are timed so that I arrive back in Newlyn just as the harbour is lit by the new sun and the last of the day-boats slip out through the gaps on their way to fish beside Wolf Rock. The station itself lies just below Penlee Point, where the coastline pushes out into the sea. As you approach it by foot it resembles a break in the landscape – a false end to the bay, which can only be reconciled as part of its wider curve if you are on a boat looking back at the land. From the sea, all of the coast's difficulties, its blemishes and pockmarks, smooth right out into one undifferentiated line of land.

The current Penlee lifeboat station, found above the small boats' pontoon at the back of the harbour car park, holds a central position in the town. Its many crew members pass back and forth through its doors each day, drinking coffee and eating cake together, yarning about the sea and discussing any recent distress signals they have answered. Apart from Patch, the lifeboat's coxswain, its crew are all volunteers – members of the community who join out of a shared understanding that the environment just beyond their homes can be treacherous and that those who face it day after day need protecting from the storms it brings. The number of people who join the lifeboat crew speaks again to the ardent belief felt throughout the town that you ought to do things for the place you live in, a fellowship that is dying out elsewhere. Those who become crew are akin to family. Cod tells me that, after his illness, while he was not well enough yet to go to sea, the lifeboat is where he would come to feel part of things.

I arrive late back at Penzance train station following a day spent in Falmouth to catch a meeting being held at the Penlee lifeboat house. The wind scrapes the air clean. Figures along the platform blow on their cold pale hands; illuminated only by the tall lamps casting stripes of light down the platform, they appear disembodied, each pair of hands rubbed together in a circular motion. The wind has picked up and, as I rush along the darkening prom, sea spray comes flying up over the low wall. Reaching the lifeboat house, I try to open the door into the poky building – set to be torn down and rebuilt with two floors and a visitor's centre in the new year – but it does not give. I push harder and hear a yelp come from the other side.

'Hang on!' comes a chorus of voices. There is some shuffling and grumbling and then the door opens just wide enough for me to squeeze through. The room steams with people. Every person I have ever met or seen in passing around Newlyn seems to be lined up along the edges of the room like a tin of sardines. I settle on the floor cross-legged to listen to the impassioned voices discuss the evening's agenda, while outside exhausted fishermen drag boxes of crab up from the pontoons in the settling dusk. Strewn across the table at the centre of the room are countless drawings and photographs of a traditional counter-stern fishing boat – a kind of lugger whose aft overhangs above the waterline – as well as an elegant glass bottle containing a perfect replica of her. The name painted on the side in curly letters is *Ocean Pride* PZ134. Tonight's meeting has been set up to initiate the lengthy process of locating and bringing her back to Newlyn, where she had spent most of the last hundred years working with Newlyn crews, until all trace of her was lost at the start of the last century.

The *Ocean Pride* was built in 1919 at Peakes shipyard in Tolcarne, an almost identical vessel to the *Rosebud*. There is a photograph of her mid-completion, the lines of her wood-carved ribcage fluent and feminine, each suture polished down until it would be hard to believe she was ever comprised of distinct parts. Every time a new boat was built at Peakes the villagers would drag her down the slip – a task sometimes requiring over a hundred people – coaxing her into the harbour waters like some part of a baptism ritual.

There is nothing half-hearted about community projects in Newlyn. If there is a case one person believes in, it rapidly becomes a town-wide concern – especially if it has anything to do with the sea or fishing. Most of the people at the meeting have some connection to the *Ocean Pride*. Each articulates how their parents, grandparents, friends, husbands fished on her or repaired her when she needed care. She was 'a lovely boat', 'a happy little thing', they say, one after another.

Every fishing vessel in Newlyn holds within it a remarkable chain of lives – intricate family trees contained within their sea-marked hulls. When I return late and see the lights of the boats in the harbour, I hear their hulls rocking mysteriously, their sails murmuring and parts clinking. I imagine these ancestors of the town telling one another stories about the places they have been, the things they have seen, like narwhals narrating their sea journeys to one another through the clashing of their horns.

It was the Brownfield brothers of Mousehole who originally commissioned the *Ocean Pride*. Nim, one of the original shipwrights who worked on her, tended to her lovingly throughout her time in Newlyn. As such he knows her every part, intimately. Her bends and keel were elm; her deck yellow pine; other parts besides were pitch pine, the type of wood for which shipwrights created the saying: 'If it lasts twelve months, it'll last a lifetime'; the rest of her locally grown oak coming from perhaps as nearby as the woods at the edge of Newlyn. These old luggers, built from natural materials sourced from the surrounding area, were as Cornish as the men who fished on them.

For the first years of her life she worked with a crew of six out of Mousehole as a long-liner and pilchard-driver – luggers designed to catch pilchards by drawing a net all the way around the shoal, similar to how Danny on the *Golden Harvest* fishes for them now. In 1937 she changed hands and was bought by George Pezzack of Mill Lane, Mousehole, and Mary Ann Tripp of Gulval. In 1948 she returned to the Brownfield family once more, bought by Joseph Brownfield, her skipper, and a Mrs Jean Herds.

Someone interrupts the line of ancestors to recount an extraordinary story about Joseph Brownfield. After he sold the *Ocean Pride* he went to work at Shippam's, the sardine canning factory in Newlyn, and ended up on one of their posters displayed at Paddington station. A young woman saw the poster of Joseph looking out of the wheelhouse window, smoking his pipe, and told her companion: 'I am going to marry that man one day'. That same summer the young woman came down on the train from London to holiday in Penzance and was surprised to run into the very man from the poster. She quickly became Joseph's 'Sweetie Pie' and they married the next year, living in Newlyn together for the rest of their lives.

In 1953 Edward Charles Downing, grandfather of Patch Harvey, the coxswain of the lifeboat, became skipper of the *Ocean Pride*, followed in 1971 by Thomas Bodilly Simons, at which point her ownership was transferred to Ian Prestage Childs from Newlyn. In 1991 she was decommissioned, along with many other fishing boats in Newlyn, as a result of new stringent laws about the number of boats that were allowed to work out of the port. Like old employees trying in vain to keep up with the newest technology in their office and at last replaced by younger, more efficient workers, these old boats slunk back to the edges of the harbour.

Once her fishing career was over, the *Ocean Pride* stayed in Penzance for a few years, operating as a pleasure boat and making leisurely trips around Mount's Bay. Finally, she was bought by someone outside the county, who sailed her out of Mount's Bay one day, then out of Cornwall altogether.

Patch sent out the first feelers in 2016 to recover his granddad's old boat, discovering her at a boatyard in Rye in East Sussex. It turned out her last owner had run out of money to restore her and moved to the Canary Islands, abandoning her there in the harbour. Patch points out the low-resolution images of the *Ocean Pride* in her current state. The photo displays a husk, a bedraggled, broken thing with decaying exposed wood, wholly unrecognisable from the photos of the glossy fishing boat sailing back into Newlyn harbour in the sixties. When he first saw those pictures of her in the muddy waters at Rye, Nim the shipwright says it just about broke his heart – 'How anyone could leave a boat in that condition. I have no idea.'

To transport her back to Newlyn harbour will be an expensive undertaking, but there is no question amongst those assembled as to whether it is worth the money or not. In the eyes of the town, to let the *Ocean Pride* fester in a Sussex harbour would be equivalent to leaving an elderly member of the community stranded far from her home on her deathbed.

In Elizabeth Bishop's poem 'The Bight' – the name for a geographical curve in the land like that of Mount's Bay – she describes the old, forsaken boats left along the shoreline: 'like torn-open unanswered letters./ The bight is littered with old correspondences'. The *Ocean Pride* lies prostrate in Rye harbour, the ink from the stories written into her body running and leaking away into the water with no one to reply to them. The simile works in both directions: each letter to friends and family back home is a boat setting out – to respond is to keep those relationships afloat, as the regions between us grow wider.

On a final weekend return to Newlyn before Christmas, I hear that the *Ocean Pride* had just returned home to Newlyn harbour and is now resting on the beachfront at Sandy Cove. It will be Nim who teaches the young shipwright coming to work on the *Ocean Pride* the art of repairing the lugger. The letter of his life as a shipwright will not be left unanswered but transmitted on to younger generations through the *Ocean Pride* herself. When I ask Nim if he has a similar personal connection to many of the other boats he worked on in Newlyn harbour. 'It's not the boats,' he corrects me. 'It's the people – the owners, the skippers, the deck hands, the other shipwrights – every person connected through those boats.'

Where the present-day Penlee lifeboat station buzzes with life in the town, the windows of the old one at Penlee Point are cracked, its once white walls discoloured and dappled by time and tide; weeds climb up its exterior. If it were not for the memorial garden and plaque set up beside the coastal path, you would be forgiven for assuming it was just another inexplicably abandoned building, like so many others stood above the sea in this part of Cornwall. But this station once housed the *Solomon Browne* lifeboat and the plaque commemorates the sixteen lives lost on 19 December 1981, a Saturday, when its crew responded to the mayday call of the cargo ship, MV *Union Star*.

The radio communication between the Falmouth coastguard and the Penlee lifeboat that night has been preserved and drills straight back through to that violent December night.

> Falmouth coastguard, Falmouth coastguard. This is Penlee lifeboat calling Falmouth coastguard.
> Penlee lifeboat, Falmouth coastguard. Go.
> We've got four men off. Hang on, we've got four off at the moment – male and female. There's two left on board.
> *There comes a cracking noise and then static.*

Penlee lifeboat, Falmouth coastguard. I understand you have four off and you say there's two left on board. Over.
Static.
Penlee lifeboat, Penlee lifeboat, Falmouth coastguard. Over.
The static comes again.
Penlee lifeboat. Penlee lifeboat, Penlee lifeboat, Falmouth coastguard. Over.

The same phrase is repeated again and again, the coastguard holding back from his voice any recognition of what the lack of response might mean. Only the progressively shorter pauses between his messages provide a hint of the rising dread that must have been felt amongst those listening back on the land. I imagine it must be similar to the feeling doctors experience when watching waves of a heart rate monitor thin out into a single line of bright silence.

When the crew of the *Union Star*, a new vessel on her maiden voyage from Denmark to Ireland with a cargo of fertiliser, found themselves in hurricane conditions, and being dragged by winds surging at up to 90 knots towards the rocks at Boscawen Point, its mayday call was picked up by the coastguard at Falmouth. On board were a crew of five, plus the captain's pregnant wife, Dawn, and two teenage stepdaughters, whom they had picked up en route.

Eight miles off Wolf Rock, the 50-foot waves reaching right over the top of the lighthouse, the *Union Star*'s engines failed. Though a salvage tug, the *Noord Holland*, known as 'the vulture of the sea', was called upon to tow her in, the *Union Star*'s captain, Henry Morgan, refused it, believing they might be able to restart the engines before matters worsened. But the waves grew higher and the coaster blew closer to the treacherous formation of rocks jutting out from the coast at Boscawen Point. When it became clear the *Union Star*'s power could not be revived, a Sea King helicopter was scrambled from RNAS Culdrose to rescue those on board.

Finally, after hearing the Sea King was unable to get close to the *Union Star*, the *Solomon Browne*, a 47-foot wooden lifeboat, coxswained by Trevelyan Richards and crewed by seven volunteers from Newlyn and Mousehole – their day jobs ranging from fishermen to telephone engineers to the landlord of the Ship Inn – was made ready. In fact, eight men responded to the call that night, but seventeen-year-old Neil Brockman was sent away because his father, assistant mechanic Nigel Brockman – the same person Nim had once tricked into believing he had to paint the Wolf Rock lighthouse – was already part of the crew and Richards did not want two men from the same family out in such dangerous and unrelenting conditions.

At 8.12 p.m. the lifeboat launched from Penlee Point to meet the coaster as it drifted amongst the rising waves out by Lamorna. It took Richards several attempts before he at last got the *Solomon Browne* alongside the *Union Star*, at which point they managed to start helping the crew to jump across from the wheelhouse, beginning with the captain's family. The very last message radioed back to land from the lifeboat was: 'We've got four off...'.

Those who were in Newlyn and Mousehole on 19 December 1981 remember what they did that day in minute detail, in that way you do when a date is wrenched out from the ordinary passage of time – each memory gone over until it becomes worn and threadbare, like a dog-eared book.

Retired fisherman and crab processor called Mike Dyer, great-nephew of Robert Hichens who survived the *Titanic*, remembers going over to Penzance to play snooker at teatime. As he drove home along the front he saw the waves flying up over the prom and when he walked in the front door he announced to his wife, Rose: 'You'll remember this night, all right, what with the wind blowing like it is.' Later that day, he got a call from a friend in Falmouth asking him if he could check whether his boat was withstanding the weather in the harbour. Once he had, Mike tells me, he got back into his car and, when he let the handbrake off the strength of the wind pulled his car along the quay on its own accord. 'It wasn't one of these light modern cars either,' he adds. 'It was a two-litre Triumph.'

'It was the saddest thing we ever knew in this village,' Pat, the former landlady of the Fishermen's Arms, tells me from her front room overlooking the harbour. 'It was terrible. Terrible and unnecessary,' she sighs, directing my gaze through the window to where the *Noord Holland* salvage tug had once been moored, which perhaps could have rescued the *Union Star* before the conditions had worsened if the captain had not refused it. 'A waste of lives.'

In his history of Mousehole, Mike Buttery suggests that he and his friend were the last people to see the stricken lifeboat in the water. That night, he says, 'We searched every rock from Lamorna to Mousehole' but found nothing. 'In our hearts we knew there would be no survivors.' The grief experienced throughout the villages around Mount's Bay was compounded by their imaginings of what had happened to the two crews in their last moments. It is thought that the *Solomon Browne* was dashed against the hull of the *Union Star*, before the two were smashed by the waves into the rocks at Boscawen. The next day Butts went to find the *Union Star's* final resting place, discovering her upside down straddling a gully. He notes that her lights were still on and 'the sound of metal grinding on rocks made some people's teeth go on edge'.

When the full extent of the tragedy became clear, Mike Dyer found he could not stay inside, doing nothing, and so he set off along the coastal path to Lamorna Cove. As he rounded the cliff path he saw the body of his friend from the lifeboat crew laid out on the rocks, beside the body of one of the daughters of the *Union Star's* captain. 'They were still together, like,' he says, along with various bits of wreckage from the *Solomon Browne* that the sea had brought up into the cove.

Two days later, the *Union Star* had broken into two pieces. 'By the end of December,' Buttery continues, 'she was in three pieces. Great lumps of her iron sides were missing and that made it easier for the waves to do the damage. By mid-January only bits of the *Union Star* could be seen at low water.' The sea dragged the tragedy out, taking its time to pull the last remnants down to its eventual graveyard.

While both villages tried to cope with what happened that night, swarms of journalists were making their way to the end of the line to broadcast the story to the world. They went from door to door, asking anyone and everyone to narrate the events that had taken place to them, how they felt and if they would give a statement for television. Even today, there is residual anger directed towards the press regarding the way they swept in that Christmas, allowing the town no time at all to grieve or process their trauma in peace. After the cameras left, a silence hung over the area. People gathered at friends' houses just to sit with each other. No one wanted to be alone, but no one could speak much either. 'It was as if the whole bay had the life knocked out of it,' David Barron remembers.

There are several fragments of poetry that Joan Didion returned to after the deaths of her husband and daughter. One of these was from Gerard Manley Hopkins's 'Heaven-Haven':

> And I have asked to be
> Where no storms come.
> Where the green swell is in the havens dumb,
> And out of the swing of the sea.

When I first read these lines they sounded like a resignation. Every fisherman I have met who has had a loved one die at sea, chooses to do the opposite: to be where the storms come, not just to live through grief, but to confront it head on, out there, in the water.

A few months later I take out a book of Hopkins's poetry at the British Library. In its printed version there is a subscript to 'Heaven-Haven' announcing its subject to be 'A nun takes the veil'. Hopkins's lines, it turns out, are not about grief but finding grace. Mount's Bay holds all of the things that have happened in Newlyn and the surrounding villages. It remembers and is marked by what the sea has taken from it and what it has brought to the shore. Storms still come to the villages along the bay. The lives they take are not hidden in silence; they are commemorated, celebrated.

The morning after the disaster Neil Brockman, the seventeen-year-old whose life was saved by the coxswain's decision not to let a father and son crew the boat that night, persuaded his mother to sign the papers that would allow him to join the new volunteer crew. With him that same day, a group of men, mostly fishermen, turned up at the lifeboat station to occupy the space left in the crew by those who had died. Brockman would go on to become coxswain of the lifeboat himself, while his son joined the lifeboat service in 2012. On 19 December each year, there is a service at Paul parish church for those lost in the Penlee disaster. Last year a new community hall was opened in Mousehole called the Solomon Browne: a name that once stood for the villagers' commitment to protect one another from the storms that come, now able to do so once again.

23

RAYMUNDO

By Saturday on the *Filadelfia*, I no longer crave the land with the hunger I had earlier in the week. Rather, my feelings have twisted back on themselves: I begin to fear the land, its discordant unruliness, the sheer number of feet that stampede across it each day. I fear the fast-approaching moment when I will have to acknowledge that not only am I not a woman of the sea, but that I am not a woman of Cornwall either. I want to stay right here, suspended above the oceans, gnawing on my time out here, my time away from the world, until there is nothing left of it.

This morning I wait for the carnival of day to arrive as it did yesterday, but the sky never opens into anything stronger than a milky pallor. The clouds, layered one in front of the other, draw the mirror image of a city skyline, whose buildings hang upside down like stalactites, but a thinly formed city, always on the verge of dissolving. The few sun rays not swallowed by the pale metropolis show in diluted strokes. The sea, too, is ashen-faced, its features made from the multiple dark whirlpools stretching out into the distance that seem to form wide eyes and mouths.

I head straight out to join the crew on the deck. Despite my oversized gloves, I gut megrims with increasing ease and even the lemons are unable to evade my grip. Noticing my progress, the men decide it is time for me to leave the small fry behind and try my hand at the next level of fish slaughter.

When Andrew first flings a tray-sized ray down before me, I can hardly bear to drive my yellow-taped knife into its thrashing body. These powerful cartilaginous fish with their knobbly spines appear more substantial, more alive somehow, than the small flatfish I was tasked with gutting previously. It instantly brings back vivid memories of a five-year-old version of myself leaning out to stroke stingrays at the London Aquarium. Following the men's advice, I flip the ray over on to its back. Its stomach is a cadaverous grey and its almond-shaped mouth gapes open and shut like the puckering of a teenage kiss. The lips are so human I am momentarily dumbstruck. Open and shut, open and shut, its mouth sounds out a wordless plea.

I shake myself from my trance and hear Stevie prompting me to make an upside-down V incision along the translucent flap of skin that conceals its vital organs. Underneath is a mess of multi-coloured pulsating guts – bright pinks, yellows and oranges. Over the roar of the engine, the men guide me to seize hold of a fistful of guts and pull them away from the ray's body. But as I do so, the ray's muscular wings start to close in upon my hand. In film footage of rays swimming, they use their wings, properly named pectoral fins, to propel themselves forward, gracefully rippling them through the water like thin material animated by wind.

The ray's last desperate bid to defend itself shocks me out of the automatic, mechanical state I usually induce in myself while gutting. In panic, I try to withdraw my arm, but its wings are still clutching me tightly. Beyond the boat, the waves have picked up and the boat slams down into the water. 'You have to stab it!' the men cry, goading me on as if we were outside the Swordy preparing for a brawl. I let out a cry and stab the ray in the heart, causing a thin trail of arrabbiata-sauce-coloured blood to seep from the wound. Its wings relax and its mouth ceases to contract. My knife hand continues shaking for the rest of the morning. While in reality ray gutting is no more brutal than any of the other work I have done, there is something deliberate and definitive about stabbing a fish in the heart.

Sebald speculates about what herring might feel during the almost eight-hour process of being gradually throttled by nylon nets cutting into their gills. By imagining that 'the peculiar physiology of the fish left them free of the fear and pains that rack the bodies and souls of higher animals in their death throes', we are able to partially console ourselves. And yet, what we do know for certain is the intricacy of their anatomy, which fishermen observe within the body of every fish they gut. If we are to recognise this complexity of their bodies, Sebald proposes, surely it is not a difficult to imagine the complexity of their minds and their propensity to feel pain. As long as I do not become desensitised to even the possibility of their pain, I make the promise to myself, I will not ever lose myself in this work.

Back in Newlyn on Halloween, Mike and Rose Dyer – who started up a crab-processing factory together and now spend most of their time playing boules for the Cornwall county team, and in the summer wake at two in the morning to take their boat down to Porthcurno to catch mackerel – had invited me over for dinner. After a decadent meal of scalding-hot tiger prawns in oil, garlic and chilli, crab salad, mussels cooked on a bed of salt, and crisped cod, all washed down with a homemade, and quite lethal, blackberry wine, Rose came to join me on the sofa, holding carefully in her hand the shell of the crab whose flesh we'd just eaten.

'Mike says you're trying to learn everything about fishing,' she said, looking down at the crab shell nestled in her palm. Since retiring, Rose told me, she had spent a lot of time considering the life she has had – one full of joy and children and grandchildren. 'Something had to give up its own life for us to have this one,' she told me seriously, gesturing around their lovely home. 'I don't think a lot of people in our industry talk about that – but I can't believe they're not feeling it somewhere in them.' She turned over the shell to reveal its pale yellow and pink interior walls. 'That's a living thing. I don't know what that means exactly, but it's important to keep remembering it.' She handed the crab shell over to me. I looked at the holes from which its void-black eyes would have peered. This was the first time I'd properly spoken to another woman about the fishing industry; there were no female 'fishermen' working in the town when I was there, though there had been one or two previously. Rose's philosophical outlook blindsided me, articulating the way in which, ultimately, fishing communities are dependent on that which they hunt – a life for a life, in its crudest terms.

The blood still runs from that first ray. I dig my fingers into its oozing mass of guts and saw at them with my knife until they come clean away in my hand. As instructed, I make two further slashes through its gill slits – the evenly spaced holes that just hours ago had allowed it to breathe freely as it glided through the water. It is only later, while watching the fishmongers at work in Stevenson's, that I learn that these disfiguring gashes have no other use than to allow fishmongers to get a firmer grip on their produce – an unnecessary, final defilement of their body. With the guts still in my hand, I falter. I lean forward as if to retch, my face growing as pale as the lifeless body before me, and then, as if to distract me, Kyle takes the intestines from my open palm and throws them against the table. He shouts 'Paintball!' as they explode bright egg-yolk yellow. And I am savage once more, cackling away with him and joining in to cause further intestinal fireworks along the silver table.

When I am back in the city I do not recognise myself as the person who drives knives through the hearts of rays. Describing the act of hunting in the Arctic, Lopez writes that 'to hunt means to have the land around you like clothing'. You are the most *in* the world that a person could be, forgetting your neighbouring companions and noticing only the thing you are hunting for. The world is stripped down to the present. 'It means,' he continues, 'to release yourself from rational images of what something "means" and to be concerned only that it "is".' If I had not allowed the sea to cover me like skin, to let myself be part of the *Filadelfia*'s world wholly and unreservedly, I would have found it much harder to make it through the trip. True hunting, Lopez suggests, exists outside linear time and space and is the closest we can come to dreaming while still awake.

As I gut, I slide between times: my own past, present, future, those of the men around me and of the fish themselves – all of us existing in this precarious world above the water, only a thin metal hull dividing us from the chasm underneath. Hands inside, amongst the bodies of fish, we are turned into haruspices, reading the future written in the straggly lines of entrails. There are hundreds, thousands of circling times chasing below us. Each species of fish is on the move – their shifting environment dictated by temperature like those Cornish surfers who emigrate each winter to chase the sun to Australia. Fishermen depend on the continuance of these intangible timelines. It is they who notice first when the world tilts slightly and a species that has never been seen before this far north is hauled up out of unseasonably warm British waters, learning the signs of climate change long before we do in cities, designed as they are to vanquish time. My physical connection to those fish, the literal opening of their bodies and directing my attention to the secrets inside of them, engenders a permanent change to the way I view fish when back on land. I notice the colour of their skin, the shape of their eyes, the way they have been filleted, and which parts of them are left behind. I imagine the men who gutted and buried them in ice, the ones who graded them, piled their bodies in boxes and sent them off upcountry.

The crew soon catch on to my complicated relationship with ray gutting – oscillating as it does between pure joy at the physical, sensuous nature of it, more palpable than with any other fish species, and a kind of prolonged horror at my own actions. It becomes a running joke: any time an especially large ray is caught in a haul, they cry up to the wheelhouse: 'This one's for Lamorna!' The feral version of me commits herself to ray gutting with verve, a maniacal expression of delight as her hands drip with guts and she slices between cuckoo rays with their round leopard spots on either side of their body, leopard rays and blonde rays – my body disappearing under the growing piles of them. Offhandedly, someone refers to me as 'Raymundo'. The name passes around the table and I adopt it for myself eagerly, delighted at last to have my very own fishing nickname. I hold it to my chest. Raymundo. I am Raymundo, the savage slasher. It feels like a badge of authenticity. I am like the Newlyn fishermen now – like Cod, like Lofty, Wordsy, Shitty, Crab Dad, Nocte, Joe Crowe, Ben Gunn.

I did not think the world had any colour left to lose, but by the afternoon shades have continued to leak from the sea and sky until they are both the same void white, the line of the horizon disappearing with it. The sky spills down into the water and I imagine the *Filadelfia* drawing up day stars in its hauls – or perhaps it is that the sea rises up into the air so that jellyfish, squid and rays dip in and out of the constellations.

I look out at my bleached cloud city, which has not budged all day, and then head over to the bench in the wheelhouse to continue reading *Arctic Dreams*. The most extraordinary mirages seen by man are those that appear at sea or in colder regions like the Arctic – Fata Morganas, so-called superior mirages. Inferior mirages occur mostly in deserts, when the distant object is inverted and doubled below its actual location, creating the illusion that there is a body of water on the ground, reflecting the object in it. Fata Morganas are much rarer projections appearing above the original object. They materialise when the temperature of the air closest to the ground is colder than that which is above it. The cold dense air causes light rays to bend upwards, tricking our minds into believing an object is higher in the sky than it truly is. The *Flying Dutchman* ghost ship is thought to have originally been a Fata Morgana – an image of a distant ship projected upwards into the sky, from which there grew a great body of maritime folklore.

True mirages are not works of the imagination, not fantastical new cities opening up above us, but merely a reflection of the known world – the ordinary raised up. These visions in the sky can sometimes be so vivid that whole land features – mountains, lakes, whole islands even – end up drawn into explorers' maps of the Arctic. Years later, when other explorers returned to follow the maps passed down to them, they found the scribbled-in landmarks had simply evaporated. 'President's Land', 'King Oscar Land', 'Petermann Land', and the Croker Mountains, were all later found to be nothing more than mirages.

On the *Filadelfia*, too, islands erupt without warning from the water. On occasion, these are faint mirages, but more often than not it is your mind playing tricks on you, expanding to fill the vast canvas it is presented with. Newlyn fisherman-turned-artist Ben Gunn told me that when fishing up near the Arctic, he found that if you stared at the ice fields long enough, they would transform into any kind of shape you wanted: 'Churches, houses, wherever your imagination takes you, you're in it. You flick your eyeballs and it's changed again.'

The places hidden from us are the points from which our imaginations flow. We do not get to see what is behind the horizon or below the surface of the water, and so impose on these unknown spaces, those unreachable things which we desire: some fishermen who have lost friends or family at sea remain convinced they are still out there. Kyle throws bottles containing his number into the water, hoping they may be discovered one day by a being who will speak across the world, across time even, back to him. Lopez writes that sometimes nature seems so illusory, so indescribable, that we cannot help but let it merge with our own fictions. When he follows a bear's tracks up to a hole in the ice, but finds no tracks coming out again, he says that one can start to understand the Eskimo's belief that 'there are bears walking around on the bottom of the ocean'. Our desires for storytelling and mythology bleed into the sea, giving it a distinctly human hue. Like my imagined abolishing of the horizon line and reconciling of sea and sky, fishermen must see themselves as becoming part of the world in which they spend half their lives, letting the water's skin be their skin.

Before dinner, Andrew takes me up to the gutting station and hands me an incredibly sharp knife – 'You're on a roll now, Raymundo. It's time you learn how to fillet.' He brings up a frosty monk, plaice, lemon and haddock from the fish room and slaps them down on our quasi-operating table. With filleting, he explains to me, you have to feel gently for the backbone of the fish as you cut through its flesh, letting your knowledge of its anatomy guide the knife through. It is a world away from the harsh, staccato stabbing of gutting. Instead you make one, unbroken movement along the centre of the fish: not a dot, but a line. Andrew starts me off on flatfish. The blade glides so easily through the plaice that if you jerk it up even a little bit, you lose half the flesh. He teaches me to caress the knife along the rough bumps of the bone, remaining attentive to the feel of it so as never to lose contact with the fish's spine.

Despite his coaching, the fillets I draw from the plaice are rough and jagged. 'Never mind,' Andrew says, throwing the limp forms over the deck to the seabirds. He chucks me a monk instead – 'much easier'. To fillet a monk, you make a nick in the skin at the end of the tail and then pull it away from the flesh, like taking a sock off a foot. After feeling for the monkfish's chunky bones, he instructs me to make a clean swipe through the meaty white flesh first on one side of the central bone, then on the other, to create two equally thick fillets. We work for a good hour, slicing through each fish and putting them into plastic bags for the crew to take home to their family and friends at the end of the trip. Just before we go back in for dinner, Andrew digs around in one of the boxes on deck and asks if I've ever eaten raw scallop. I shake my head and he breaks one open with his knife, spearing it and passing it over to me. Sweet and delicate in flavour, it tastes of the sea.

The late-night haul around eleven is always the wildest. Outside it is 'as dark as a dog's guts', as Don puts. The sea seems to absorb all else into it. If I fell in now, I think, I would not hit water but disappear without a sound into its depths. The bodies of fish, illuminated by the trawler's lights, gleam white. They stand in two large heaps, like treasure. Now and then, a roving fish eye is caught in the same lights and flashes demonically. Sea-dwelling hunters have an easier job seeking out their prey at night. Drifting along the seabed, they search the moonlit waters above them for dark patches, which indicates where its prey hides. Certain species have evolved to overcome this shortcoming. The bobtail squid, closely related to the cuttlefish, has a unique adaptation to avoid being seen at night. It participates in a symbiotic relationship with a variety of bacteria that is bio-luminescent – a living organism that emits light. These bacteria gather in the squid's light organ, where they are fed an amino acid and sugar solution. In return, the glowing bacteria allow the squid to mimic the moon and stars' milky glow so that its shadow body is hidden under cover of light – an optical illusion called counter-illumination.

Several gnarled spider crabs scuttle across the *Filadelfia*'s deck and I give them a wide berth. Sea urchins roll from left to right across the sodden wood, curled up into protective spheres dotted with spikes so sharp that they can pierce through gloves. And everywhere there are the dismembered legs of starfish that found themselves tangled in the net and ripped apart. Alongside them too are sea-beaten cans, pieces of plastic and hats. I am amazed by how many hats are pulled up by trawlers, mainly caps, but the odd beanie too – and once an old boot. The scene resembles the aftermath of a violent battle.

Beyond the detritus scattered across the deck are the cuttle-fish, writhing in their boxes and sending out sudden jets of black ink that add blood spatters to the scene of devastation. Andrew tells me that you get to know from holding them exactly when they're about to squirt from the particular way their body tenses. 'Like this,' he says, and demonstrates by pointing a cuttle at Kyle, drenching him a moment later in black ink. It streams down his face and he wipes it away with a glove, still grinning. On the gutting table tonight are also a couple of massive ling, once the most common fish caught by fishermen, but these days seen rarely and worth nothing. I decide they are my least favourite fish. Their long, thrashing bodies are reminiscent of eels and, when they die, their innards come up through their mouths so it looks as if they have vomited bright pink sausage meat.

Before I head down to bed, I look out of the wheelhouse window to check whether the cloud city is still hanging there. You can just make it out in the night, looming above us, the bright stars piercing it like the lights from flats. I think of Newlyn. I think of home. All of a sudden it doesn't feel so far away anymore.

24

VORTEX

Before the end of my last stay in Newlyn I wake to a text from Nathan. It says he'd come back to land unexpectedly during the night and would be free for an hour on his boat before they head off again, if I wanted a last chat before I go home to the city. I dress quickly and sprint down to the harbour to meet him on the *Resurgam* – 'I will rise again'.

After days dissolved in sea mists, Newlyn harbour is shot through with sunlight this morning. Only the thinnest belt of soft cloud hangs above the horizon line. The water gleams and the fishing boats' colours glare as if brand new – reds, blues and greens. They move differently in weather like this; each vessel seems to be propelled along with the sea, rather than fighting against it as they do in choppy seas. The suspicious looks I get from engineers and fishermen as I dash past no longer bothers me, as I leap over an upturned red crate on my way to the North Pier. There is no one on deck when I arrive at the *Resurgam*. I wait a while and then give an awkward yell, 'All right?' The heads of several sleepy-looking fishermen pop up from behind windows and out of wheelhouses on nearby boats, ducking back down again as soon as they realise the shout was not for them. A moment later, Nathan sticks his head out of the *Resurgam*'s galley, wearing a grey knit jumper and holding a mug of coffee. He waves, calling down to me – 'All right, jump on board and have a cuppa' – before disappearing again.

The boat is moored further away from the harbour wall than I am used to and I'm not sure I trust myself to make the jump.

I close my eyes, uttering a silent prayer as I fling myself towards the birdshit-varnished deck. Somehow, I make it onto the narrow bar of the rail that rounds the boat and grab a hanging rope to stop myself falling over the side and into the muddy waters, before finally jumping down onto the deck. In the homely galley I find a new crew sitting around the table, each with a huge mug of milky coffee before them. The stench of rolling tobacco transports me straight back to the *Filadelfia*.

I have never before gone for tea on a trawler in the harbour at eight in the morning and find myself privy to that period of quiescence just before the men leave the harbour, when they feel themselves no longer quite on land or yet at sea. Some of the men read, others scroll glumly through phones. Nathan passes me over a pint of coffee. Up close, I see he has that knackered look that all fishermen carry for the first few days back on the land.

'I didn't tell you last time, did I, that my old man was a fisherman?' he says, pouring milk into my mug. 'You probably don't remember anyway, you were pissed!'

Nathan's father moved down to Newlyn from Grimsby along with many other northern fishermen in the 1970s seeking better fishing grounds. But, unlike many of the other fisherman fathers who trained their boys up to join the family business as soon as they could walk, Nathan's father forbade him from even hanging around the harbour when he was young. 'He didn't want me following the same paths through life that he did,' Nathan says. 'He thought the fishing industry was too hard a way of life.' As a result of this ambivalent relationship with the sea, Nathan's father devised a plan to leave fishing and find a less precarious job, like trucking. And then, in early November 1997, a few weeks before he planned to hand in his notice, a message was received by the coastguard that the twin-beam trawler Nathan's father was working on, the *Margaretha Maria*, had sunk fifty-five miles off the Lizard. When the wreck was discovered near Lizard Point, underwater surveys reported that there were four tonnes of shells and sand caught in her nets, suggesting that she must have capsized after her derricks heaved up such a weight.

The whole crew went down with her. Nathan was eleven when it happened. His father was never found, but the remains of the skipper's body were picked up by chance three months later in the nets of another fishing boat.

Before the advent of technologies such as AIS, during stormy weather fishermen's wives would climb up to the top of a hill overlooking the town known as Mount Misery, the highest point in Newlyn. From there, they would watch for sails arriving over the horizon and pray one of them would be their husbands' boat. Somehow, I have never noticed Mount Misery before. When I look back towards Newlyn from the sea, my eyes are drawn first to the harbour and behind that the mouth of the town with its many rows of crowded teeth. Even further back Mount Misery looms behind, a dark green shadow haunting the town, the one place that has not been built upon. I imagine the Newlyn fishwives in their long skirts, necks craned and hands shielding eyes from the morning glare, holding each other together on that sloping hill.

Almost every person I meet in Newlyn has lost someone to the sea. Each fishing death reshapes the social fabric of the town, causing ruptures in the family lineages that most residents can trace back for generations. Told years later, the twists of fate leading to these tragic events grow yet more pronounced, their impact on the rest of the town fanning out like concentric rings from an object dropped in a lake. Reweaving sea tragedies into prophetic tales becomes a way of challenging their arbitrariness. If Nathan's father had quit fishing just a few weeks earlier, his death may have been avoided, and perhaps Nathan would never have become a fisherman. Ben Gunn tells me one such tale. One morning his late wife had woken up in a cold sweat. 'You must promise me not to go to sea today, Ben,' she begged him. Surprised by her vehemence, he agreed and they spent the day in the Star together. That night, the news came that the vessel Ben had been destined to sail on that morning had foundered without warning on its way out to sea and all those on board were lost.

When Mike Dyer was still a boy, his father left the fishing industry to start coasting, conveying oil or coal from port to port around Europe. At school one afternoon, his teacher passed around forms for students to fill out detailing which of their parents were coming to parents' evening the following week. Mike recollects clearly thinking to himself: 'Well, my da's not coming; I've only got my mum.' As soon as that thought crossed his mind, Mike wondered what had prompted it – his dad was meant to be back from sea by then, why was something telling him it would just be his mum? Barely an hour later, a hall monitor came into his classroom and told Mike to go to the headmaster's office. The headmaster did not even lift his gaze from his papers, Mike remembers. 'You better go home boy,' he said. 'Your father's died at sea.' Mike sped back home, pedalling his bike all the way up Paul Hill.

In *The Year of Magical Thinking,* Joan Didion describes a sensation she calls 'the vortex effect', whereby any chance mundane event might trigger particular memories of her lost loved ones. These vortices from the past overwhelm her, like a camera whose back falls off and the entire length of film spools out onto the floor at once. Didion tries to avoid all possible places that might stir up painful vortices but it is almost impossible: every place, person and object contains some trace of her family.

Without quite meaning for it to come out, I hear myself asking Nathan how someone would go to work in the same industry and same environment that was in some way responsible for their father's death. Surely the sea would be the most consuming memory vortex of all? 'I cannot imagine being able to face the water after that,' I say.

'Nah, I had to find out.' Nathan breaks off with a laugh and looks away. 'It sounds stupid now, but I had to find out what was out there beyond that horizon in case it was him – in case he was still out there somewhere.'

A pause. His words seem to shimmer and hang there in the galley, mixing with the plumes of smoke from the men's cigarettes. *'To find what was out there beyond that horizon.'*

'You know, hope and all that crap.' Nathan has a way of expressing the most poignant thoughts with a shrug, as if they were the most mundane sentiments, as if they meant nothing at all and, if you are not paying attention, you might miss the underlying truth in them.

The border of a black hole is called an event horizon. Events occurring beyond this boundary line can have no effect on an outside observer; nothing that occurs inside the black hole can impact the future events of the space outside it. It is a point of no return, the shell surrounding the region whose gravitational pull is so great that to escape from it is impossible. There is no coming back, no selkie's coat or avian transformation from mythology that might let it be undone. If there is an astronomical equivalent to the Christian heaven, it is surely this: the one realm we have not been to and the one we cannot return from. When I try to imagine what happens after we die, I see where the sky meets the sea, where they greet each other, these two great regions touching cheek to cheek. I think that is hopeful enough.

After his father's death, Nathan says, 'the only thing I could do was go out there and make a man of myself – see what it was like for my dad'.

By discovering those same things your loved one saw out there in the water, these men tell me, you are able in some way to stay with them, to know them beyond their death.

Nathan laughs again. 'Course, first week out there it was a force 10 and I soon realised all that was a load of bollocks.'

That first week at sea changed him, altering the composition of his body in some way he could not quite articulate. Still a teenager, he had never worked so hard in his life before, and, while still angry about his father's death, it became an energy that he found he could harness at sea. It was this same anger that spurred him on to get all his skipper's tickets at such a young age. 'I know he'd be proud, but he'd be pissed off because he didn't want me to do it. He wanted me to be a lawyer or a doctor, and I was like, "I haven't got the grades for that shit, dad!" – I did A levels and everything, but it just wasn't me.'

Mike, too, knows his father would never have wanted him to go fishing: 'He would've wanted me to be like my brother, go to university and all,' he tells me, 'but I'd sooner be mucking around with boats.'

The compass point to which young men in Newlyn are sent is always the sea. Over the years Nathan has become better at expressing his emotions, the way his own father was never able to do. 'I know so many fishermen who are pretending to be strong. I kind of get the idea that every fisherman is a screaming boy inside, wanting to talk to somebody, and the alcohol is just masking all these problems.'

The image of the hyper-masculine, unwaveringly solid fisherman has only been bolstered over the years by the various literature and reality TV shows that have appeared about trawlermen. Just like Weil's squirrel's cage that traps man within work, this rigid characterisation of fishermen can be a poisonous prison. Nathan's father dealt with such strain the way many fishermen do: by retreating to the pub once back on land. 'I don't blame him for it,' Nathan tells me. 'I don't resent him for it. He did what he had to. But I'm going to tell my son everything, every feeling.'

You become reflective while out on a fishing boat: finding yourself alone in the midst of an empty ocean in a great chasm of silence. When you look into the water, sometimes it is hard not to believe that it holds everything within it – the whole past and future of the universe. Just before I leave the *Resurgam*, I see *The Book of Dust*, Philip Pullman's prequel to *His Dark Materials*, poking out from under someone's thick, knitted jumper. I ask who the book belongs to, as I am reading it myself. Nathan says he's just bought it because he was a fan of the other ones – 'Slicing into all those other worlds with that knife and crazy animals with wheels for feet... What the fuck, you know!?' He and his crew read tonnes at sea. There's never the time on shore, but out there with all those vacant stretches of time on watch, they can get through many books in a week, he says. Another of the crew, whom Nathan calls 'a bit leftfield' and who has travelled around the world twice, is reading a holographic-covered book on trances and out-of-body experiences.

I clamber up the harbour wall while the crew are still con-
spiratorially discussing where they should fish for the next few
days and guessing what the rest of the Newlyn fleet will be up to.
I think about the absolute quiet Nathan will find on the *Resurgam*,
in which grief cannot be blanketed as it is by the noise and glare
in cities. If you stare at it long enough, fishermen tell me, you can
see anything. Alone at night, during the Dog Watch, thoughts fly
out across the sea. Dark shapes in the water refigure themselves
into vague human forms and the shadowy clouds above swim
with memory.

The vortex Didion comes back to again and again is that
memory of her and her husband swimming in the cave below the
Portuguese Bend in California. 'The tide had to be just right,' she
writes. 'We had to be in the water at the very moment the tide
was right.' I return to imagining the men at sea checking the time
on their tidal calendar for when they can go home and the fat-
cheeked moon on the tidal clock at Michael's Mount. I think of
my grandmother, who had not observed the tide closely enough
when out with her young children and all these years later, my
repeating of her error. Returning to that moment one last time,
Didion writes: 'If we are to live outside ourselves there comes a
point at which we must relinquish the dead, let them go, keep
them dead. Let them become the photograph on the table. Let
them become the name on the trust accounts. Let go of them in
the water.' She continues – the abstract 'them' turning, as always,
back to him, back to John: 'Knowing this does not make it any
easier to let go of him in the water.' I think of all those fishermen
and the families of fishermen, who have gradually learnt how to
let go of their loved ones in the water, to accept that they are gone
to that 'great wheelhouse in the sky', as Larry puts it.

Back on land, I reread *His Dark Materials*. Leafing through *The
Northern Lights*, I find a passage about the voyage to the north
in which Lyra's daemon, Pantalaimon, distracts her from her seasickness by becoming first a storm petrel and then a porpoise.
I catch myself wishing I could have had a daemon to combat the
menace of my own seasickness. While at sea, a seaman tells Lyra

of an old sailor he knew, whose daemon had settled as a dolphin. Because of this, he could never go ashore again. 'He was never quite happy till he died and he could be buried at sea,' Pullman writes. There is always a danger of giving yourself too much to the sea, of leaving a part of yourself out there in the water.

After my pint of coffee on the *Resurgam*, I join Paul, a police sergeant who moonlights as a birdwatcher and whose excursions with tourists I found advertised online during a hunt for rare spoonbill wading birds across the coasts. My uncle was an avid 'birder'. When with us in Lelant, he would spend most of his days watching the skies. Now and then as a child I would go to sit with him above Hayle estuary and look out for birds, growing bored as our tea cooled, while he insisted on staying for several more hours to look – just to look, I would think, the exasperation barely disguised from my young face – out at the marshy, colour-less flats around which a grey B-road now runs.

What I found most torturous about my uncle's hobby was that he did not seem to mind what he saw: he was just as delighted at observing eighteen black-headed gulls as he was a kingfisher or a purple sandpiper, or an unexpected exotic bird escaped from the nearby bird sanctuary. I did not understand then the uncom-plicated joy of observing: to observe the world, not in the sense of watching it, but of practising, of upholding, maintaining just through witnessing its variation, not to impress upon it, not make any contact with it, just to count it. One seagull, two, three, eighteen ...

The wind rips across the harbour and down the Strand, causing plastic bags to rattle like loose teeth. People are reduced to dark outlines, as much of their skin covered as they can possibly manage, heads bent. I hurry over to the market car park to meet Paul. His online blog is called 'Ornitholosism II – It's a Religion!' Paul, wearing khaki and a baseball cap, comes to shake my hand and ask if I have brought my own binoculars. I ashamedly reply no and he tells me he has several spare pairs anyway, his look somewhat disappointed, as if recognising that his latest client has faltered at the first hurdle and is not a true bird enthusiast. We head straight down towards Jubilee Pool, set just above the sea, with sloping white tiers like a jelly mould and fronted by a wrought-iron gate, and gaze out at the revealed rocks where birds tend to sit when the tide is out. I cannot help but let my binoculars wander from the algae-bluish rocks and out towards the horizon, trying to decipher the blurry registration numbers and what they're catching and how the swelling winds might be affecting the boats just returning to harbour.

'If any word could be found engraved around my skull, just above the ears and eyebrows,' Ted Hughes writes of growing up in Yorkshire, 'it would probably be the word "horizon".' As Paul watches for birds, I watch that sloping line, which is not actually a line at all but the empty, undrawn moment where two regions of being meet, and I realise that this is my addiction now. Though back on land, I cannot bear to look away from the horizon. Hughes imagines the horizon between the moor and the sky as 'the outlook of a bottle floating upright at sea': its faded-plastic perspective of the world 'consists of simple light and dark, the light above, the dark below, the two divided by a clear waterline'. The horizon is nothing more than a contrast of shades, simple light and simple dark, but this makes it no less seductive.

Paul has birded since he was a child; he does not remember a time when his life was not devoted to winged creatures. Any moment he can get away from the police station in Falmouth, he races off in his car to follow the birds. At night he likes to stand out in his porch and watch redwings, his favourite birds, migrate to the UK for winter from Russia and Scandinavia. You can hear their wings like pages of a book leafed through by the wind's fingers and occasionally see the flash of red on their bellies picked up by a street lamp. He tells me that though he forgets the details of everyday life and the things he has read, he has a photographic memory for birds and remembers perfectly every bird he has ever seen and where. There is a sky map in his head, a constellation of feathers.

Along by Jubilee Pool we see purple sandpipers and turnstones. The origins of bird names tend to be satisfyingly straightforward; the little turnstones spend their days turning stones over, searching for worms. Their wings are mottled brown and their legs bright orange. Purple sandpipers are not purple, and have puffed-out bodies and stride about importantly, much like little bird policemen I think, but I do not tell Paul in case it offends him. Paul, who does not express his excitement with exclamations or flutters, but through more concentrated looking through binoculars and bringing his weight forward as if to get as close as possible to the bird he is watching, spots a kingfisher. Even I know this is a significant sighting. I wave the binoculars around frantically but cannot seem to find the bird. They do not wait to be noticed, flitting away as they please with little care for who sees them and who does not. Paul once more carefully lines me up and at last I see it. Their turquoise bodies seem to glow, bright against the milk-stained white sky and shore. Their bodies possess a marmalade colour that shadows around their eyes too. I have just a moment to take him in before we lose him. He does not fly away, I don't think, but seems to melt from the air.

Then we are off in Paul's Chevrolet across the headland to Hayle estuary. I keep my hands wafered between my thighs, trying desperately to warm up. Paul tells me that Cornish birders seem to him particularly competitive and often won't declare their sightings. It maddens him, as he has an egalitarian approach to birding, constantly posting sightings. Like hurricane-chasers, these khaki-wearing, deep-pocketed, floppy-hatted men and women speed off in their cars as soon as they hear the news of something special.

Once we get to the estuary, we pass a man tending to his hedge. As we walk past, he shouts out through the wind: 'Looking for her again, are you, Paul?' My eye darts across the estuary and down to Lelant beach below. A spasm passes through my chest as I realise it has been almost exactly two months since I've seen my mother, the longest I have ever been away from her.

'There she is!' Paul jabs his finger towards the low waters along the estuary where once my uncle would look out with his tea. The spoonbill is a large, fluffy white bird, like the inside of a punctured pillow. Her legs are dark and dainty, her dark elongated bill opening up into a perfectly round disc, which she hypnotically sways from left to right, scanning for food amongst the shallows.

Driving back towards the south coast, Paul points out Hell's Mouth, a group of cliff faces between Hayle and Pentreath whose cavities look like an enormous paw has ripped away parts of the coastline. Hell's Mouth was once a notorious spot for smugglers. Now, Paul tells me as we observe the dark shadows it casts over the sharp rocks below it, it is better known as a suicide spot, a place policeman dread to receive emergency calls from. 'I don't know why they don't just change the names of places like that,' he says. And yet, I don't think it can be that simple. It is not the name that draws those who are unhappy towards it, but something larger and more profound, which is to do with the geography of the place. Mount Misery, too, does not retain its footprint of sadness because of its name, but because the mount is the highest place in Newlyn, from where fishermen's wives could look out, hoping to see their husbands' boats returning through the storms.

According to the Office for National Statistics, 234 people took their own lives in Cornwall between 2014 and 2016. That works out as sixteen suicides for every 100,000 people, the third highest rate in the country, behind only Middlesbrough and Corby. When I tell my friends back home how prolific suicides are in Cornwall, none of them can believe it. We find it hard to imagine death in beautiful places. I ask Paul why he thinks there is such a high number of suicides in Penzance in particular. 'It's the end of the line, isn't it?' He replies. 'The very last place you can come to.'

We stop one last time just past Penlee Point to follow the hedged path down into Sandy Cove. The foliage knits above our heads, creating a subway of thick, heavily scented greenery that seems to cut out both light and sound. I've passed through undergrowth like this before in Cornwall, on my cross-country trips from one coastline to the other. Once in them, there is no opportunity to stop, to doubt the way, you can only go onwards. I tell Paul that when I'm in these tunnels I feel like I'm being carried through dimensions, right out of time itself. There should be a name for them, I say – these tunnels that take you between worlds. 'There is', he replies. 'They're called holloways.'

For the final flourish of his tour, Paul gets out his iPhone and starts to play recordings of bird calls, a modern-day Pied Piper sounding them out from their hidden nests in the thick foliage beyond Newlyn's edge. Dusk comes at the same time they do: goldfinches, firecrests, black-tailed godwits, their arrival signalled by a cacophony of chirrups.

25

A PASSIONATE RAGE

I heard the news that a Newlyn fisherman had committed suicide my first day on the *Filadelfia*, when another fisherman messaged us on the VHF to ask if it was really true. After Don confirmed it, the other fisherman did not speak for a while. Eventually he answered, sounding almost exasperated: 'But I had a drink with him the day before yesterday.'

Every person I speak to has a story about the tall, joyful figure, universally loved in the town and who was only in his thirties. When I met Nathan for a drink on the day of my birthday, as soon as we sat down he said: 'So my mate, he just topped himself.' I said I'd heard, but that I'd never met the man.

'Yeah, twat,' Nathan replied, before explaining that it was this fisherman who got Nathan his first berth on a gill-netter, having met him at some rave somewhere, who trained Nathan up and was one of his closest companions in the industry. The tragedy has left him blindsided. Several people speculate that the taking of his life was partly to do with the fact that he had been landlocked for months with an injury. 'I knew he was unhappy,' Nathan says, 'everyone knew he was unhappy. I'm just angry the way he's done it.'

The young fisherman's funeral is the day before I return to London. That morning, there are many more boats in the harbour than usual as skippers have chosen to delay trips or return early for the service. In *The Aran Islands*, Synge describes how the grief he witnesses at the funeral of an elderly member of the community on Inishmaan is not a 'personal complaint for the death of one woman over eighty years'. Rather, that funeral contains 'the whole passionate rage that lurks somewhere in every native of the island. In this cry of pain the inner consciousness of the people seems to lay itself bare for an instant, and to reveal the mood of beings who feel their isolation in the face of a universe that wars on them with winds and seas.' This seems to me the most beautifully articulated observation. I feel it could have been written about Newlyn.

The fishermen walk solemnly up the hill towards the parish church at Paul, dressed not in their usual oilskins and wellies, but in smart dark suits and polished shoes. I think of the rage I have encountered in Newlyn. It is a rage that builds up, not just in response to the sea's violence, but as a result of continuously feeling unheard. It is a rage that grows from seeing large companies take over the fishing fleet; a rage as once more fishermen read in the newspapers that the government will ignore their pleas for a fairer division of quotas and more thorough up-to-date analysis of fish populations; a rage as each family-run shop is taken over by a homogenous national brand; at the floods of tourists, who arrive in summer months to stay in expensive holiday cottages that simultaneously push up house prices and locals out; rage at the lack of jobs for young people save for seasonal tourism and fishing; rage at having to watch those things that had once seemed essential to life in Newlyn being eroded away. It is this tide of rage that has driven the people of Cornwall eight times now to London over the last few centuries, demanding no longer to be ignored by politicians in matters that affect them directly. It is a rage that springs from helplessness. You can feel this rage in Newlyn's alleyways, down by its harbour walls, kept at bay until, at desperate moments, it bursts forth with overwhelming intensity.

I watch as the funeral party snakes its way back down into the town from Paul church. A trawler leaving through the Gaps, where the Christmas lights have already been strung up ready to be ceremonially turned on the next weekend, blows its foghorn. The sound, usually loud and indignant, today sounds plangent – a wail of mourning sent out to the sea. There is a time-honoured ritual in Newlyn that after funerals everyone walks back down to the Red Lion for a piss-up. Danny, the skipper of the *Golden Harvest,* says they have already factored in a day off pilchard fishing tomorrow because it's likely to be such a big night. Always in Newlyn there is this finest of lines between tragedy and humour. As each storm at sea is followed soon by a day of flat calm, so each tragedy merges celebration with communal grief.

Synge writes of this change after the funeral of the elderly woman. 'We walked back to the village, talking of anything, and joking of anything, as if merely coming from the boat-slip or the pier.' After funerals on the Aran Islands great quantities of poteen would be consumed. Synge hears that one night, after the funeral is long over, 'two men fell down in the graveyard while the drink was on them. The sea was rough that day, the way no one could go to bring the doctor, and one of the men never woke again and found death that night.'

Looking back at my time in Newlyn, all moments seem to converge on this last day: a hundred river mouths flowing into the same area of new sea, their waters mixing with the salt water, groomed through by the waves. Devastation that springs out of the quotidian cannot be rationalised. 'Even the report of the 9/11 commission,' Joan Didion writes, 'opened on this insistently premonitory and yet still dumbstruck narrative note: "Tuesday, September 11, 2001, dawned temperate and nearly cloudless in the eastern United States".' I think of how one such ordinary cloudless day became the day that Nathan's father's boat sunk, just weeks before he would have left fishing forever; the ordinary day when a whale washed up on Long Rock; the ordinary day we set out on the *Filadelfia* that was the same morning a young Newlyn fisherman hanged himself.

That night, I go to the Star to say goodbye to everyone before my early train home the next morning. Debbie has transformed the Star into a decadent Santa's grotto with gleaming gold and green decorations hanging off every available surface, the pub now crammed with those from the funeral party, who have drifted down the hill from the Red Lion to continue celebrating the dead fisherman's life. In some ways the mood is like any other day in the Star. There are the usual waves of laughter punctuated by long yarns, the habitual silliness and play interspersed with more serious musings on life and losses. 'No matter what,' one fisherman tells me, 'when you lose someone at sea, or to the sea, or whatever...' He pauses. 'Well, you just gotta look out for each other after a tragedy like that.'

26

'Ome

When I imagined my time at sea, I never saw it raining. My mind retained some childish logic along the lines of: there's so much water out there already – how could there be more? But my final day on the *Filadelfia* is marked by torrential rain. Its needle-thin lines draw slants across the sky, rendering the sea's once smooth surface rough and scaly.

In his meditation on architecture, the *Poetics of Space*, the French philosopher Gaston Bachelard writes of his amazement that even for the snail, a creature whose entire life is experienced from within the confines of a shell, 'the great cosmic rhythm of winter and spring vibrates nonetheless'. The universe's rhythms seem to vibrate almost more profoundly in those who are shut off from the everyday passage of time. As a blind person is better attuned to their other senses, we feel keenly each word from the land that pierces our sea cocoon. Time does not melt away at sea, as one fisherman warned me early on, but arrives in sudden vibrations sent skipping out from the land like a skimming stone across a lake.

On the *Filadelfia* we watch the six o'clock news each day, and though the stories seem muffled as if coming from a long way off, they shock us back momentarily to the concerns of the land. We rear our heads from our metal shell to feel the freshwater rain droplets splash our faces and, in that moment, are returned to the coastline: an image of Denise rushing outside to bring in her sodden washing springs to my mind, then cuts to an image of the jam-pink stone of Penzance prom, which appears to become diluted in downpours, dribbling pink streaks into the sea.

The rain blurs the work on the boat, causing moments to run into one another. Hauls leads to more hauls; the guts from indeterminate fish mix together on the silver table before being hosed down and thrown back into the sea. And yet, the mood on the boat has altered since yesterday. Moments of levity arrive with increasing frequency, flooding in like the sudden opening of a sluice gate after much time barricaded down. The men break into spontaneous song in the fish room; they skip across the deck; grins pass over their faces as the glints of particular memories of home catch their minds' eyes. We are almost ready to go home.

That morning I watch Don leafing through papers, making notes and filling in his online skipper's log, which details the fish we caught this week and the time of our hauls. He sighs into his coffee as he punches in one calculation after another, swearing under his breath when the antique computer freezes for a third time. There is something disquieting about seeing a fisherman's face lit up by a computer screen. Many of them lament how the growing bureaucracy presiding over the industry has forced them to become paper-pushers, and they hark back to the times when they could roam the sea freely. In the short story 'Poseidon', Franz Kafka reimagines Poseidon as forever buried under paperwork. 'What irritated him most,' he writes, 'was to hear of the conceptions formed about him: how he was always riding about through the tides with his trident. When all the while he sat here in the depths of the world-ocean, doing figures uninterruptedly.' There are still hoops fishermen must jump through, lines and boundaries demarcating their passages through the sea. Kafka's tale ends with Poseidon becoming bored with the sea and returning to dry land at last. 'He let fall his trident. Silently he sat on the rocky coast and a gull, dazed by his presence, described wavering circles around his head.'

All week the crew have been avidly discussing their tactics for making the most money possible at the market when we return. We learn through snatches of conversation on the VHF when other boats are planning to land this week and what the prices are looking like at auction. In the past, buyers have been known to work out between themselves what prices various fish should go for before the auction, leaving the fishermen completely at their mercy. 'People shouldn't just play on other people's livelihood like that,' one trawlerman tells me. There are weeks, too, when you just might be unfortunate and barely catch anything. In these times, morale on the boat reaches its lowest. 'There's nothing worse than that feeling,' Don tells me, 'and, as the skipper, it all comes down to you. Your men are all depending on you for their pay packet.'

This week, we've been lucky. None of the other trawlers at sea with us are going to harbour on the same day. The only other large boat landing for the Tuesday morning market is a gill-netter, which does not target the same species as us (tending to catch mainly hake and turbot in their static nets), so is unlikely to have a dramatic effect on our prices. While I watch Don growl at the computer once more, I imagine his very first days on a fishing vessel as a decky learner, before all the legislation came in and the sea was a watery region full of promise.

He looks up from his writing, noticing me watching him. 'What you going to call this book, then?' Before I can start to reply, he answers for me. 'What about: *Don*,' he mimes the unfurling of a banner, '*Part I*?'

Around two o'clock, Don starts preparing his much-anticipated weekly roast dinner, the meagre size of the galley's oven and lack of surfaces in no way limiting his culinary ambitions. Every dish, pot, pan, tray and flat surface in the galley is made use of, often at least twice with a quick wash in between as its previous contents are decanted into another bowl. As soon as one element is boiling, it is rotated with another pot, the stove constantly spilling over with flecks and spittle from various gravies and juices. It is an acrobatic procedure; Don skilfully twists and twirls like a ballet dancer in his slippers, now chopping, now stirring, now peeling – and, miraculously, managing to navigate the boat and conduct three successful hauls in the meantime.

Each time I offer to help chopping some vegetable or other, Don yells territorially: 'You siii'down!' It is his galley and this is his special supper. He wants no interferences or challenges to his authority. He does, magnanimously, allow me to observe his making of the cheese sauce for his cauliflower cheese (from scratch) so that I will be able to replicate it myself in the future. There is no end to my learning on board the *Filadelfia*. This involves the most furious, sustained beating of butter, flour and cheese I have ever witnessed, overlaid throughout with colourful language.

The end result is one of the best meals I have ever eaten. From the oven, Tetris-like, comes a steaming tray of golden roasted 'fuckin'' potatoes, swede mash, Yorkshire puddings, an overflowing pot of cauliflower and broccoli cheese, perfectly crisped, honey-roasted parsnips and tender strips of beef. On the stove bubbles a great cauldron of thick gravy, as well as pans of peas and carrots. We each take our place around the table with our enormous mounds of food. Silence falls over the galley as everyone concentrates on the feast before them. Every now and then one of us wipes our brow or stretches, willing our bodies to fit in more, before continuing with the task at hand. At last, every plate is mopped clean, and Kyle has, somehow, managed to finish off most of the leftovers too.

While we sit nursing our bloated bellies, the TV is turned back on and we find ourselves confronted with Johnny Depp's eyeliner-smudged and darkly tanned face swinging the wheel of the *Black Pearl* with gusto. There will probably never be a more appropriate environment for watching *Pirates of the Caribbean* than shoulder to shoulder with four fishermen as you push through the running sea on a wet night. The crew guffaw and slap the table as the pirates run rings around the Royal Navy officers. And when Elizabeth Swan joins the buccaneers, exchanging her corset for a pair of men's trousers and a sword, I cannot help but glance down sheepishly at my fish-stained tracksuit and think of my yellow-stripped knife hanging up on the deck. We watch the film right through, snug from the winds and rains drawing around the boat, the heat from the oven fogging up the galley windows.

Before my last haul, I join Kyle in the wheelhouse to find him doubled up with heartburn from wolfing down his food before the watch. In a fair amount of pain myself, I lie down on the wheelhouse floor, feeling the vibrations from the engine travel through me, as they had that first night, and imagining that the *Filadelfia* has absorbed me right into her so that I can no longer be said to be my own separate entity. I close my eyes, considering it to be for just a second, but when I open them again, Don is standing above me, giving me a weird look – 'Last haul. I hope you've been praying it's a good one!'

I scramble up quickly and take my customary position beside Don as the derricks moan at the immense weight they must draw out of the water one last time. As the fish slosh onto the deck, Don climbs on to his tiptoes, hitches up his loose tracksuit bottoms and sticks his head out of the wheelhouse. 'What you got for me, boys?' By now, I am as caught up in the process as the rest of the crew. Like waiting for our lottery numbers to come up, I bob up and down beside Don with my fingers tightly crossed that this will be the haul with which we beat our turbot record.

It turns out to be the best haul of the trip. The men fill up three and a half buckets of oozing cuttlefish – alone worth around £500 – and as the heap of fish is shifted, we make out five large, gleaming turbot hidden amongst the other bodies. The whoops from Kyle celebrating rise up to the wheelhouse; he was on watch for this haul and so, by rights, takes full credit. 'We are going with the tide, that's why it's so good,' Don explains sagely.

Perhaps it is the heaviness of the roast dinner, but, as I watch the men work in synchronisation below us, a tremendous shudder of exhaustion passes across my body. I get no more than a few steps towards the ladder down to my waiting sleeping bag when Kyle and Andrew shout from the deck: 'Lamorna! Look out the window!' Almost as soon as I wake each morning, Andrew would smugly announce that I should have stayed up because he had seen a whole school of dolphins right by the boat just after I had gone to bed. Initially, my response to these reported sightings was to give a howl of frustration and vow to stay up later the following night. But as the week drew on and my bed-time got later and later, I still apparently missed the dolphins each night, and I grew suspicious that Andrew, the prank-master, was winding me up all along.

Suspecting this to be one final joke at my expense, I pull the heavy wheelhouse door open reluctantly and go out into the night. I gaze out at the choppy waters, their serrated crests lit brilliantly by the boat's floodlights. With each glimpse of a dark patch of sea or arching wave, my head whips round. My eyes squint out at the ensuing darkness, but I can pick out nothing. 'Ha ha!' I call down, making to head back in.

'There!' the crew call again, gesturing with their blue gloves to the disturbed sea by the nets. 'Right there!'

When I do at last see them, they are unmistakeable. Right by our gear, a whole school of dolphins, many more than I had seen while on the *Three Jays*, appear from the depths like silver commas, arcing over the waves, before diving back into the water without a splash a second later. I wish I could follow the paths of their streamlined bodies under the water, see the mirror image of the curved shape they make above the water. Like Melusine with her tail in the bath, I imagine the dolphins transforming into something beyond human comprehension below the sea's surface, their sleek bodies spreading out, perhaps, in the way that a dress billows in wind.

Their motion is so captivating that I forget to join the men on the deck for my final gutting as Raymundo. I watch for a long time, my eyes straining to pick out their crescent-moon dives. And then, as when they came, I am no longer certain whether what I am seeing are dolphins or the crests of waves. The cold strikes my face once more and I remember the tiredness in my legs. I count a minute in my head, promising myself to go to bed if I don't see them again. Like Lopez's Fata Morganas, my eyes attempt to transform the empty landscape into what I desire to see. I count another sixty seconds; the sea remains vacant. One more...

'It's deceiving,' Andrew says, joining me on the balcony. 'Look at it long enough and you'll start to see all sorts … Go on, get yourself to bed now.'

No one sleeps much that night. The fishermen call it 'channelling': when thoughts of your missus and your children and your home at home swim through your mind all night, waking you repeatedly from sleep. When I first heard the term, I assumed it came from the idea of a channel as a watercourse, connecting two greater regions of water together, but another fisherman tells me it is drawn from channel in the spiritual sense: to convey the message of a spirit from another world to this one. The *Filadelfia* herself is the medium in this sense, providing the link between the men's two worlds, the sea and the land. Our channelling seems to fill the whole cabin, as if Newlyn were radiating out from our bunks, each of our personal images of it merging together into a single, shimmering image at the room's centre. We wake from our half-dreams, bleary-eyed. While we have been rocked and tossed in our sleeping bags, the sea has grown impatient, and by morning resembles a threatening mass of dark waves like a herd of buffalo waiting to charge.

'See, I told you,' Don announces as I enter the wheelhouse. 'You always pay for good weather sooner or later.' I track the gradually worsening conditions through the surface of my coffee, its usual concentric circles of activity developing into a whole tidal movement in my mug that occasionally spills over the rim and onto my now blackened and gut-sodden tracksuit bottoms. I go to the fridge to make myself a ham and cheese sandwich for breakfast and a pack of butter leaps out at me from inside and hits me square in the face. Several cold Yorkshire puddings follow it out, like the more cowardly members of a gang coming in for a final beating once I'm already down. When it is rough weather, Andrew likes to tease the men watching the waves nervously by saying: 'You pay thirty quid to go to Alton Towers, and out here you get it for free!'

All those months before, during my final night on the *Crystal Sea*, I similarly saw the predicted Force 8 storms begin to transform the sea. The gentle rhythms of the waves picked up into a violent lurching motion, shifting from 'milk' to 'smoking' – when the wind is so fierce it knocks the tops off the waves, creating something that looks like smoke. I stayed up in the wheelhouse the whole way back to land during the ghostly period of the Dog Watch, gripping onto the sides of my seat, not daring to move. To take my mind off the brewing storm, the crewman on watch, a Newcastle man named Jimmy, recited to me his favourite conspiracy theories as we drove back to shore. In those unslept hours before the sun rose, I began to imagine it was his words that were making the seas churn – chimeras surging out of the blackness and slamming against the square wheelhouse windows, while his yarns become wilder. Jimmy told me that at the centre of the earth there existed a nether region where aliens lie dormant, waiting for some sign or final act of destruction upon the earth by humans before they reveal themselves and save our planet from us. The Pyramids were actually nuclear sources that power alien spaceships, each story becoming more plausible as the storm blew outside. His final tale, he claimed, he had seen with his own eyes. 'On a raging night, much like this,' he narrated in a prophetic tone, 'a creature believed to be no more than a myth appeared right beside the boat.' A white vortex with a black circle at its centre surfaced slowly from the water. The black circle flicked around to stare right at Jimmy and, to his horror, he realised he was being watched by the humongous, globe eye of a giant squid. The eye watched him; he watched the eye. He yelled out to the other crew, but the gale swallowed his voice and the eye disappeared back into the sea. No one ever believes him, Jimmy told me, but he knows what he saw.

Back on the *Filadelfia*, it is Kyle who is on watch for the three hours it takes us to return to shore with our seagull companions littering the deck and flying alongside us like streamers. When he tells me that once we are exactly five miles from the land, our phone service will return and with it the whole mood of the boat will shift, I am unconvinced. After eight days, the crew feel akin to my family and I cannot believe such closeness is merely one of proximity and lack of other options. 'Any second now,' Kyle announces half an hour later, his eyes glued to the radar. 'Yep, here we go.'

I can feel my phone burning through my pocket, imagining the strips of light darting across it with each new message. All vows to keep myself from it are forgotten. I should at least text my parents, and what if something had happened to a friend while I was away? I reach into my pocket and turn it on.

A myopia descends upon the whole crew simultaneously. Our smiles turn inwards as our home lives open outwards. At once, Kyle and I, who have yarned and prattled together all week, lapse into silence, transfixed by our screens. Our fingers caress the smooth, clean surfaces of our virtual lives and in each of our eyes shines a reflected blue oblong. And, like that, the community of the past eight days fractures. The *Filadelfia*, moments before the only world that mattered, is no more than a place of work once more, or a vehicle to convey us back to our real lives. I find myself already trying to condense eight days' worth of life into digestible anecdotes for friends. I send long, apologetic texts to my frantic parents, who, not knowing I would have no signal, had gone into panic mode when I suddenly went silent – they later admit that they called both the Harbourmaster's Office and Stevenson's and tracked every second of my journey back on the AIS, their daughter represented by a small green arrow making zigzags across the oceans.

The land comes as a genuine surprise. I don't think I had imagined it as a single, unbroken entity the whole time we were at sea; I was only able to conjure up pieces of it, isolated in time. We sit in the galley eating crisps, looking from our phones to the views beyond the galley windows and back again, our eyes resting briefly on each recognised landmark along the scabrous cliffs. There is Land's End, where I am reminded each year by my parents that I threw up in the car park when I was seven because the road to it is so winding; there is Porthcurno with its telegraphy history; the tumbling granite terraces of the Minack Theatre; my namesake, Lamorna, which, from a sea distance, appears insignificant and grey.

At this point on the voyage home, Don calls his brother Shane. Their conversation is brief. Shane, an ex-fisherman who works on Newlyn's fisheries patrol boat, lets him know that things are all okay on land; Don fills him in on the success of the fishing trip. After the call, Don tells me he and his brother made a pact when they were boys to call each other on the way home every time either of them were coming back from sea. Don and Shane lost their brother at sea when he was a teenager and their father, a fisherman too, died when they were just children. And so now they make this weekly call, just to say, 'Hello. I'm okay. I'm coming back again.'

We round the next bend in the coastline and see St Clement's Isle, the small cluster of rocks where a hermit once lived, at which I have stared at drunkenly for many happy hours from the Old Coastguard in Mousehole. And then, as we reach the final jut of shoreline before Newlyn, my gaze lingers upon the forlorn shape of the old lifeboat station at Penlee Point, hanging out above the sea. I remember Roger the geologist telling me that beneath this extrusion in the land is a dolomite foundation. It is this foundation that provided the bay with a natural shelter, allowing the first people to be protected from the desolate conditions of the Cornish coast. This means, Roger had informed me with a wry smile all those months before, that the very basis for Newlyn's existence, the reason it ever became a fishing port at all, was geological.

As it was with our departure, the sun is just going down behind Mount's Bay on our return. Where before the panorama opened up to show us the whole sky and every moment of the sun's descent, now the sun disappears quietly again behind Mount Misery. I find myself feeling bereft, almost, as I realise that my perspective will be bracketed by the land once more – for who knows how long this time. I ask Don, who has taken over from Kyle to moor the *Filadelfia*, if it is still exciting for him to see Newlyn emerge along the coast after all these years. 'You see the Mount,' he replies solemnly, 'and it doesn't matter whether the trip was the best you've ever had or a pile of crap, you think "I'm home".'

The 'h' of home is swallowed, the contracted word pronounced with great meaning, like a word of prayer. 'Ome.

The other men and I, without seeming conscious of our movements, have gravitated towards the very extremities of the deck, the same position from which Newlyn fishermen have for hundreds of years leaned out as they steer back towards the harbour; at this point, they too, like Don but with an even thicker Newlyn accent, would cry out: 'I'm 'Ome.' Andrew sees me craning my neck, my eyes squinting to make out Denise and Lofty's cottage and calls out to me: 'It's a good sight!'

And for hundreds of years too, wives, parents and children have hurried down to the harbour as soon as news spread that their fishermen are about to return. Kyle talks excitedly of seeing his beloved dog and missus, who has promised to bring him several of his favourite sandwiches; Stevie's wife will pick him up with their daughter; Andrew's brother is coming straight down onto the boat to pick up his promised fish and drop off some blackberry wine; Don will stay the latest, sorting out all of the business of the boat, before seeing friends briefly, if he's not too exhausted, and then heading home to his flat.

The *Filadelfia* passes the welcoming red and white lighthouse at the entrance to the harbour and makes it way over to the market, where I can already see Stevensons' employees waiting to unload her catch. I had not expected anyone to be waiting for me, but when we are a hundred metres or so away from the harbour wall, I see a tall figure leaning against a mooring pole. It is Lofty, still wearing his work fleece, hands in his pockets. I race across the deck to greet him, oily-faced engineers peering down in surprise at the girl brought in from the sea.

The last moments on a fishing boat are always anticlimactic. The men, their work not yet over, sigh, stretch and climb back down to the fish room to start attaching boxes of frozen fish to cranes up on the market level. I watch the stream of action occurring around me and feel redundant once more, alone in the middle of the deck.

On the *Crystal Sea,* one of the crew had warned me of a strange pull that might prevent me from leaving the boat once we reached the harbour. I felt this almost immediately: the everyday world beyond the boat became overwhelming – vast, loud and filled with bodies bustling about. To delay re-entering the fray I stayed with the crew on board for a few hours. Sitting in the belly of the boat with nets sprawled across the floor, I observed the crew skilfully weaving net needles in and out of the loose fabric, replacing deteriorating sections with new, diamond shapes. The heterogeneous texture of these nets, composed of variously aged and coloured threads, told the history of the *Crystal Sea*'s journeys and of the many hands that have worked together on the boat. At last David the skipper picked up my bag, placed a firm hand on my back, as if he had encountered this reluctance with other visitors to the *Crystal Sea* too, who had in those few days out on the water forgotten where they were from and had to be gently reminded, and guided me back over the harbour wall.

When I ask Don if I can do anything to help on the *Filadelfia,* he replies: 'No, you take yourself home now,' and gives me a quick hug. 'I'll see you tomorrow, all right Lamorna?'

'Right, yeah. See you tomorrow, then…' I say, disorientated. 'And thank you!' I call down to the crew. Andrew climbs back up to hand me the plastic bag filled with the fish I filleted. Kyle tells me he always keeps a few crabs back after a trip so that if you're pissed and don't have any money for a Stones Taxi, you can barter with seafood. 'Couple of crayfish and you can get a nice bottle from the offie, too,' he advises me and then also hugs me goodbye.

I heave myself up the harbour ladder from the sea, practically falling into Lofty's arms when I reach the top. In *Tristes Tropiques,* Lévi-Strauss writes that when, after a whole month at sea, the men at last saw Martinique appear on the horizon, they did not cry: 'Land! Land!' but, 'A bath, at last a bath tomorrow!' It is only then, when coming face to face with Lofty, that I realise quite how rancid I smell. 'You need a shower!' Lofty laughs.

I stagger down the quay, swaying like a drunkard and almost falling over several times, unused to the land's stillness.

The town is quiet and dark, the sun now fully submerged behind Mount Misery. Outside the door to Orchard Cottage, I look up at the stars, scanning for the lasso constellation I saw every night at sea, but am unable to find it. Once in, I go straight to the shower and stand right close to the showerhead so that the water pours down my face. I keep my head under until the last entrails of unspecified fish have washed down the plughole, gasping at the strength of the water pouring down on me, my hand placed against the blue tiled walls to keep my balance. And then, still wrapped up in my towel, I collapse into bed.

Most extraordinary to me in Lopez's account of the narwhal is the fact that their earliest ancestors, and of whales too, were insect-eating terrestrial creatures. After 330 million years facing the sea from the land, they slipped away to start new lives under the skin of the water. I wonder if the narwhals carry any memory of what it was like to walk upon the land and if, in the great passage of time still to come, they might ever return to the solid earth once more.

27

FISHERMAN'S BLUES

All that first night back on land my ears are full of the drone of the *Filadelfia*'s engine. I dream I am back in the shower, washing yet more fish guts from my hair. They splatter onto the white base of the bath like a crime scene and get stuck in the drain. More guts pour down, coming not just from my hair, I realise, but from the showerhead itself: guts, and then whole fish, fish within fish. And the water is dark, salt. It fills the bath and goes over.

Next morning the world still has not realigned itself. The sounds are all wrong, the ground below me still suspiciously motionless, the lack of distance oppressive. It is as if I am viewing my life through the porthole in the *Filadelfia*'s toilet, the world outside just the flicking images of a kinetoscope. I call my parents again, unsure what else to do, but when they answer, I don't know what to say. Each time they ask me for a detail of the trip, my answers come out jumbled or half-finished. I break off and try again, growing more mumbling with every attempt. Eventually I say something like: 'Sorry, I don't think I'm properly back yet, actually,' and hang up on my poor, bemused mother and father.

I try to remember the normal things one does on the land. I send a few letters, do some washing, pick up groceries, nervously peek at my email account with my hands over my eyes and, overwhelmed by the sheer volume of detritus gathering in my inbox, shut it. I return to bed, exhausted. There is a saying that goes: 'I'm in the harbour again.' It announces to the world – I'm safe, I survived, I've come home. Returning from sea doesn't feel that definitive. Though your body is in the harbour once more, for a long time your mind is still at sea.

I must have fallen asleep because an hour later I wake to a call coming in from Don. 'You'll never guess what!' he yells down the phone as soon as I answer (after a day without direction, it is a relief to hear his gruff tones once more). 'We got a boat record at the auction this morning: fifty-four and a half grand!'

'Fifty-four?!' I say, 'Jesus Christ, congratulations!'

'Don't forget the half!' He bellows. And then, joyfully, 'So we're getting pissed, tonight. All right?'

Before I can reply, he hangs up.

Cabarouse – a 'noisy frolic' or 'drinking bout' – is a term that comes to feel as essential to understanding Cornish fishermen as any other dialect word relating to fishing in Nance's *Glossary*. By the time I roll into the Star at around five, Don and Andrew are already a few pints down. Our first greeting is uncharacteristically formal, almost awkward, as we take in each other's clean, land-appropriate appearances. Don has had his hair cut and wears a smart jacket; Andrew has brown leather shoes and jeans; I've washed my hair and put on a little make-up – back on the *Filadelfia* Andrew joked that I'd turn up in high heels and a skirt and no one would recognise me. Our collective stuttering is broken as soon as Don shouts: 'Come 'ere!' and pulls me into an embrace. Andrew joins in and we huddle together in a circle, rejoicing over the victory at this morning's market.

I take a look around the Star. There is a smattering of bodies: an old man in a cowboy's hat leaning low over his drink at the bar whom Debbie is cleaning around; a tired fisherman smoking in the doorway; a petite, bald man running his finger down the side of the jukebox, and Rob and Ellen, a retired couple who are good as gold. It doesn't surprise me that Stevie hasn't joined us – he doesn't like to waste precious time in the pub anymore when he could be with his wife and young daughter – but I keep expecting Kyle to appear. Back in the wheelhouse, he would regale me with innumerable landing-day-pints stories, each wilder than the last. Just yesterday morning, he boasted that he'd probably be in the pub by lunchtime and I'd have to catch up. I ask Andrew and Don if they know where Kyle is, but they say they haven't heard from him all day, and meanwhile set to buying drinks for the entire pub.

We gather cosily around the wooden table in front of the window that looks out to the harbour, where I have sat so many times before with Denise and Lofty. There is a grating of wooden chairs as Rob and Ellen, and the few others who have joined us, dutifully settle in opposite us to play audience for the night. Every time someone in Newlyn told me their story, I wished I had one to tell back – a single story that was not of school, or university, one not set against some kind of institutional backdrop. This is the first thing I have done. It's the first story I'll tell about myself.

The room descends into a reverential hush, broken now and then by a gasp or burst of laughter let out in between punchlines. We allow each heroic moment from the *Filadelfia* to swell outwards like oats in water. I find I am no longer speaking as myself, but my alter ego Raymundo, as I viciously slash through fish with a great sword. Don wrenches a great ship's wheel around, which has been transported from its position in the warm wheelhouse to the rain-lashed deck, in hot pursuit of a shoal of turbot. The *Filadelfia*, our girl, responds to his every touch, nimbly galloping over the waves. The spectators drink in our adventures greedily, remarking on our boldness, our bravery and demanding more.

The pints flow, the three of us seeming almost to glow like gold saints as the evening draws on. The old days of fishing are not lost yet, I think; narratives of brave men returning from the wild, running seas with a bounty to feed the village persist. Of the 'grey poteen' drink that one could not avoid among the pubs on the Aran Islands, Synge writes it 'brings a shock of joy to the blood' and 'seems predestined to keep sanity in men who live forgotten in these worlds of mist'. Our drinks in the Star that night have a similar palliative effect. We step out of the sea of mist, letting its cloak slip off our backs, and recover the parts of ourselves that we had left behind us. We relax once more into the world. And yet, we are fallible heroes, our tales rambling sideways as the drink takes hold of us.

At last Kyle appears. He does not rush over but lingers there in the doorway as if deciding whether or not to break through some invisible barrier that separates him from us. We draw up a chair for him, hooting his name and clapping him on his back. Everyone waits, but the wide grin that had brought a certain lightness to hard moments at sea does not break across his face. Instead, he looks solemnly into the pint that has been pushed in front of him.

'Drink up, lad! You earned it!' someone shouts.

Kyle sips slowly, lost in thought, seeming not to notice us at all. When he finally speaks, all he says is: 'Weird day', repeating it several times and shaking his head. None of us presses him after that. Those monosyllables are words enough to articulate the way that the troubles of the present can rush back over you the moment your feet touch solid ground, often coming to a head as soon as the men step back through the front door. Kyle leaves after only an hour, making a short, muttered apology.

Drink can never really be the cure to keep 'sanity in men who live forgotten in these worlds of mist' that Synge imagines. At the most it is a perfunctory painkiller, another cloak of mist that we temporarily cover ourselves with. Most men of the sea have families to support and responsibilities to take care of that are far more urgent than attending landing-day pints with the crew.

And then, without my quite realising it has happened, there is a round of tequila shots before our now depleted number. Andrew insists we all down them immediately. I check the time on my phone – 6.30 p.m. It is suddenly very apparent that this will not just be a 'couple of pints and call it a night' kind of celebration. I don't check the time for the rest of the evening. The hours wheel frenziedly, while we sway through them. Other fishermen just back from sea trickle into the Star to join us. The slightly older couples leave, seamlessly replaced with Andrew's girlfriend and a younger crowd who share our desire for a big Tuesday night. We all squash around the table, pints and spirits piling up around us like tower blocks. In Newlyn, whoever is there, regardless of their age or walk of life, becomes your crew for the night. Whatever happens, you support them loyally, downing shots together, arms around shoulders, proclaiming soppy, meaningful statements about friendship into their ears. The one requirement is that you're 'up for it'. This speaks to a larger value system that pervades the whole town – no individual is too old, too drunk, too unhappy to be shut out from the goings on of the place.

The latecomers tell their own stories as the night grows darker. Andrew's girlfriend teases him about the self-assured, Lothario status he likes to cultivate. She didn't grow up in Newlyn but has lived here for years now. It is because of nights like these, she tells me, when the fishermen come home and bring life to the pubs, that she has stayed so long in this place – 'On a Friday or Saturday night, the pubs might be empty as anything, but you get a rogue Tuesday like this and they're the most alive places in the whole world.' Fishermen are still Newlyn's spirit, its faith system, its beating heart. If the fishing industry were to collapse, I wonder what would happen to these pubs. There is a young woman who came to Newlyn on a whim as a teenager, and has never left; a middle-aged man with a long beard who has travelled the world multiple times, but always finds himself back here somehow; an elderly ex-fisherman whose voice is so husky I couldn't tell you any of his life story, but his gesticulations and expressive eyebrows suggest it was filled with many twists and turns of fate.

Eventually, Debbie has had enough of our rowdiness and turfs us out so she can close up, and we pile along en masse to the Swordy. This is a regular osmosis in Newlyn; once you've got drunk in the Star, you stagger a few doors down to the Swordy with its slightly rougher atmosphere that is more appropriate for later nights.

Once in the Swordy, our gang of reprobates get more shots in at the bar, and someone turns the jukebox on. Sensing that the party is finally kicking off, Andrew jumps up on a table, and is instantly asked to get down again by the bar man. 'Don't worry,' I say enthusiastically, 'that was still awesome.'

We form a sweaty bunch in the middle of the room, stomping our feet and spinning each other about the room headlong. Don and I jump up and down to 'Hotel California', a song we had listened to together back on the trawler. We yell along to each song – old, new and everything in between – pints sloshing over the floor together with the more vigorous arm movements. It no longer matters that most of us have never met before. In the heat of it all we are together – one stumbling, teasing, shoving gang, getting our well-deserved thrills on a Tuesday night.

The first few rousing chords of a folk song come on and a huge cheer reverberates about the pub. I ask what song it is and am met with shock. 'You don't know "Fisherman's Blues" by the Waterboys?' someone asks. 'This *is* the song of Newlyn.'

The crowd sings the words to 'Fisherman's Blues', with such conviction that I feel each line belongs to Newlyn, their lives plainly expressed in lyrical form. The narrative of escape – wishing to leave it all and become a fisherman – promised by the song is especially pertinent this night. Its longing plea echoes the shared amnesia experienced by the Newlyn fishermen, who after only a few days on stable land seem to have forgotten the harsh nature of their work and start to crave the purifying waves of the sea once more.

By its third rendition, I know 'Fisherman's Blues' well enough to join in, tunelessly, and we bellow the words louder and louder until you can no longer hear the music beneath our hoarse cries. Andrew takes my hand and we do a rollicking jig together. 'We're friends now,' he shouts into my ear. 'Doesn't matter how long it is until we see each other next. Could be a year, could be ten years. You and me will be friends still, right?' We shake on it and the bell for last orders goes. 'It'll be the same.'

We grab one last shot each, play 'Fisherman's Blues' a final time, and pull each other into passionate hugs goodbye as the barman shuts the door behind us.

Outside, we are met by darkness and the brackish winds racing down from the harbour. There is a moment of hesitation, as if the night might go further if only someone were to take the lead, before each of us slinks off into the night. I am no longer scared, as I was the first few months in Newlyn, to walk home along in the extreme blackness, so unlike the shoplit nights of London. It can be dark in Cornwall, yes, but it is the same darkness that you see when you shut your eyes, knowing that, when you open them again, it will be light once more.

When I see any of these figures again before I leave Newlyn the following week – queuing at the Co-op, waiting for a bus, walking along the prom – we give each other a brief nod and a smile, remembering that Tuesday night when none of us could have been closer.

28

Holloways

The *Filadelfia* is set to cleave the men from the land once more only a few days after our return. That afternoon I make my way along the Strand and up to the bench that sits above the harbour, from where one can see its several quays and pontoons growing out from the town like weeds. Nestled between two other rusting Stevenson's trawlers I can just make out the *Filadelfia* sitting low in the water, her aged body leaning heavily in towards the harbour wall. After scanning her for signs of life and finding none, I check my watch. It's five, the time Don had texted me to say would be call time this voyage around. I hear Andrew in his mocking tone: 'But is that Don Time, or actual time?' – my Don, Father Time, whose time does not correspond to the rest of ours, but is tidal time, is a whole wilderness of time beyond the comprehension of us landfolk. And then, from my elevated position, I see the *Filadelfia*'s floodlights blaze on, casting galaxies across the black harbour water and illuminating several pairs of glistening oilskins rushing about the deck and readying the gear. I hear her engine growl into life, see more lights flashing on, off, on, and the oilskinned men taking their positions at the front of the boat. One fisherman told me he never looks back as the boat leaves the harbour. He won't turn around until the land is a line too far away to make out.

I track the *Filadelfia* as she makes her way along the row of sleeping trawlers and out through the Gaps. How can they be doing it again so soon, when they've only just come home?

And then, a pang that I had not expected to come brings with it another question: how could they have gone without me?

'As we get older,' my friend Isaac writes in one of his letters to me in Newlyn, 'I think we learn to say goodbye to places and people less dramatically.' When we're young, we shake off the past like wet dogs until only a few droplets remain clinging to our skin, those last glimmering fish scales glued to a fisherman's jumper. It is only as we grow older that we learn to look back at people and places while we walk away from them, saying: 'See you soon. I will come back to you.' Perhaps we teach ourselves to greet places with more grace as we get older, too.

When I first arrived in Newlyn, I tried desperately to mould the town to my shape, to make it fit as a place I could imagine I had come from – my own creation myth. And yet, the more I come to know Newlyn, the more I recognise that smothering a place with admiration does not make it yours. I cannot keep wishing to have been born to Cornwall, to Newlyn. That desire, by its very nature, forces a kind of flattening onto the place. Instead, I try to notice Newlyn's ways, discovering more bits of it every time I come back and, in doing so, letting it become a place, not to which I belong exactly, but that feels like a friend I can return to. In his letter Isaac continues by telling me he's planning to return to Newlyn, the home he has said goodbye to many times now, for a longer stint than usual this summer, working full-time as crew on his father's fishing boat. His father may retire soon, he writes, and if he does not learn the family trade soon, generations' worth of knowledge passed from father to son through boats will be lost. To know himself, to know the place he comes from, he must follow his ancestors out into the seas.

The *Filadelfia* steams off without me, her yellow bird wings folding down once more. The darkness seems to lead from the sea outwards as she passes beyond Penlee Point and into the arms of the ocean, the halo of light just beginning to show around her almond-shaped body. I imagine the crew climbing down below to dream their last land-touched dreams, while Don, at her helm, cigarette in mouth as always, begins the tiring process of wiping himself blank once more. Near the end of *Moby Dick*, Ishmael wonders more broadly what will happen to the whales of the world in future generations: he asks 'whether Leviathan can long endure so wide a chase, and so remorseless a havoc; whether he must not at last be exterminated from the waters, and the last whale, like the last man, smoke his last pipe, and then himself evaporate in the final puff.' Over a hundred and fifty years later, the whale is an endangered species, hunted almost to extinction in the first half of the twentieth century. I worry how the sea's shape will change over the next 150 years, what impact the changing climes will have on it, and whether there will still be men like Don battling against its remorseless waves, just keeping their heads above the water.

I stay on the bench overlooking the harbour a while longer, saying goodbye and see you again to each part of the bay, now and then allowing my eyes to drift back out towards the *Filadelfia* as she readies herself to plunge below the horizon line. I try to hold in my head what my time on the *Filadelfia* was. And yet, fishing, like the sea itself, is not one thing. There is not some illusive kernel that, when got at, will open up to reveal its essence. It is the staccato rhythms of the physical work at sea, pulling glistening guts out of unsuspecting fish and scattering ice upon their bodies; it is every shared meal, every unusual thing pulled up in the nets; it is the music from Don's sound system, the sea dreams, the gulls doggedly following us; it is in the sparks of intense joy and closeness felt between the crew, as well as every melancholy note of loneliness; it is the stories we tell afterwards, the yarns we drew out in the warm interior of the Star amongst a forest of half-drunk pints; and it is my own retelling of my experiences to friends and family back in London, too. Somewhere amongst all that, along the scummy tide mark left on the shore that fishermen call the *seech*, I begin to catch a sense of what it is to be at sea.

Much of the past comes to be replaced with cardboard cutouts. We don't notice it happening at the time: the budgets get smaller, the set designers swapping whole vistas with backdrops and flatpack buildings. When we return years later to a memory that matters, we find we can no longer look at it the whole way around. And yet, while many of the events from my time in Newlyn start to loosen from my mind, like the sound of waves in a seashell that you know is really only echoing the blood pumping in your own ear, the rhythms of the town and the sea beyond it stay with me somehow.

Once home, I listen to 'Fishermen's Blues' on repeat as I lie in bed beside my half-unpacked suitcase on top of which are many of the keepsakes I've brought back from Newlyn: the fistful of rough amber dragged up from the seabed by the *Filadelfia* and given to me by Kyle, speckled rocks from Newlyn beach collected with Roger, a toy trawler with tiny silver fish dangling below it that flicker and cast torn light across my wall, which Denise and Lofty gave me for my birthday, and the crumpled sugar-paper life drawings of the man who may have been a fisherman, through whom I had first come to see how you might be able to understand a place like Newlyn. Like items washed up on the *seech*, these are the things I have gathered along the line between Newlyn and London. They are ways through; they are holloways.

BIBLIOGRAPHY

Most of the works referenced in this bibliography were read contiguously with the writing of *Dark, Salt, Clear*. Many of the authors listed here – such as Joan Didion, John Steinbeck, Elizabeth Bishop, Barry Lopez and Virginia Woolf – have helped me understand how it might be possible to bridge life, observation and imaginative thought.

PROLOGUE

For John Steinbeck, see *Cannery Row* (London: Penguin Classics, 1945, 1994). Every few months I return to its first pages with a new student, and each time it opens itself up to me in new and surprising ways.

END OF THE LINE

For Virginia Woolf's childhood visits to St Ives Bay, see her diary of August 1905 in *A Passionate Apprentice: the Early Journals 1897–1909*, ed. Mitchell A. Leaska (London: Vintage Books, 1992, 2004).

WAY DOWN TO LAMORNA

For Marlow Moss, see Sabine Schaschl, Lucy Howarth and Ankie de Jongh-Vermeulen's *Marlow Moss: A Forgotten Maverick* (Berlin: Hatje Cantz, 2017). One of the few images of Moss is a photograph taken c.1937, around the time she first moved to Cornwall. She is standing below a signpost indicating 'Lamorna 1 [mile]'; her pose is strong – left leg forward, gloved hand on hip, her short hair slicked back. She does not look towards the camera but follows the direction of the sign pointing across towards Lamorna Cove.

VESICA PISCIS

For Paul Valery, see *Sea Shells* (Boston, MA: Beacon Press, 1995). For Herman Melville, see *Moby Dick: or, The Whale*, (London: Penguin Classics, 1851, 2003). For Maggie Nelson, see *Bluets* (Seattle: Wave Books, 2009). For Joseph Conrad, see *The Nigger of the 'Narcissus': A Tale of the Sea*, ed. A. H. Simmons, (Cambridge: Cambridge University Press, 1897, 2017).

GUTS

For W. G. Sebald, see *The Rings of Saturn*, trans. M. Hulse, (London: Vintage, 1995, 2002). This book was recommended to me by Isaac. Before reading it, I hadn't known you could make a kind of non-fiction that was so strange and rich, and trod a path so close to the realm of fiction. Thomas Browne's *Garden of Cyrus* (1658) is quoted in *The Rings of Saturn*. For Barry Lopez, see *Arctic Dreams* (London: Vintage Classics, 1986, 2014).

THE SING OF THE SHORE

The Morrab Library is an extensive archive of specifically Cornish writing; several of those who work there study the Cornish language, preserving it for future generations. For R. Morton Nance, see *Glossary of Cornish Sea-words* (Federation of Old Cornwall Societies, 1963). The words included in this slim volume have more life to them than any English ones I have heard: *Lagas-awel* – 'the weather dog, a fragmentary rainbow'; *Skubmaw* – 'splinters of wreck in pieces'; *Zawn or sawan* – 'deep fissure in the cliffs caused by the wearing away of softer rock'; *muzzicky* – drizzling (a word especially common in Newlyn, Nance tells us); *Durks* – 'the period where there is no moon'.

LINES THROUGH ROCK

Almost all that I initially discovered of Cornwall's geology was first narrated to me by Roger on the rocky beach between Penzance and Newlyn, and then expanded upon through my own research. For the Wherry Mine, see Arthur Russel, 'The Wherry Mine, Penzance, its history and its mineral productions', *The Mineralogical Magazine*, Vol. 28, no. 205 (1949). For Walter Benjamin, see 'On the Concept of History', in *Walter Benjamin: Selected Writings, 4: 1938–1940,* eds H. Eiland, M. W. Jennings (Cambridge, MA: Belknap Press of Harvard University Press, 1942, 2006). For Joan Didion, see *The Year of Magical Thinking* (New York: Harper Perennial, 2005, 2006). This is a book which, in the past, I have given to friends experiencing bereavement: I never know what to say in these circumstances – words do not seem to exist for it – but Didion comes the closest to expressing how loss redraws the landscape of one's life.

WILD BEASTS

The majority of what I learnt about the various types of boats and methods of fishing came first hand from the fishermen of Newlyn. Lawrence 'Larry' Hartwell, in particular, is an invaluable source of information on all things boats and fish: though retired from his fishing days, he rises before the sun most mornings to watch the boats come in and the catch unloaded at Newlyn market. The Falmouth Maritime Museum and its archives is another excellent resource. For Elizabeth Bishop, see 'At the Fishhouses', in *The Complete Poems* (London: Chatto & Windus, 1969). My thanks go to Andrew, a close friend, for letting me borrow his copy when I returned to Newlyn a second time (and my apologies for still not having given it back). For South Pier's foundation stone celebration, see *The Cornishman*, 2 July 1885. For Mike 'Butts' Buttery, see the Newlyn Archive for his catalogue of boats, and *Mousehole: a Documented History* (Redruth: Palores Publications, 2012). For 'Newlyn fishermen have quite often counted over fifty large trawlers', see *The Cornishman*, 1963. For the *wondyrchoum,* see Pet. 51, Edward III, 1376–77 quoted in J. W. Collins, 'The Beam-Trawling Fishery of Great Britain, with notes of beam trawling in other European countries', in *Bulletin of the United States Fish Commission* (1887).

FISH THROUGH FINGERS

For Walter Benjamin, see 'The Storyteller', in *Walter Benjamin: Selected Writings, 3: 1935–1938*, eds Eiland and Jennings (Cambridge, MA: Belknap Press of Harvard University Press, 1936, 2006).

MISWAYS

For Woolf, see her diary of August 1905 in *A Passionate Apprentice*. For Daphne du Maurier, see *Vanishing Cornwall* (London: Virago, 1967, 2012). My mother keeps a copy of *Vanishing Cornwall* at home, its jacket bleached out and ripped in places. For the purpose of her book, du Maurier and her son motored around the whole of the Cornish coast, stopping off at each ancient stone formation, well and 'secret place'. The Gerard Manley Hopkins is quoted in Robert Macfarlane and Jackie Morris, *The Lost Words* (London: Hamish Hamilton, 2017). For the rescue of a boy drowning off Newlyn, see *The Cornishman*, 1927.

FISH WITHIN FISH

Fishing legislation in Europe is not only intensely complex, it also shifts as frequently as fish populations do across the seas. Much of my knowledge about the industry comes from fishermen and experts based in Cornwall, supplemented by various newspaper and journal articles. For Epeli Hau'Ofa, see 'Our Sea of Islands', in *A New Oceania: Rediscovering Our Sea of Islands*, eds Eric Waddell, Vijay Naidu, Epeli Hau'Ofa (Suva, Fiji: the University of the South Pacific School of Social and Economic Development, in association with Beake House, 1993). Hau'Ofa rejects the deliberate lines drawn around the world by Western explorers and map-makers who conceive of Polynesia and Micronesia as tiny, isolated islands in a faraway sea. When the sea-faring peoples of Oceania consider their world, he writes, they do not think only of the islands, but 'the surrounding ocean as far as they could traverse and exploit it, the underworld with its fire-controlling and earth-shaking denizens and the heavens above with their hierarchies of powerful gods and named stars and constellations that people could count on to guide their way across the seas' – a sea of islands. Though Cornwall is a county in the UK and not a continent,

I found Hau'Ofa's image of a land that does not end with the land but extends out into the waters a powerful tool with which to consider Newlyn and Cornwall more generally. For Garrett Hardin, see 'The Tragedy of the Commons', in *Science*, Vol. 162, no. 2859 (1968). For Elizabeth Bishop, see 'The Fish', in *The Complete Poems*. For Joseph Conrad, see *The Nigger of the 'Narcissus'*.

CAREWORN

For Dylan Thomas, see 'Quite Early One Morning', in *Collected Stories* (New York: New Directions, 1945, 1967, and London: Weidenfeld & Nicolson, 2014). For Simone Weil, see *The Need for Roots* (Abingdon: Routledge, 1949, 2001). For J. M. Synge, see *The Aran Islands* (Dublin: Maunsel, 1906, 1912). Much of Synge's text takes the form of reported speech from the stories Aran islanders, told to him in pubs and out on boats. *The Aran Islands* continues to be one of the most brilliant, illuminating and empathetic pieces of embedded anthropological research I have encountered.

SEA-HAB

For Walter Benjamin, see the 'Nordic Sea' in *The Storyteller: Tales Out of Loneliness* (New York: Verso, 1930, 2016).

BEATEN COPPER

For Georg Büchner, see *Woyzeck*, trans. Gregory Motton, (London: Nick Hern Books, 1913, 1996). For Annie Dillard, see *Pilgrim at Tinker Creek*, (Norwich: Canterbury Press, 1974, 2011). For the Deep Scattering Layer, see the ship's log of the USS *Jasper*, quoted in 'Blue-sea thinking: technology is transforming the relationship between people and the oceans', in *The Economist Technology Quarterly*, 10 March 2018.

LOCAL

For Synge, see *The Aran Islands*. For Woolf, see her diary of August 1905 in *A Passionate Apprentice*. For Plath, see 'Ocean 1212-W'. For Ralph

Waldo Emerson, see *Nature* (Boston: James Munroe and Company, 1836).

A FEAST OF SEABIRDS

For Pam Lomax and Ron Hogg, see *Newlyn Before the Artists Came* (Penzance: Shears and Hogg Publications, 2010). For Sebald, see *The Rings of Saturn*.

ROSEBUD

I am grateful to Michael Sagar-Fenton, who lives in Penzance, for telling me the story of the *Rosebud*. His book, *The Rosebud and the Newlyn Clearances* (Saint Agnes: Truran, 2003), is highly informative and includes the quotations from news publications published around the time of the clearances. For Richard Carew, see *The Survey of Cornwall* (New York: A. M. Kelley, 1602, 1978). For Polydore Vergil, see *Anglica Historica*, 1535. For 'joyned-in-hands', see *Thomason Tracts*, E.445, (tract 28), 'A Letter from the Isle of Wight', June 1648, quoted in Mark Stoyle, 'The Dissidence of Despair: Rebellion and Identity in Early Modern Cornwall', in *Journal of British Studies*, Vol. 38, no. 4, (1999).

DROPPED THINGS

For Claude Lévi-Strauss, see *Tristes Tropiques*, trans. John and Doreen Weightman (London: Penguin Classics, 1955, 2011). For Walter Benjamin, see 'The Storyteller' in *Walter Benjamin: Selected Writings, 3*. For Melville, see *Moby Dick*. For news of Marconi's telegraph station, see 'Daily News Reporters', *Cornish Evening Tidings*, 20 February 1904. For Marianne Moore, see 'A Graveyard', in *Complete Poems of Marianne Moore* (London: Faber and Faber, 1968). For Lopez, see *Arctic Dreams*.

SOME OLD RESIDENTS

For 'Some old residents of Newlyn', see 'Newlyn Wagonette-men' in 'Correspondence', *The Cornishman*, 14 April 1926. For Edwin

Chirgwin, see *The Rustic Jottings of Edwin Chirgwin (1892–1960)*, *Cornishman* (Bodmin: John Chirgwin Jenkin, nd). For Plath see 'Ocean 1212-W'.

GRAVEYARD

For Jack the Giant Killer, see Dinah Craik, 'Jack the Giant-Killer', in *The Fairy Book* (Gloucestershire: Echo Library, 1870, 2007). For Geoffrey of Monmouth, see *Historia Regum Britanniae*, (1136). For Elizabeth Bishop, see 'On Being Alone', in *Elizabeth Bishop: Prose* (London: Random House, 1929, 2014). For Marianne Moore, see 'A Graveyard', in *Complete Poems of Marianne Moore*.

STORMS DO COME

For Elizabeth Bishop, see 'The Bight', in *The Complete Poems*. For Buttery, see *Mousehole: a Documented History*. For Gerard Manley Hopkins, see 'Heaven-Haven', in *Poems and Prose*, ed. W. H. Gardner, (London: Penguin Classics, 2008).

RAYMUNDO

For Sebald, see *The Rings of Saturn*. For Lopez, see *Arctic Dreams*.

VORTEX

For Joan Didion, see *The Year of Magical Thinking*. For Philip Pullman, see *The Northern Lights*, (New York: Scholastic, 1995, 2017). Pullman's *His Dark Materials* series continues to teach me much about imagination and integrity as I reach my mid-twenties; there is surely no better, nor more appealing, literary invention than the daemon. For Ted Hughes, see 'The Rock', in *Writers on Themselves*.

A PASSIONATE RAGE

For Synge, see *The Aran Islands*.

'OME

For Gaston Bachelard, see *The Poetics of Space*, trans. Maria Jolas, (London: Penguin Classics, 1957, 2014). For Franz Kafka, see 'Poseidon' in *The Complete Stories* (London: Vintage Classics, 1920, 1992). For Claude Lévi-Strauss, see *Tristes Tropiques*, trans. John and Doreen Weightman (London: Penguin Classics, 1955, 2011).

FISHERMAN'S BLUES

For Synge, see *The Aran Islands*.

HOLLOWAYS

For Melville, see *Moby Dick*.

ACKNOWLEDGEMENTS

If you want to write, it turns out you have to live at the same time. And if you decide to make a go at living, in turns out you need a lot of people to help you along the way. As such, my list of thanks would probably stretch as long as this book – longer even. But for now, here's an abbreviated version, which I have made roughly chronological for the sake of ease.

Thank you to my mother, Zelah, for each wet and windy walk we've taken across Lelant beach together. Thank you to my father, Francis, for helping me through every crisis of confidence – and there were many – with tremendous patience. To my brothers, Georges and Simon. To Nick and Sara Williams for opening up their home to me and being my ballasts on the north coast. To my friends, including, but not restricted to: old friends, new friends, school friends, university friends, friends I've lived with, worked with, danced with, kissed, pined after, lost and laughed with; it is you who have shaped these first few, unsteady years of adulthood, and so, in a way, have shaped this book too.

Thank you to those at *TLS* for giving me the opportunity to write in their paper – I learnt so much from you all. I am eternally grateful to my editor Michael Fishwick for taking a chance on an unknown quantity and for supporting me every shaky step of the way. Thank you to Lilidh, Lauren, Emma and everyone else at Bloomsbury. Thank you to my brilliant agent, Cathryn Summerhayes. Thank you to my copy-editor Kate Johnson, whose thoughtful, discerning edits transformed this book and whose every phone call I look forward to immensely.

Thank you to the town of Newlyn for letting me stay a little while. Thank you to every fisherman and individual involved in the fishing industry who took the time to give me an insight into their livelihoods – Nathan, Andy, Cod, Roger, David, James, Danny, Kyle, Andrew, Stevie, Freddie, Nick, Mike and Rose, Harry, Simon, Larry, Nicky, Shane, Rob, Nocte, Mad Dick, Alan, Ben Gunn, Tony, Chris, Lucy, Elizabeth, among others. To every member of the community who made me howl with laughter in the pub and showed me it is possible to love your neighbours fiercely. Thank you to Isaac – the conversations we had about home, about identity, became the bedrock of this book. To Don, for providing *Dark, Salt, Clear* with its hero and for being the best skipper in the southwest. To Lofty and Denise, for whom there do not exist words enough to say thank you properly: it meant everything living with you those months. Denise, Newlyn's Dancing Queen, I will never forget you.

ABOUT THE AUTHOR

Lamorna Ash is an education worker at the charity IntoUniversity and is a freelance writer for the *Times Literary Supplement* and *TANK* magazine. She has a degree in English from Oxford and a masters in Social and Cultural Anthropology from UCL, and has written numerous plays that have toured Edinburgh, Oxford and London. She can gut most kinds of fish, quite slowly. *Dark, Salt, Clear* is her first book.

A NOTE ON THE TYPE

The text of this book is set in Linotype Sabon, a typeface named after the type founder, Jacques Sabon. It was designed by Jan Tschichold and jointly developed by Linotype, Monotype and Stempel in response to a need for a typeface to be available in identical form for mechanical hot metal composition and hand composition using foundry type.

Tschichold based his design for Sabon roman on a font engraved by Garamond, and Sabon italic on a font by Granjon. It was first used in 1966 and has proved an enduring modern classic.